ID0975832

PRAISE FOR

UNJUST

"An elegant and thoughtful dismantling of perhaps the most danger-ous ideology at work today. Modern social-justice thinking tears away at our most cherished ideals and institutions. Noah Rothman has done a tremendous service in cutting through the sloganeering and getting to the heart of the matter—the elevation of crude iden-tity politics at the expense of decency, merit, and truth."
>   —**Ben Shapiro**, editor in chief, The Daily Wire

"Reading Noah Rothman is like a workout for your brain, and this book also tugs at your heart. Noah calls upon all of us to remember our common identity first—we are Americans. He suggests we start acting like it."
>   —**Dana Perino**, press secretary to President George W. Bush

"Noah Rothman makes it clear that Americans have just two choices before them. They can fulfill the beautiful principles that were out-lined in the Declaration of Independence and were then extended by those who fought for the right to their 'promissory note,' or they can descend into grievance-mongering, identity politics, and sectar-ian strife."
>   —**Charles C. W. Cooke**, editor, NationalReview.com

"Identity politics is corrupting the American ideal of e pluribus unum. 'Out of many, one' has been replaced by 'from one into many.' In this robust endorsement of our nation's timeless founding prin-ciples, Noah Rothman says the things that need to be said but that too few people have the courage to say."
>   —**James Kirchick**, author of The End of Europe: Dictators, Demagogues and the Coming Dark Age

"Noah Rothman examines a movement more focused on political retribution than the search for justice, explaining with great insight how it has poisoned our politics, coarsened our culture, and turned us into a nation of victims."

—**Joe Scarborough**, host of MSNBC's *Morning Joe*

"Noah Rothman's pointed, eloquent, powerful, and necessary *Unjust* marks the distinguished beginning of what will surely be a remarkable career as an author of books."

—**John Podhoretz**, editor, *Commentary*

"Noah Rothman's first book (of many, I hope) shows how social justice ideologues, left and right, are rejecting the uniquely anti-tribal nature of the American experiment that has allowed us to rise above the tit-for-tat tribal temptation that has marked—and wrecked—so many past civilizations."

—**Jonah Goldberg**, author of *Suicide of the West: How the Rebirth of Tribalism, Populism, Nationalism, and Identity Politics Is Destroying American Politics*

UNJUST

Unjust

SOCIAL JUSTICE AND THE UNMAKING OF AMERICA

Noah Rothman

REGNERY GATEWAY

Regnery Gateway™ is a trademark of Salem Communications Holding Corporation
Regnery® is a registered trademark of Salem Communications Holding Corporation

Cataloging-in-Publication data on file with the Library of Congress

ISBN 978-1-62157-792-8
ebook ISBN 978-1-62157-905-2

Published in the United States by
Regnery Publishing
A Division of Salem Media Group
300 New Jersey Ave NW
Washington, DC 20001
www.Regnery.com

Manufactured in the United States of America

10 9 8 7 6 5 4 3 2

Books are available in quantity for promotional or premium use. For information on discounts and terms, please visit our website: www.Regnery.com.

For Jace and Elias.

CONTENTS

INTRODUCTION

There is no better time to visit the former Soviet Union than the dead of winter. After all, if you're going to learn anything about a people, it will not be when conditions are optimal. And winter conditions in Ukraine are far from optimal.

On a February afternoon in Kiev, I joined a group of Western journalists seated across from Yuri Lutsenko, the chief prosecutor for the government of Ukraine, a country that has been ravaged by conflict since the overthrow of its pro-Russian regime in 2014. The education in post-revolutionary politics he provided us was as enlightening as it was chilling.

As Lutsenko explained in perfect English that it was not and should not be a government priority to prosecute those who might be implicated in revolutionary violence but were loyal to the current government—a pro-Western government, we were pointedly reminded—I was overcome with a sense of foreboding. This was not justice he was describing. This was payback, which can only foster resentment, cycles of violence and counter-violence, corruption, and tribal animosities that span generations. Lutsenko surely knew that as well as anyone, but we are all hostages to the currents of history. Some of us are simply more resigned to it than others.

One of our guides described Ukrainian politics as a contest of personalities. At any given time, there are five or six strongmen who command the support of this or that political bloc. Parties are built around these personalities. Alliances form and dissolve with no grander objective than keeping everyone else off balance. Exogenous events, such as the occasional Russian invasion or a corruption crisis, alter this balance, but the fundamental dynamic does not change. That dynamic is about power: securing it, maintaining it, and exercising it.

This is not how politics works in the United States—a blessing we take for granted. Americans can be cynical about their political culture, but America's institutional and conventional checks on the ambitions of demagogues should be a source of great pride. The United States is a mature republic founded upon ideals, and its two dominant political parties are united more by ideological convictions than personalities. At least they were once.

The American tradition of political idealism is imperiled by a growing obsession with the demographic categories of race, sex, ethnicity, and sexual orientation—the primary categories that are now supposed to constitute "identity." As groups defined by these various categories have come to command the comprehensive allegiance of their members, identity alone has become a powerful political program. As it turns out, it is not a program that appeals to the better angels of our nature.

Identity has always been a part of our political culture, but lately the practitioners of identity politics have been less interested in continuity and legitimacy than in revenge. This retribution is antithetical to the conciliatory ideals by which injustices perpetrated in the name of identity were once reconciled. The authors of this vengeance reject the kind of blind, objective justice toward which Western civilization has striven since the Enlightenment. They argue, in fact, that blind justice is not justice at all. Objectivity is a utopian goal, a myth clung to by naïve children. We are all products of our experiences and the conditions into which we were born, whether we like it or not. Those traits set us on a course that is in many ways predestined.

The identity-obsessed left believes that Americans who are born into "privileged" demographic categories—male, white, and heterosexual, among others—will have an easier time navigating life than their underprivileged counterparts, among them women, ethnic minorities, and the LGBT. Those on the right believe the opposite is true: the historically marginalized have had the scales tipped in *their* direction. The so-called "privileged" majority not only has lost its privileges but is often stripped of its essential rights.

The paranoia which can ensue from this division is the venomous progeny of identity politics. Its practitioners call it *social justice*.

This idea of social justice has developed into a way of life. The study of identity long ago ceased to resemble an academic discipline. Its tenets are as inviolable as any religious dogma. The diversity industry is populated by con artists, some of whom have shifted from advocating diversity solutions to pitching themselves as experts on why diversity solutions so often fail. They have bloated the administrations of already top-heavy organizations, such as large businesses and universities, while failing to achieve even their stated objectives.

You would think this charlatanism would bother social justice enthusiasts. Oddly enough, this parasitic relationship seems to annoy only their critics. Often those who display even token obeisance to the diktats of identity politics escape censure, no matter how deserving of condemnation their behavior may be. So enamored with their own virtue are these social justice advocates that they cannot see the injustices they are abetting.

The creed forming around social justice idealism is shaping our every daily interaction. It influences how businesses structure themselves. It is altering how employers and employees relate to one another. It has utterly transformed academia. It is remaking our politics with alarming swiftness. And its self-appointed inquisitors make sure that there are consequences for transgressors.

Every society wrestles with its past, and it is judicious to try to right historical injustices perpetrated on the basis of race, sex, ethnicity, and class. No virtuous society ignores the petitions of the genuinely wronged, and social justice can be the recognition of the legitimacy of particular grievances. Absent a limiting principle, though, the pursuit of social justice becomes the pursuit of retribution. Societies that dedicate themselves to that objective without circumspection become like Lutsenko's Ukraine, convinced of the righteousness of its own prejudices.

Social justice is a theory of human relations that predates the modern age. It mandates that agrarian societies transitioning to industry and urbanization provide a soft landing for the displaced, that a widow should not be separated from her children because she lacks the means to provide for them. It recognizes that racial disparity in American prisons is a symptom of a broader social malady with roots that go back centuries, that the effects of ethnic and sectarian discrimination, sexual disparity, and prejudice are expansive and overlapping, shaping our perception of the world in ways most of us cannot fully comprehend. It demands that we have difficult conversations, examine our own assumptions, and build coalitions toward truly noble ends: honesty, recompense, and reconciliation.

But social justice in its modern form encompasses the idea that an ill-defined class of persecutors and oppressors is due for a reckoning. The same idea animated the Jacobins in France, the Bolivarians in Latin America, and the Bolsheviks in Russia. It is an idea that inculcates in its most militant devotees an uncompromising bitterness, twisting its adherents into petty, vindictive specters of their former selves. The thirst for revenge against those who allegedly benefit from the repression of the past is powerful and corrupting. Retribution rarely resolves conflict. Often, it fosters more of it.

Has the pursuit of this retributive social justice made us better people? I will argue in this book that the answer, by and large, is no. I hope to demonstrate that a preoccupation with identity becomes a mania when it forms the basis of an ideology, and that ideology blinds its devotees to certain inopportune realities. This book will illustrate how social justice is producing a society full of activists who revel in an impotence that they insist has been imposed upon them. They eschew agency, wallow in helplessness, and project their shortcomings onto others. This book will show that this kind of ruinous politics is dumbing us down and, in our weakness, leading us to lash out violently. Finally, it will offer a way out of this cycle of madness.

I attack social justice as a governing program and the identity politics that serves as its underlying ethos with some passion because the problem is urgent, but this book is not a polemic. If you are looking for red meat, there is no shortage of butchers. Rather, this is a condemnation of an embittering ideology, not of social and racial awareness or self-actualization.

Social justice is a creed born of grievances, some of which are undoubtedly valid. I make no effort, though, to litigate the legitimacy of those individual grievances; to do so would be beyond the scope of this book. This is a defense of the principles that gave birth to America's democratic republic and were subsequently adopted by much of the civilized world. Every person on Earth has a God-granted right to succeed by virtue of his or her abilities and labors. In the abstract, this remains an uncontroversial notion, but that perspective is changing in practice. It is a change that must be resisted.

Those who seek to acquire influence and authority that their aptitude alone cannot secure will resent these conclusions. Social justice is divisive, and division has always empowered the unscrupulous. The rise of revanchist elements within both major political parties in the United States bodes ill for the future of the country. Left unchecked, these elements will stoke revolutionary sentiments. Given time, revolutionary sentiments eventually give way to terror and tyranny.

Identity politics is not limited to any one political party or socio-economic class. Many of those who have embraced the philosophy that animates the most militant practitioners of identity politics may not even recognize the trap into which they have fallen. The objective of this book is to define social justice so that readers may be better able to identify it when it masquerades as patriotism, nationalism, or progressivism. It will seek to demonstrate why the present iteration of what activists call social justice is a toxic ideology—one that saps the United States, in particular, of its republican character. Finally, it will appeal to our collective sense of generosity, humility, and modesty. The absurd and dangerous aspects of this new fanatical militancy deserve to be consigned to the dustbin of history.

CHAPTER 1

Identitarianism

K-Sue Park volunteered with the American Civil Liberties Union as a law student, but by the time she was a Critical Race Studies Fellow at UCLA a few years later, she had concluded that the ACLU "should rethink how it understands free speech." Its "narrow reading of the First Amendment," she wrote in the *New York Times*, blinds it to the illegitimacy of "hate-based causes." "More troubling," Park continued, "the legal gains on which the ACLU rests its colorblind logic have never secured real freedom or even safety for all."[1]

This is as naked an expression of hostility to the rights enshrined in the First Amendment as you're likely to find. Park sees American society as so stratified that an absolutist commitment to free expression is no virtue. "Colorblind logic," she insists, is a naïve pretense that should be discarded.

Park wrote in the wake of a heavily publicized violent clash between white supremacists and counter-demonstrators in Charlottesville, Virginia, that left one young woman dead—a horrifying episode that prompted many people to reconsider the limits of free speech. Park's argument is a familiar one, but it is incompatible with the civic traditions that buttress the right of all Americans to engage in free expression and assembly. In effect, Park argued that the only cure for the ills of bigotry is more bigotry.

"For marginalized communities, the power of expression is impoverished for reasons that have little to do with the First Amendment," she continued, citing the power of money, fifty years of Supreme Court precedents, and the history of exploitation and violence against minorities. First Amendment rights, she concluded, conflict with the demands of a just society. "Context" is vital, and that "context" should be racial. What she called "spurious claims of 'reverse racism,'"—that is, the notion that anyone, not just women and minorities, can be subjected to persecution—must be dismissed without a second thought. "Sometimes standing on the wrong side of history in defense of a cause you think is right is still just standing on the wrong side of history," Park concluded.

Unabashed arguments for race-based discrimination intended to thwart economic, legal, and social fulfillment were once rarely encountered in the wild. Sadly, the views expressed in Park's op-ed seem to be becoming increasingly widespread.

Writing in the *Los Angeles Times*, Laura Weinrib of the University of Chicago Law School agrees that the ACLU has lost its way. Once dedicated to protecting "free speech as a tool of social justice," the ACLU now protects the rights of not only neo-Nazis but corporations and public-sector employees who don't want to contribute dues to unions of which they are not members.[2] The rogues!

Weinrib argues that the ACLU's commitment to protecting the rights of white supremacists in the twentieth century was not a matter of principle but a deft political gambit designed to support Democratic political causes by giving the public a good look at their unsympathetic opponents. In Weinrib's view, free expression and assembly are valuable only insofar as they advance progressive policy goals.

Even many of the ACLU's own staffers no longer believe in the organization's absolutist commitment to free speech. More than two hundred employees signed a letter in late 2017 asserting that the ACLU's statement of purpose conflicts with its objectives. "Our broader mission—which includes advancing the racial justice guarantees in the Constitution and elsewhere, not just the First Amendment—continues to be undermined by our rigid stance," the letter reads.[3] These and other "racial justice" advocates have convinced themselves that their objectives are incompatible with the Constitution. One or the other has to go.

Park and Weinrib are remarkably candid advocates for social justice. In their view, principles must be tempered in partisan fires. For them, "colorblind" is a four-letter word. Free speech isn't an unalloyed good if it is applied universally and, therefore, licenses the wrong sort of behavior by the wrong people. This is a curious definition of "justice," but it is one with a growing constituency.

For these and other activists, getting on the "right side of history" requires that we recalibrate the scales of justice to favor the "marginalized" and their descendants. But who has a legitimate claim to such a privileged status? Identity politics prescribes a particular moral code, but it is not a governing program. It is merely the philosophy. Social justice is that philosophy in practice.

Social Justice

If we think of the objective, blind justice associated with the rule of law as analogous to free-market capitalism, modern social justice is the equivalent of a command economy. In such a system, justice is a finite commodity, like aluminum or wheat, but there is no supply chain. If one person has it, another is deprived of it. Therefore, it falls on a society's most enlightened to distribute justice to the most deserving. The phrase "social justice" itself would seem to describe a value-neutral proposition to which anyone in his right mind would subscribe.

It is, in fact, less a theory of justice than a new way of thinking about how society should be ordered.

The definition of social justice has evolved over the decades. Retributive social justice developed out of the utopian theological movements of the nineteenth century, but it only became an element of the left's governing program in the mid-to-late twentieth century.

The identity politics practiced by today's social justice activists has retained its vestigial quasi-religious traits. Though this dogma has traditionally been most attractive to the collectivist left, it has recently found an audience on the populist right. Those who see themselves as members of a "marginalized" class and who seek payback against their perceived oppressors through both state and non-governmental institutions are social justice advocates, whether they know it or not.

Many who dedicate themselves to social justice are pursuing a noble goal: equality and reparation for genuine historical crimes. But harboring a grievance is toxic, and in the hands of an influential set of activists, social justice has turned poisonous. It appeals to our pettiness and stokes envy. It compels us to think of ourselves and those around us as victims inhabiting a complex matrix of persecution. While robbing us of our sense of agency, it entices us to take out our frustrations on our neighbors. It demands that we define people by their hereditary traits and insists that we take subjective inventory of the "privileges" we acquire at birth. It rejects as folly the idea that we are free to rise as far as individual aptitude and merit allow. For social justice's devotees, the American idea is a lie.

Millions of Americans, even savvy and ideologically astute political observers, assume that the tenets of social justice are just another extension of the American creed. Equality and fairness—what's so un-American about that? Some might even see attempts to compensate the victims of real historical injustices as a necessary precondition for broader social reconciliation. That's a decent impulse, but that project has been terribly mismanaged.

American liberals have allowed their movement to be hijacked by an ideology that mimics their style but betrays their traditional values. Liberals appreciate diversity within a cohesive whole; social justice advocates resent assimilation into American culture. Liberals cherish equality; social justice advocates see objective notions of equality as inherently unfair. Liberals support free expression; social justice advocates think free speech normalizes intolerable ideas. Liberals treasure nonconformity; social justice advocates view a failure to conform to certain precepts as a threat.

So how was an ethos of equality and egalitarianism across lines of class, race, and sex transformed into a bitter ideology that resents classically liberal policies? The mixing of identity consciousness with the precepts of social justice seems to have a lot to do with it. As inherited or ingrained traits supplant experience and deeply held principles as sources of identity, a new kind of identity politics has arisen. When this identity politics is fused with the obligations that social justice activists see as vital collective imperatives, you get something that resembles a religion.

The Cult of Identity

To tell his masterly short story "Harrison Bergeron," Kurt Vonnegut needed to encumber his characters with a familiar plot device: the ubiquitous and inflexible Big Brother. Published in 1961 and set 120 years in the future, the tale explores the dystopian nature of any society in which everyone is equal. Here, however, equality is measured by incapacity. Every person bears an impairment forced on him by a remote bureaucracy—a mask for the exceptionally attractive, leg weights for the athletically gifted, constant acoustic distractions for the highly intelligent, and so on.

Vonnegut's story illustrates the moral hazards of ensuring not just equality of opportunity but equality of outcomes. At a time in which Moscow seemed set on exporting Marxism-Leninism to every corner of the globe, Americans recoiled from such hostility to individualism. Vonnegut reasoned, therefore, that such a bleak form of social organization must at first be imposed on a population. Only after it knew no alternative would it turn freely to dreary uniformity as a remedy for freedom's natural inequities. Vonnegut was wrong. Compulsory homogeneity does not have to be forced on the public by Big Brother. Today, it is being imposed from below and by popular demand.

As the totalitarianism of the twentieth century recedes from living memory, some have begun to look favorably upon alternatives to classically liberal laissez-faire republicanism. Some of today's most popular alternatives—populism and tribalism—are the primordial ooze out of which despots crawl.

The *New York Times* is not in the habit of publicizing arguments that appeal exclusively to the fanatical fringe. The sentiments expressed by people like K-Sue Park, who holds a law degree from Harvard and a Ph.D. from Berkeley, are sentiments with broad purchase. The definition of "diversity" in terms of inherited traits has made those who fancy themselves diversity's most dedicated champions less tolerant of genuine diversity. Those who adhere to a regimented code of identity politics have confused a punitive, retaliatory ethic with a kind of karmic fairness.

This is the final result of a fanatical devotion to identity politics. It exhibits the traits of a religion, and that is how I intend to treat it. "Identitarianism" suffices to describe a set of values and beliefs based on the politics of personal identity.

In Europe, Identitarianism is the opposite of egalitarianism, and it's closely associated with militant right-wing movements. In France,

Génération Identitaire is the youth wing of the Bloc Identitaire party. Members of the German New Right proudly call themselves Identitarians. In the United Kingdom, Generation Identity is a self-described Identitarian movement ostensibly dedicated to the preservation and defense of Europe. It has adopted the Spartan Lambda as its symbol and warns that "self-destruction through a multicultural zeitgeist" is bringing about a Muslim conquest of Europe. This disparate transnational movement is united by the belief that immigration from outside Europe is dangerous, that Islam is incompatible with European values, and that the European Union is a corrupt vehicle dedicated to the destruction of the European identity.[4]

These sentiments represent only one strain of Identitarian thought. But they are what you get when a political movement commits to abandoning "colorblind logic." Perhaps the ACLU's social justice activists don't realize that they are mirroring the racially anxious nationalist right in Europe and America, but they are.

The Pace of Change

Today, the behavioral imperatives of the social justice movement can be seen everywhere, from the absurd behavior of America's cultural elite in the boardroom to its youth on campus. From imposing restrictions on speech to weakening the very foundational notions of English common law—most notably the presumption of innocence—social justice is altering the American compact right before our eyes.

According to the New York City Commission on Human Rights, it can now be considered a civil offense punishable by termination and a fine of up to a $250,000 to fail to "use a transgender employee's preferred name, pronoun, or title."[5] Ignorance is no excuse. Malice is presumed. Therefore, it is recommended that the public make use of fabricated "gender-free" pronouns like "ze" (singular) and "hir" (plural). Forcing made-up words loaded with ideological connotations on the public with the threat of punishment represents nothing less than ideological coercion by the state.

The demands of social justice in the workplace long ago expanded beyond diversity consulting and equal employment opportunity compliance. Firms as large as Comcast and as small as Silicon Valley startups have begun factoring lost productivity resulting from their employees' political engagement into their operating costs. Following the onset of the pronounced recession that began in 2007–2008, for example, Citigroup began offering its prospective employees the opportunity to defer their work responsibilities for one year to do philanthropic or volunteer work in exchange for 60 percent of their salary.[6] This was not a decision based in altruism. Millennials were simply less interested in a career in the financial services sector if it did not make allowances for their heightened sense of social conscience.

Some firms have begun providing their employees with paid time off specifically to engage in political protest, as long as it is the right kind of political protest. The clothing company Patagonia, for example, will even provide bail money for its employees who are arrested while peacefully protesting environmental issues, a category that is loosely defined by the progressive firm. Patagonia employees are also eligible for paid time off for court appearances and meetings with their lawyers. "We hire activists," said Patagonia's vice president of human resources, Dean Carter. "If you're hiring a wild horse because of its passion and independence and then you keep it in the pen, that's ridiculous."[7]

Of course, the social justice left is pretty particular about the forms of political expression it sees as valuable. Particularly on American campuses, some speech is considered so dangerous that it must be suppressed.

In 2015, the University of California system provided its professors with a list of "microaggressions"—modest slights, as the prefix "micro" suggests.[8] Often, students are instructed not to shrug off these irritations but to dwell on them and exaggerate their importance. Among the sprawling list of "microaggressions" are expressions that we used to consider boilerplate patriotism:

- "America is the land of opportunity."
- "Everyone can succeed in this society if they work hard enough."
- "When I look at you, I don't see color."
- "Gender plays no part in who we hire."
- "I believe the most qualified person should get the job."

These phrases promote what the UC system dubbed the "myth of meritocracy." It is the social justice left's inviolable conviction that prejudice is a shackle around the ankles of women, minorities, the transgendered, and homosexuals. They are taught that they cannot rise above prejudice without the aid of benevolent progressive authorities.

That conviction has also led its adherents to attack those who do find success, particularly if they do not check the right demographic boxes. Consider the ordeals of the scientists Tim Hunt and Matt Taylor. Sir Richard Timothy Hunt received the Nobel Prize in physiology and medicine in 2001. Taylor, a British astrophysicist, helped design and land a man-made object on a speeding comet in 2014. By all rights, these men should be celebrated for their triumphs. Instead, they were brought low by organized attacks executed by those who did not share their talent but were devoted to social justice dogmas.

"Let me tell you about my trouble with girls." These were the words that cast Hunt into a maelstrom. He uttered them at a scientific conference in South Korea hosted by an organization dedicated to promoting women in the sciences. "Three things happen when they are in the lab," he continued. "You fall in love with them, they fall in love with you, and when you criticize them, they cry. Perhaps we should make separate labs for boys and girls."⁹

Hunt was talking about his wife, a fellow scientist, whom he met in a laboratory. He concluded, "Now, seriously, I'm impressed by the economic development of Korea. And women scientists played, without doubt, an important role in it. Science needs women, and you should do science, despite all the obstacles, and despite monsters like me." This line revealed the joke for what it was. Even absent nonverbal cues that the deliberately obtuse ignore to make a point, these were obviously the self-effacing remarks of a seventy-two-year-old man. They probably would never have attracted any notice if it were not for a spiteful colleague in the audience. In dispatches from the conference, Connie St. Louis, the director of the master's program in science journalism at New York's City University, eagerly and intentionally misrepresented both Hunt's quip and how it was received by the audience. The phantom of overt sexism having been invoked, the press jumped at the opportunity to turn St. Louis into a star and Dr. Hunt into a pariah. For a Western media establishment that caters to the perpetually aggrieved social justice left, it was a story too good to temper with mitigating context. Despite no obvious malicious intent, Hunt was forced to resign his honorary professorships at University College London and the Biological Sciences Awards Committee of the Royal Society.

Taylor, too, found himself humiliated by those whose spitefulness was matched only by their lack of scruples. Giddy after his history-making achievement of landing a probe on a speeding Kuiper belt object, he appeared on a broadcast discussing his team's achievement wearing a shirt adorned with cartoonish images of women in bathing suits. "No, no, women are toooootally welcome in our community," remarked *The Atlantic*'s technology writer Rose Eveleth with theatrical sarcasm, "just ask the dude in this shirt."[10]

Her comment produced a familiar cyclone of recriminations and denunciations. The scolds who condemned this accomplished scientist made no allowance for the fact that the shirt was a gift from a female friend who had hoped to see it on television. Within days, Taylor was forced to reappear on camera, this time in tears. He had been humiliated, and the rabble was satisfied to see him suffer.

As we will see, much modern social justice activism takes the form of simply cutting the successful down to size. This movement's more ideologically committed members justify their antipathy toward the thriving and prosperous by convincing themselves that success is an ill-gotten gain. Accomplishments and failures are not earned but bestowed upon someone by higher powers. The idea that work yields reward is just a comforting fable.

For the social justice left, meritocracy isn't the only myth that must be stamped out. Objective truth is another.

Vulgarity and Seduction

"Historically, white supremacy has venerated the idea of objectivity," reads an open letter composed and signed by students at the five-school Claremont Consortium in California. "The idea that the truth is an entity for which we must search, in matters that endanger our abilities to exist in open spaces, is an attempt to silence oppressed peoples."[11]

What prompted this pseudo-intellectual orgy of self-indulgence? A scheduled appearance on the McKenna College campus of Heather Mac Donald, the author of *The War on Cops*, an important work of research in defense of America's police. Some 250 Claremont students found her work intolerable and mobilized to prevent their fellow students from hearing her conclusions. Mac Donald didn't get to speak; those who wanted her silenced were considered too volatile, too dangerous. Mac Donald's suspicion of the Black Lives Matter movement, regardless of her argument's merits, was an unendurable heresy.

In an ironic twist, the students who led that protest were so racially enlightened that they opted to segregate themselves. Protesters who marched against Mac Donald placed "white accomplices" at the front of the line to serve as a buffer against police, who they believe have an itchier trigger finger when confronted by African-Americans.

Racial separatism in service to solidarity and safety is a common feature of demonstrations dating back to the civil rights movement of the mid-twentieth century. In isolation, this amounts to a nostalgic reenactment that would not be worthy of much note, except that police don't seem all that reluctant to pepper-spray unruly white protesters. But this phenomenon is not exclusive to protests and demonstrations. Benign ghettoization is making a comeback, particularly on college campuses, and it has nothing to do with protest culture.

Columbia University recently cordoned off areas of campus exclusively for use by lesbian, gay, bisexual, and transgender (LGBT) and minority students. President Morton Schapiro of Northwestern University penned an op-ed in the *Washington Post* defending racially segregated cafeteria tables, insisting that lunchtime isn't the place for "uncomfortable learning."[12] Students at the University of Michigan recently demanded the establishment of African-American "safe spaces" on their state-owned campus that could not be penetrated by state-run police. Because the state's police union had endorsed Donald Trump, the students insisted that "placing us in the police's care is an act of anti-Black violence."[13]

We're no longer talking about separate living conditions for students who want to steep themselves in lifestyles that complement their fields of study. The idea that *study* has anything to do with it is a pretense that has finally been abandoned.

In early 2017, Frank Furedi, a professor at the University of Kent, stuck his neck out by protesting the "safe space" movement on campuses. He said that this concept led faculty and administrators to defend the idea that Jews, conservatives, African-Americans, Asians, LGBT students, and others cannot interact with one another without feeling menaced. "The popularity of identity politics among insecure Millennials threatens to fracture campus life to the point that undergraduates are inhabiting separate spaces and leading parallel lives," he wrote.[14] He's right. In the name of Identitarian social justice, the next generation has embraced racial, religious, and political segregation and censorship. This isn't progress. It's regression.

In much of the rest of the world, identity politics is just called "politics." In nations forged over millennia with a distinct ethnic or religious heritage or in countries without an egalitarian tradition, personal identity is largely indistinct from the national or subnational character. The United States is different. This is a nation built not upon heritage but a common idea. It is an idea built upon the concept that all men and women are created in God's image, equal and free. The standards it sets for itself often go unmet, but America's ideals have nevertheless guided its political evolution since the Founding.

Today, as a virulent form of identity politics gains broad and bipartisan credence, that idea is under attack. A bastardized notion of equality has compelled Western elites in politics, media, and academia to view the accomplished with suspicion. Since victimhood, not capability or achievement, opens doors, claims of victimization are proliferating. Americans are being divided into two perceived and often overlapping classes: aggressors and their victims. This division has heightened tensions among individuals and groups that brandish competing claims to victimhood. The inevitable result of this trend will be tribalism, oppressive communitarianism, and the perception that individuality is a dangerous form of deviancy.

From the legitimate scholarly examination of cultural distinctions, social power dynamics, and trans-generational memory, a poisonous brand of social justice was born. It is the very antithesis of justice. It is a doctrine that infantilizes its adherents while making them belligerent, and it is exclusive to no political creed. It has Identitarian devotees on the left and the right. It professes to value equality, but its central tenet is vengeance. It is as vulgar as it is seductive.

The vindictiveness and envy inherent in modern social justice can be made to seem less obviously contemptible when festooned with academic pretensions. It's no wonder, then, that so many men and women of letters have devoted their careers to concocting a dubious scientific doctrine around unfalsifiable claims. Arguably the most famous of these is the feminist doctrine of intersectionality.

Intersectionality

Social justice has birthed a variety of complementary splinter ideologies, but few have been as successful as intersectionality. Even its most devoted adherents disagree about its definition, but the basic idea is well-defined.

Institutional racism does not run parallel to patriarchal discrimination, intersectional theorists contend. Anti-gay bias is not completely distinct from class-based persecution. These pathologies are interrelated; they "intersect." Practically, "privilege" is enjoyed by those with one or more of the following traits: white, wealthy, heterosexual, male. Those who lack at least one of those traits suffer some discrimination, but prejudice is doled out in degrees. A gay white man suffers less prejudice than a black heterosexual woman, to say nothing of a poor, disabled, Native-American lesbian, and so on. This is intersectionality.

The scholar Kimberlé Williams Crenshaw has done more than most to formalize and popularize intersectionality. In a 2016 TED Talk, she describes the theory as an effort to break up an old model of civil rights and social activism, which she derisively calls "a trickle-down approach to social justice." Writing in the *Stanford Law Review* in 1991, she provides a real-world example to help define intersectional theory in practice: the "Clarence Thomas/Anita Hill scandal."[15] Crenshaw argues that Hill was disadvantaged because of her status as a black woman alleging sexist harassment by a black man:

> This dilemma could be described as the consequence of antiracism's essentializing Blackness and feminism's essentializing womanhood. But recognizing as much does not take us far enough, for the problem is not simply linguistic or philosophical in nature. It is specifically political: the narratives of gender are based on the experience of white, middle-class women, and the narratives of race are based on the experience of Black men.

The notion that Hill's accusations did not receive a fair hearing both in the press and on Capitol Hill seems divorced from any empirical assessment of reality, but that's not the only bit of objectivity that intersectionality tosses out the window.

In an academic context, intersectional theory is a perfectly legitimate conceptual framework for understanding prejudice. As an organizational philosophy, however, it resembles a Marxist ideal: all struggles against discrimination are linked because they all originate from the same fundamental source of inequality. For Marx, that source was class. For intersectional feminists, it's identity.

In theory, intersectionality is a source of strength for the social justice left. It unites otherwise disparate elements of the liberal activist base in a common cause. In practice, however, intersectionality is a trap that saps its enthusiasts of legitimacy, as the corruption of the Women's March of 2017 demonstrated.

When Donald Trump won the presidency, hundreds of thousands of angry activists took to the streets, marching for days on end. This movement was not blemish-free, and on Inauguration Day, violence in its name erupted across the country. The Women's March was the antidote to these destructive passions.

For two days in January, millions of people marched in opposition to Trump. The demonstration was peaceful, powerful, and, most importantly, sympathetic. It was not long, however, before the inter-sectional feminists who organized this event sullied their group's reputation.

Among the Women's March organizers was the self-described feminist and Palestinian-American activist Linda Sarsour, who enjoyed tremendous cachet on the left. The ACLU, Demos, and other left-leaning organizations praised her effusively. Democratic Senator Kirsten Gillibrand dubbed her one of the "suffragists of our time." Sarsour repaid these favors by putting her supporters in the awkward position of having to defend her frequently aberrant behavior.[16]

Though supposedly a feminist, Sarsour has essentially endorsed Saudi Arabia's medieval treatment of women. She has said that Riyadh's formerly tight restrictions on the rights of women, like driving a car, were offset by the state's paternalistic welfare policies. Moreover, this was a tradeoff that any woman would be silly to turn down. "I wish I could take their vaginas away," Sarsour wrote of female activists like Ayaan Hirsi Ali. A Somali-born Dutch-American lecturer and writer, Ali was a victim of genital mutilation at an early age. "You'll know when you're living under Sharia Law if suddenly all your loans [and] credit cards become interest-free," Sarsour wrote. "Sounds nice, doesn't it?" These are the intellectual compromises demanded of those who would surrender to authoritarianism, and Sarsour seems eager to submit.

Most neutral observers would conclude from all this that the drawbacks of associating with Sarsour outweigh the benefits, but the logic of intersectionality forbids prudent dissociation.

As long as her activism resonated with the left, Sarsour's liberal allies were content to ignore her excesses. While delivering the keynote address to a Muslim-American conference in 2017, however, Sarsour violated this unspoken compact when she insisted it was the duty of Muslims to engage in "jihad" against President Donald Trump.

Rather than chide Sarsour for this reckless instigation, her compatriots went to the mattresses to defend it. Bizarrely, they claimed that only Sarsour understood the true Quranic meaning of the word "jihad." The word denotes only peaceful dissent, they insisted, not warfare or violent resistance. Never mind that this alleged misapprehension is apparently shared by a good portion of the Muslim world— many adopted Sarsour's line uncritically. "Right-Wing Outlets Read Violence into Sarsour's Anti-Trump 'Jihad,'" the website The Daily Beast declared. "Muslim activist Linda Sarsour's reference to 'jihad' draws conservative wrath," the *Washington Post* insisted. "The people disagreeing with [Linda Sarsour] clearly don't understand what Jihad means," Professor Marc Lamont Hill of Temple University postured.

However heavy the burden of defending Sarsour and the tarnished Women's March, the logic of intersectionality prevented the social justice left from abandoning her. The same phenomenon is observed in the movement's veneration of Assata Shakur, whose birthday the Women's March celebrated in 2017 as a day of "resistance." Shakur is perhaps better known by the name that appeared on court documents when she was convicted of the execution-style murder of a New Jersey state trooper: Joanne Chesimard. A black-power activist implicated in a variety of violent crimes and robberies, Shakur was convicted of eight felonies in 1977, including first-degree murder, before she fled the United States. She currently lives in communist Cuba, a fugitive from American justice.

Several months later, the organizers of the Women's March, Tamika Mallory and Carmen Perez, defended their organization's association with the Nation of Islam's anti-Semitic figurehead, Louis Farrakhan. "People need to understand the significant contributions that these individuals have made to Black and Brown people," Perez said of "Minister Farrakhan" and his associates. "There are no perfect leaders."[17]

Intersectional ideology unites those who would be mounting otherwise disparate and disorganized campaigns of resistance against discrimination, but it also forces its adherents to surrender discretion. Maybe Sarsour is friendly toward the most repressive aspects of patriarchal Islamism, but she hates Donald Trump and she calls herself a feminist, so she's "one of us." Sure, Shakur robbed, vandalized, incited violence, and killed a cop, but she also hates white supremacy and capitalism. She too is one of us. To abandon one is to abandon all. Intersectionality has rendered the "Sister Souljah moment" obsolete.

Flowers for America

In the spirit of Vonnegut, more and more university students are attempting to make up for the supposed inabilities of their peers by neutralizing the advantages of others. Anyone who disagrees too loudly with this enforced leveling is subject to ostracism or worse. Students of assumed "privilege" are taught that their contributions are inherently less valuable and that the fruits of their labors are never entirely their own. The power to crush fragile young psyches is attributed to challenging words and ideas.

America's young adults are eagerly enlisting in a new war against transgressing speech and conduct. This crusade has matured beyond the standards of "political correctness," a term that describes behavior that is downright quaint compared with that which aggravates today's censorious radicals. These young adults and the stultified elders who teach them intolerance are still largely confined to academic institutions and liberal opinion journals, but this self-imposed isolation won't last. Their grievances are being adapted for mass consumption.

The information age has seen the destruction of barriers that once impeded entry into elite political debates, and good riddance to them. This development has, however, proved to be a double-edged sword. There is a largely beneficial stigma associated with tuning out of politics and current events; apathy is not a virtue. But not everyone is inclined to do the homework necessary to understand and opine on politics with any insight. It takes work to know what you're talking about. Identity politics and social justice provide a convenient method by which the ill-equipped can engage in politics and be taken seriously.

From the "social awareness" of commercial brands to the latest Marvel comics superhero film; from the faces that grace American currency to "race mixing" in fantastical young adult fantasy novels; from the chauvinism of "Taco Tuesdays" to the potentially traumatic imagery evoked by the surname "Lynch," trivialities preoccupy the minds of American social justice advocates.

This isn't politics or policy. It has little to do with the direction in which society will develop. At most, this is a substitute for substantive political engagement. These and other controversies made for the social media age produce the illusion for social justice advocates that they are engaging in genuine political discourse. In fact, they're only obsessing over popular culture.

Wanting to engage in politics in an informed and sophisticated way is commendable. It should be encouraged. Unfortunately, those who once served as gatekeepers to that discourse have abdicated their responsibility to ensure that it remains erudite. In service to the dictates of social justice, the barriers to entry into political dialogue have been lowered to the point of virtual nonexistence.

This phenomenon could be dismissed as trivial had it not matured alongside the idea that victimhood not only deserves sympathy and redress but also confers virtue. The value attached to historical grievance has led to the proliferation of grievances. Everybody's got a claim to persecution, and he's submitting that claim for reimbursement.

Piety and Prejudice

Otto Warmbier was just twenty-two years old when he died. The former University of Virginia student had been held captive in North Korea for seventeen months before the regime unexpectedly released him. When American authorities received him, however, Warmbier was in a virtual coma. He was unresponsive to stimuli and showed signs of physical abuse at the hands of his captors. While in captivity, Warmbier also suffered at the hands of his countrymen back home.

The regime arrested Warmbier for allegedly stealing a North Korean propaganda poster as a souvenir—a "crime" that his roommate said never happened. For this alleged insult to the dignity of the Democratic People's Republic of Korea, Warmbier was sentenced to fifteen years of hard labor in a gulag. Meanwhile, among Western social justice enthusiasts, there was little sympathy for the young captive. Instead, upon his capture, Warmbier was mocked and attacked for having the temerity to offend the world's last Stalinist dictatorship.[18]

"It's just tough for me to have much sympathy for this guy and his crocodile tears," said former Comedy Central host Larry Wilmore. The comedian mocked Warmbier for evincing "privilege" by presuming he could commit what he sarcastically referred to as the "international crime" of poster theft. "This might be America's biggest idiot frat boy," the left-wing web-based magazine *Salon* wrote of Warmbier. *Huffington Post* contributor La Sha chided the student for the "reckless gall" he displayed in upsetting the Kim regime, behavior she attributed to his "being socialized first as a white boy, then as a white man" in America. Never mind the fact that North Korea held at least three other American citizens in captivity at the time of Warmbier's release, all of them of Korean heritage.

It didn't matter that Warmbier was being abused by a despotic regime that was using him to advance its geopolitical prospects at America's expense. For Warmbier's critics, all that mattered was their presumption that he had probably behaved with the carelessness they believed to be typical of his race and sex. In any other context, we'd call that prejudice.

Among the plotlines to which social justice advocates cling with religious conviction is that of the United States as an inherently bigoted and sexist nation. Lingering prejudice pervades virtually all its institutions. Even prominent Democrats like Hillary Clinton have advanced this notion by blaming her 2016 loss, in part, on America's misogyny. This is an article of faith shared by many of her fellow progressives.

To test this proposition, researchers devised an experiment. Two professors of educational theater were enlisted by the international business school INSEAD to memorize the behavior, mannerisms, and dialogue of both Clinton and Donald Trump in their three presidential debates. Clinton would, however, be played by a man, while a woman would portray Trump.

The results of that experiment shocked even its designers. Audience members discovered previously unknown wells of sympathy for Trump's voters because his message struck them as "more precise" when delivered by an assertive woman. By contrast, Clinton's caution and timidity were dubbed by one audience member "punchable" when

displayed by a man. It never previously occurred to these rooms full
of urban liberals that Clinton might have failed on her merits rather
than as a result of American misogyny.

A *New York University News* review of the experiment concluded
that the test had raised "as many questions about gender performance
and effects of sexism as it answered."[19] Foremost among those "questions" has to be why the social justice left's assumptions about gender
bias manifest in ways that so closely resemble bigotry.

Too often, what is obviously stereotyping to outside observers is
written off as a necessary evil by those who indulge in them. Blanket
statements and generalizations may be unfair to individuals, but they
highlight grander historical trends and are, therefore, valuable. It
doesn't seem to faze the activist class that their "greater truths" are built
on a foundation of lies.

"The Right to Be Believed"

Another belief that thrives today among advocates of social justice
is the idea that America somehow condones sexual violence. These
activists correctly note that ossified private institutions have historically shielded serial offenders in their midst from punishment. That
is a real and long-standing injustice that society is slowly recognizing
and correcting. But these activists do not stop there. They contend
that we live in a "rape culture"—a society so forgiving of violence
against women that its institutions cannot be trusted to mete out
proper justice.

Those who decry this alleged "rape culture" have a habit of
demanding that evidence-based prosecutions be subordinated to
empathy. For years, college campuses heeded this demand. There,
secret tribunals adjudicated criminal cases to achieve a result preferred
by social justice advocates, even if that made a mockery of due process.

"To every survivor of sexual assault," Hillary Clinton wrote amid her quest for the Democratic Party's presidential nomination, "You have the right to be believed."[20] Nothing should so offend an American as the idea that an accuser has "the right to be believed" because of a status conferred at birth. It is an assault on the rule of law. Wars have been fought to rid mankind of these shackles.

Clinton was not describing accusations of harassment or discrimination but felonious brutality. She was not talking about claims against public figures or deliberations in the court of public opinion but allegations that should be the exclusive province of the criminal justice system. "The right to be believed" exposes the lie that the social justice left seeks only fairness. In practice, the "right to be believed" is a notion that has led to the destruction of many innocent young male lives.

One of the most notorious beneficiaries of the "right to be believed" was Crystal Magnum, an African-American stripper who in 2006 accused a number of young white men on Duke University's lacrosse team of gang rape. The investigation into this incident was a debacle. The prosecutor, Mike Nifong, was fired, disbarred, and spent a day in prison for his unethical efforts to convict the accused despite a lack of incriminating evidence. Still, the lives of the men Magnum accused were permanently damaged. Many of the victims of that scandal have found it difficult to secure or retain employment. One was compelled to change his name. Magnum was later convicted of stabbing her boyfriend to death and sentenced to fourteen years in a North Carolina prison.

The lessons of that episode were lost on *Rolling Stone*'s reporter Sabrina Rubin Erdely. In 2014, she penned a (literally) unbelievable tale for her magazine in which she "exposed" a gang rape initiation ring within a University of Virginia fraternity. Her implausible yarn of systematic sexual assaults on women, one of whom was allegedly violated repeatedly atop a pile of broken glass, was eventually retracted in its entirety. The students accused of mass rape sued their school for overreacting to that story, which had suspended the charter of not only the fraternity in question but all fraternities on campus. Today, Erdely is disgraced, and her story cost the magazine that once employed her $1.65 million in damages. Still, these young men will find their reputations scarred, perhaps for the rest of their lives.[21]

The Duke lacrosse players and the Virginia fraternity brothers were only some of the highest profile targets of a culture of social justice. Theirs is the wrong identity—young, male, white, and born into comfortable surroundings. These innocent lives were to be sacrificed to an ideological objective. The fact that their cases had to become national scandals before their names were cleared is sobering. How many more victims of a petty, vindictive, ideological crusade don't make national headlines?

The great jurist Sir William Blackstone wrote that it is "better that ten guilty persons escape than that one innocent suffer."[22] Not everyone agrees. "If I was running [a college], I might say, 'Well, you know even if there's a 20 to 30 percent chance that it happened, I would want to remove this individual,'" Governor Jared Polis, a Democrat from Colorado, averred. "If there's ten people who have been accused, and under a reasonable likelihood standard maybe one or two did it, it seems better to get rid of all ten people."[23]

For classes of unfortunate birth, guilt is presumed. They call this progress.

The "Job Interview"

In the autumn of 2018, the confirmation process for the Supreme Court nominee Brett Kavanaugh, which had almost reached its predictable if contentious conclusion, suddenly exploded in a storm of social justice activism when Kavanaugh was accused of having committed sexual assault at the age of seventeen. The accusation itself was the beginning and end of the evidence against him, but the arbiters of political discourse seized the opportunity to explore their own experiences and let their own preconceptions lead the way.

Along the way, something snapped in the national psyche, and the antisocial dogmas that underlie ideological social justice were laid bare—an affinity for racial hierarchies and race-based preferences, antipathy to due process and the presumption of innocence, reduction of individuals to nondescript representatives of their taxonomic class. Prominent reporters, editors, political professionals, and celebrities displayed with absolute self-confidence what can only be described as bigotry.

Testifying before the Senate, Kavanaugh defended himself against accusations that had progressed from the unsupported to the absurd. Although his obviously unfeigned indignation persuaded many, his enemies portrayed the understandable passion of a falsely accused man as the unsavory behavior typical of his race and sex. "It's not just that white men are allowed to be angry and women are not; it's that white men's anger can be used to their benefit," the columnist Rebecca Traister wrote.

Judge Kavanaugh, whose thirty-year career was unspotted by even a hint of impropriety, was now accused of gang rape, but Maureen Dowd of the *New York Times* branded him as one of the "entitled white men acting like the new minority, howling about things that are being taken away from them, aggrieved at anything that diminishes them or saps their power." The *Times'* news editors headlined the report of his testimony, "Kavanaugh Borrows from Trump's Playbook on White Male Anger."

Matthew Dowd of ABC News urged his fellow "white male Christians" to "give up our seats at the table." Senator Mazie Hirono passionately concurred. "Just shut up and step up," she roared in the direction of "the men in this country."

The economist Paul Krugman said Kavanaugh's performance was not about the existential threat that being found "guilty" of sexual assault in a mock courtroom would pose to the judge and his family but "the rage of white men" and the "threat to their privileged position." The *Boston Globe*'s Renee Graham compared Kavanaugh's "white male superiority complex" to the pathology that led the infamous Nathan Leopold and Richard Loeb to kidnap and murder a fourteen-year-old boy for fun. Christine Fair of the Georgetown University faculty insisted that Kavanaugh and those "entitled white men" who look like him deserve "miserable deaths" involving posthumous castration.

The former tennis star Martina Navratilova insisted that Kavanaugh represents "the epitome of White Male Privilege," while the actress Margaret Judson declared that "white male privilege was palpable" in the room as the judge attested to his innocence. The novelist Stephen King wrote that Kavanaugh's picture should accompany the dictionary definition for "white male entitlement."

Those who defended Kavanaugh from the unsubstantiated claims against him were not spared this repulsive treatment. When Donald Trump said the ordeal to which Kavanaugh had been subjected had been traumatic, John Harwood corrected him in the *New York Times*: "[M]ore accurately," he wrote, the judge's behavior was indicative of "trauma for white men unaccustomed to trauma." Senator Lindsey Graham's heated condemnation of his colleagues' conduct was simply an attempt to beat back the challenge from feminists and people of color "demanding a seat at the table." To the columnist Alexis Grenell, Senator Susan Collins's forty-three-minute speech elaborating on the thinness of the claims against Kavanaugh was the act of a "gender traitor." Collins and the "white women" like her were acting to "uphold a system that values only their whiteness."

The critical mass of influencers who engaged in these public displays of chauvinism could be confident that their prejudices were shared by the members of their professional class. There would be no repercussions for their transgression against not only fairness but basic good taste. They had internalized social justice's nostrums, convincing themselves that judiciousness was found not in a dispassionate evaluation of the evidence before them but in a subjective assessment of race, sex, and collective power dynamics.

This was no longer about Brett Kavanaugh. It wasn't even about sexual assault. It was about vengeance.

The Identitarian Right

Mark Lilla, an outspoken liberal critic of the Identitarian left, has observed that identity politics has destroyed the art of argumentation. "Classroom conversations that once might have begun *I think A, and here is my argument*, now take the form, *Speaking as an X, I am offended that you claim B*," he writes.[24]

Lilla has since broadened his critique of Identitarianism to include much of society outside the classroom. What began as a humbling and enlightening quest for racial and cultural awareness has become a competition among victimized classes to determine who is the most oppressed and to capitalize on that status. Thus, Lilla observes, the left has established that it is impossible to truly understand the experience of anyone with discrete racial, cultural, biological, or sexual traits. And if we cannot understand others' experiences, we cannot truly empathize with them. And empathy is the acknowledgment of shared human traits and conditions. It's all that stands between us and sociopathy.

The right has long known that this kind of divisive identity politics is ugly, anti-intellectual, and deleterious to national comity. And then, in 2016, it forgot.

In many ways, Donald Trump beat the social justice left at its own game. Trump inculcated in his supporters a sense of grievance that was philosophically alien to conservatism, convincing his most enthusiastic voters that forces greater than they were responsible for their lot in life. Their identity—be it white, conservative, Christian, or whatever you like—was not just looked down upon by elites in positions of power, but also discriminated against.

By appealing to Identitarianism to win the Republican presidential nomination, Trump drove an eighteen-wheeler through the standards that had governed political discourse on the right. Out of this breach cascaded a familiar horde that went by a new name: the "alt-right."

The alt-right was not a conservative movement. Its members were not shy about condemning conservatism as a philosophy that had failed to "conserve" much of anything—at least, the idealized, bygone America that they thought was worthy of conservation. Its members were nakedly hostile toward non-white immigrant groups, and its leaders did little to tamp these base sentiments down. The alt-right rejected the idea of limited government, and some of its admirers mocked reverence for the Constitution as mere idol worship.[25] The alt-right is hostile toward an extroverted foreign policy, preferring instead to retrench behind the walls of Fortress America. It has no use for what it sees as the pompous religiosity, false moralizing, and self-defeating decorum of social conservatism.

Some on the right might contend that this movement was a natural response to a political vacuum. Writing in February 2015, the conservative columnist Ramesh Ponnuru observed that the sprawling field of Republican presidential candidates had no use for immigration hawks, despite the unpopularity of permissive immigration regimes among the party's grassroots voters.[26] The Federalist's Ben Domenech noted that a populist counter-reaction to the false consensus on immigration policy Ponnuru identified should have been anticipated: "If a large...portion of the country wants existing bipartisan immigration laws to be enforced, and one party tells them 'Yes,' but means 'No,' and the other party tells them, 'No' but means 'You're a racist,' then it's only a matter of time before some disruptor is going to emerge to call them out for their game."[27] Trump's ascension wasn't predicated on Identitarianism; it was a legitimate response to a blind spot almost universally shared by the political class in Washington. To those who longed for it, though, Trump's rise presented an opportunity to legitimize white identity politics.

The alt-right is a funhouse-mirror reflection of Identitarian movements on the left. White nationalism is perhaps the primordial form of identity politics in America, and its program is social justice for white people. Its members revel in self-pity. They are hypersensitive to perceived slights against their race or their culture. They are convinced that society has erected insurmountable obstacles in their paths to success because of their heritage. They seek only fairness, they contend, just as their progressive counterparts do.

There is a case to be made that Trump's attack on liberal speech- and thought-policing was a necessary antidote to the left's excesses. That may be the kind of resentment politics that satisfies many conservatives, but it is still resentment.

Some conservatives will see these admonitions as just more political correctness—"virtue signaling" for the benefit of an effete coastal audience. Maybe they don't agree with Trump on everything, and maybe they find his willingness to tolerate the intolerable off-putting. Yet for many on the right, he is the avatar of an overdue backlash against a dominant cultural ethos that resents them and their values.

That is undoubtedly a sincere belief, but it also concedes that Trump contributed to precisely the same Balkanization of the American electorate that the right resented when the left was doing the Balkanizing. Conservatives cannot reject the identity politics practiced by their adversaries while simultaneously adopting a style of it for themselves. Only the most cynical would knowingly embrace such hypocrisy.

How Republics Fail

Although they may be indistinguishable to outsiders, warring tribes in close geographic proximity are consumed with their relatively modest distinctions. Identitarians on the left and the right are those undifferentiated neighboring tribes, and they are coming to blows. This may not be a fleeting bout of national hysteria either. Intellectual foundations are being laid to legitimize political violence.

College administrators and professors advocate forcible censorship on the grounds that certain types of speech are just not productive. The editors of college newspapers from the *Harvard Crimson* to the Georgetown *Hoya* to the *Oberlin Review* publish works with no loftier objective than validating their student body's worst impulses. Ostensibly responsible political actors whitewash brutality as a legitimate response to the trauma associated with distressing speech.

It is increasingly common to hear social justice activists equate discomfiting or objectionable speech with acts of violence, and not in a metaphorical sense. Those activists are just as liable to view reactionary activities—including public disturbances, property destruction, and even the physical harassment of their opponents—as alternative forms of expression. Since they conflate offensive speech and violence, a violent response to speech isn't just reasonable; it's necessary. It's practically self-defense.

From the massacre of editors and cartoonists at the offices of the satirical French magazine *Charlie Hebdo* to the attempted slaughter of provocative cartoonists in Garland, Texas, a disturbing number of self-described liberals—ranging from cable television hosts to figures as prominent as the secretary of state—thought these acts were at least understandable, if not entirely warranted.

From the darkest corners of the alt-right's online haunts to the ivy-covered halls of academia, language that dehumanizes political adversaries, depicting them as one-dimensional creatures of singularly malevolent intent, is rampant. It is inevitable that that kind of incitement will yield real violence.

Media outlets devoted extensive coverage to acts of violence committed by Trump supporters against anti-Trump demonstrators in 2016. Perhaps the most under-covered story of that election year, though, was the organized violence targeting Trump supporters. In city after city, gangs took revenge upon persons attending pro-Trump events. The attacks by both sides portended a grim future typified by street violence. Even after Trump's inauguration, the fighting between Identitarian factions on the right and the left did not abate. Indeed, it only grew worse.

What Went Wrong?

The miracle of America is that its egalitarian spirit and capitalist value system have produced the most powerful engine of social and economic equality humanity has ever witnessed. Progress toward true equality in America is a project that will, in all likelihood, never be complete. Striving toward that goal is noble even if the ideal is unattainable. Furthermore, the study of cultural and individual distinctions and social inequities is perfectly legitimate. But from a healthy awareness of identity and the desire for self-actualization a strain of crippling self-pity has emerged. Identitarian activists have made paralyzing victimization a virtue.

The social justice movement and its ill effects didn't materialize overnight. The United States is, in a way, the culmination of the enlightened principle which states that the legitimately oppressed are entitled to redress. That was a relatively novel innovation in the late eighteenth century. It was a product of ideals enshrined in America's founding documents, which were themselves the paradigmatic revolution brought about by Enlightenment thinkers like Immanuel Kant, John Locke, and David Hume. In that sense, the modern social justice movement is not an aberration but an extension of America's magnanimity. That does not, however, render this movement's excesses any less dangerous.

Identitarianism and social justice can be understood only through the lens of history. These related ideologies were shaped and, in many ways, bastardized by generations who sought to remake the honorable American ethos in their own image. Distinguishing the conventionally Anglo-American conception of justice from the bitter vendettas that masquerade as righteousness and equality could not be more urgent. The perversions that today's modern activist class calls social justice have roots in centuries of Identitarian thought in America. We must evaluate that history critically if real egalitarian virtue is to be saved from association with and corruption by this thing that calls itself justice.

CHAPTER 2

A Nation or a People?

I dentity politics in America is not new, and it has always conflicted with the founding ideals of the republic. The contradictory notions of egalitarianism and slavery were baked into America's founding documents. Human nature is such that identity will always play a role in the conduct of political affairs.

In some ways, the pursuit of social justice is perfectly compatible with the principles of the American founding. The way in which social justice has been perverted to mean censorship, thought-policing, and inequality in the name of social leveling is a scandal, but it is a scandal that was centuries in the making. Social justice in theory is markedly distinct from social justice as practiced by its modern devotees.

The history of social justice and Identitarianism in the United States is a fascinating and often sad story of unscrupulous operators and missed opportunities. To avoid repeating the mistakes of the past, we must learn from them.

The Gospel Truth

Spend any time in the vicinity of a committed social justice activist and you are bound to walk away with the impression that his is an almost religious commitment. That religiosity isn't a figment of your imagination. It's a vestige of the time in which social justice was an entirely theologicial concept.

Amid the increasing nationalistic fervor of nineteenth-century Europe, as revolutionary reunification movements gained steam in the Italian peninsula, the conservative Papal States and the Catholic Church that governed them committed to a philosophical revival. Catholic scholars looked to the teachings of St. Thomas Aquinas for an alternative to the liberal ideals espoused by Enlightenment thinkers. After all, the Catholic experience with the Enlightenment was not the British experience. The Church passed through the fires of the French Revolution; its priests were slaughtered and its sanctuaries defiled with idols dedicated to self-worship. The Church and its adherents had every reason to fear what men driven by the cult of "pure reason" were capable of reasoning themselves into.

Among the Church's more prominent theorists at the time was the Jesuit philosopher Luigi Taparelli d'Azeglio. "Taparelli's aim," writes Thomas Patrick Burke, "...was to develop a conservative and specifically Catholic theory of society that would be an alternative to the liberal and laissez-faire theories of [John] Locke and Adam Smith."[1] Locke, Smith, and their contemporaries advanced ideas that Taparelli viewed as products of the Protestant Reformation. For him, formulating an alternative to their vision of social organization wasn't just a political imperative but an ethical one as well. Smith's "invisible hand" was, to Taparelli, an abomination. Sound morals and communitarianism were the font from which social goods spring, not individualism and naked self-interest.

To counter the challenge of Protestant Enlightenment thinkers, Taparelli and his collaborators settled on an argument based on paternal authority, which is conferred by God and God alone, and an acknowledgment that men are inherently *unequal*—not as a species, but as individuals. The notion that political power is transferred from one man to another by virtue of a piece of parchment, Taparelli argued, was not only a novel idea but an unnatural one. The right to rule a society is conferred by divinity upon whoever brings order to that society.

In 1843, Taparelli became the first to use the phrase "social justice" ("giustizia sociale") in a way that is rudimentarily consistent with its modern definition. His philosophical approach to developing a theory of social justice was informed by the revolutionary movements of the late eighteenth century and their secular character. He saw the Lockean vision of the rights of man and property being secured only through eternal conflict with one's neighbors as tyranny by another name, which is why a collection of his essays on the subject was aptly titled *Tyrannous Liberty.*[2]

"[S]ociety is in a perpetual antagonism where each one offers the minimum in order to obtain the maximum," Taparelli wrote. "[S]ociety is a war of all against all: war among the producers, war of the producers against the buyers, war of one nation against another in order to absorb its wealth by means of customs duties." As such, governments (including but not limited to the Catholic Church) were obliged to insert themselves into private affairs to secure the revenue that was their lifeblood. To argue otherwise is to close one's eyes to reality.

Taparelli's case for social justice was not explicitly economic—indeed, he rejected the contention that charity should be the province of the public sector alone—but we can see the outlines of a collectivist theory of social organization in his work. "Taparelli did not seek to overthrow classical economic thought but rather to supplement its naturalism with a more coherent anthropology," writes Thomas Behr. "He sought to 'baptize' economic science as he found it and return it to its place as a sub-discipline of ethics and politics, without diminishing its value as a positive science of the production, consumption, and distribution of wealth."³ Taparelli argued that governing was a moral enterprise. All affairs of state—the meting out of justice, the administration of an economy, and the conduct of the art of state-craft—must be subordinated to the demands of ethics.

Taparelli's teachings were reflected in the works of other influential Catholics, notably the Jesuit philosopher Matteo Liberatore, who was instrumental in drafting Pope Leo XIII's seminal 1891 encyclical, *Rerum novarum*. This address on the "rights and duties of capital and labor" shaped the thinking of social justice advocates over the course of the following century, establishing the notion that social justice was a moral theory of societal and economic development. This idea will be discussed further in the chapters that follow.

Our Glorious Republic

These nineteenth-century theories of social justice sound familiar to us, but something is missing—the identity politics that animates today's activists. Identity politics is bound up in the history of the American republic. Early nativist movements and the institution of slavery ensured that there was no period in which the United States was free from identity's distorting influence on ideology. And yet, that's not how citizens of the early republic would have seen it. They might have contended, with reason, that their political affiliations were organized around shared principles.

Caitlin Fitz demonstrates in her book *Our Sister Republics: The United States in the Age of American Revolutions* that the early nineteenth century was typified by gauzy idealism and the heady debate over whether anticolonial revolutionary republicanism should be exported elsewhere in the Western hemisphere. There were ethnic and religious tensions in the early United States, but they failed to dominate the American imagination in the way they soon would.

Fitz observes that such animosity as there was in the nation's press toward Latin American revolutionaries was less a matter of race than of religion. The Catholic Church of the early nineteenth century was hostile toward the Lockean ideals on which the American Constitution was based, and the feeling was mutual.

Newspaper editors in Louisiana, Baltimore, and New York, for example, hoped that revolutionary movements would throw off Spanish chains, but they were nevertheless skeptical that the priesthood would allow it. "The clergy of Spanish America, whose influence is every thing, cannot be friendly to equal rights," wrote the St. Louis *Gazette's* editors about the insurrection in Venezuela that led to independence in 1811.[4]

This sentiment was, however, more or less limited to the Federalist faction in early America. These believers in centralized authority argued that the American Revolution was a self-contained phenomenon. As the French Revolution's bloody descent into despotism confirmed, the American Revolution could not be duplicated, much less exported. Jeffersonian Republicans, idealists that they were, disagreed. Though they were no doubt as cynical about what they perceived to be the backwardness of Iberian Catholicism, they did not believe that the Jacobite plague that had consumed France would find new hosts on the American continent.

Fitz's study of the Fourth of July toasts of the period, as recorded in local newspaper accounts and the documents of planning committees, reveals that by 1812 more Americans had begun to see Latin American revolutionaries as brothers in arms. Of course, as the persistence of human slavery in the United States demonstrates, equality in this period is a relative notion. But for many in the early republic, the South Americans' revolt against the Spanish crown was itself evidence of their enlightenment.

Agents of revolution who came to the United States from South America seeking support were surprised to find that many Americans did not regard them as white, even though they perceived themselves to be and were treated as whites at home. Those diplomats who left behind records of their American sojourns were, however, still able to navigate elite society. By espousing the ideals of revolutionary republicanism and anti-colonialism, they successfully advocated their interests and won the support of wealthy benefactors and policymakers alike.

The wealth of some of these emissaries surely helped. Describing the mission to America of Antônio Gonçalves da Cruz, a "swarthy" Portuguese-speaker from Pernambuco, Fitz cites the Brazilian adage "o dinheiro embranquece"—money whitens. "If Cruz told anyone about his African ancestry, they kept quiet, leaving the nation's adoring white legions to welcome Cruz into their ports and homes without so much as a shrug."[5]

Early America's republican egalitarianism was a function of its relative isolation. Before 1820, immigration was modest and records were sparse; most U.S. population growth up to that point was the result of domestic births. By 1830, however, federal records keepers began accumulating passenger ship logs, which allowed a more accurate accounting of immigration. From 1820 to 1845, between ten thousand and one hundred thousand immigrants arrived in the United States annually. In the 1830 census, two hundred thousand Americans described themselves as foreign-born. A decade later, on the eve of the potato blight that would send an unprecedented wave of Catholic immigrants across the ocean from Ireland, the number had surged to eight hundred thousand. By 1850, nearly 10 percent of the American population had been born on foreign soil. All the while, an early American Identitarianism was taking shape: nativism.[6]

The Origins of Identity

They had secret rituals and rites of passage. They took oaths of loyalty and swore to their racial purity. They formed small clubs dedicated to anti-Catholicism and the preservation of America's Anglo-Protestant identity. And if you asked them about any of this, most were obliged to reply, "I know nothing."

In the mid-1820s, "Know-Nothing" political chapters had begun claiming elected offices by rallying voters against the non-Protestant immigrant groups that were dominant in their particular regions. As the Whig Party began to crumble under the weight of its internal differences in the 1850s, most of which orbited around the issue of slavery, Know-Nothing organizations filled the void. They avoided the slavery trap by focusing their energies on immigration. They favored draconian anti-Catholic policies, including mandatory Protestant education in schools, a twenty-one-year naturalization period for all immigrants, and barring practicing Catholics from public office. Despite all this, or perhaps because of it, the nativists experienced some remarkable successes over a short period.

While American nativist sentiments have evolved since the mid-nineteenth century, the thematic notes struck by the Know-Nothing movement's leaders ring familiar today. The views of Thomas Whitney, the son of a New York City tradesman and the author of the Know-Nothing mission statement "A Defense of the American Policy," would be familiar to those who are drawn to the alt-right today. People are "entitled to such privileges, social and political, as they are capable of employing rationally," he insisted.[7] Rationality was presumed to be the province of white Protestants.

Whitney and his followers steeped themselves not only in nationalism and religious chauvinism but also in their own working-class identity. Immigration, they believed, was a boon to elites alone, robbing the native-born of work. Of course, that depends on how you define elite. Irish immigrants of the period were often pitted against African-American freedmen in the North, as both struggled to secure the lowest-paying, most undesirable jobs. The Irish would be employed to perform the most menial of tasks—often by those who could hardly be called elite—because they would work for less than the average black laborer. When the Irish bucked their tasks or demanded higher wages, African-Americans would be brought in as strikebreakers—that is, where they were paid any wage whatever.

Meanwhile, in Europe, the series of crop failures that sent scores of Catholics from Ireland and mainland Europe across the Atlantic were also fueling political unrest. By 1848, the increasing appeal of popular liberalism, nationalism, and antipathy toward the old aristocratic structures that still dominated Europe gave rise to a year of popular revolutions. Though he was inclined to look more favorably upon liberalism and democracy than his predecessors—and certainly more than neo-Thomists like Taparelli—Pope Pius IX was not inclined to support the kind of anti-monarchist rabble that made up the bulk of the 1848 revolutionaries.

The Pope's refusal to support an Italian nationalist war of liberation against the Catholic Habsburg Empire and his mistrust of the constitutional revolutions of 1848 served as a pretext for American nativists to claim that Catholic immigration to the United States was the product of a vast papist plot. This flimsy premise provided Know-Nothings, now organized under the banner of the Native American Party, with a superficially valid political grievance. They began to recruit even non-nativist Protestants to the cause. The excuse of 1848 helped to legitimize American nativists' otherwise unsavory antipathy toward Irish and German Catholic immigrants.

The nativist fever began to break when the issue the Know-Nothings tried so hard to avoid became unavoidable. The Compromise of 1850 allowed select territories vying for statehood to resolve the slavery question on their own. That compromise made it easier for Southern slave owners to retrieve their "property," fueling the Dred Scott case— a national scandal that dominated American headlines off and on for years. Four years later, the idea that slavery should be a matter for "popular sovereignty" to resolve led to the outbreak of a proto-civil war in Kansas. In October 1859, John Brown led a raid on the federal arsenal at Harpers Ferry, which foreshadowed the cataclysmic clash of arms to come.

By 1860, the issue of slavery had proved more urgent than unregulated immigration. As the Republican Party gathered under the "Wigwam" in Chicago to nominate Abraham Lincoln for the presidency, the political irrelevance of the once formidable American Party, as the Know-Nothings had been renamed, became obvious.

At the convention, Carl Christian Schurz—a refugee from Prussian militarism, a member of the Republican platform committee, and a future U.S. senator and secretary of the interior—rose in defense of immigrants. Schurz endorsed a resolution protecting the rights of "emigrants from foreign lands" and rejecting changes to naturalization laws. Pointedly referring to their status as "citizens," Schurz declared that the party must "be washed clean of the taint of Know-Nothingism."[8] Though they had just rejected a resolution endorsing the extension of voting rights to free black Americans, the Republicans in attendance eagerly approved this measure.

Though it was short-lived, the American Party enjoyed some remarkable triumphs in a relatively short period. Practitioners of Identitarian social justice being nothing if not opportunistic, the political success of nativist organizations, strangely enough, set the stage for an Identitarian backlash.

The Urban Machine

The art of strategically molding unrefined potential voters into disciplined blocs organized around class or racial identity was perfected by the earliest urban political machines. The most notable and most effective of these was New York City's Tammany Hall.

In its earliest days, Tammany was a nativist organization. Membership was restricted to "native-born patriots," and its mission was to preserve the political privileges enjoyed by the city's Anglo-Protestant establishment. Tammany's true calling arrived in the form of a mob of Irish protesters.

In April 1817, angered by the organization's efforts to uphold a code of conduct that kept Catholics out of public office, what the New York *Evening Standard* called "a boat of adopted citizens"—two hundred or so—invaded a meeting of Tammany's general committee before it had even convened. A bitter war of words ensued between Tammany loyalists and the Irish upstarts, who had quite effectively demonstrated their organizational skills and political potency. Fists started flying, along with whatever furniture that wasn't nailed down.[9]

Though egos and flesh were bruised, the melee made it clear who would soon become the real power brokers in New York City. "[T]he Irish had made their point," writes Terry Golway. "They had left behind a country where they were routinely denied access to power. They were not about to let that happen again."[10]

When immigration made Irish Catholics the city's largest voting bloc, Tammany shifted gears, ostensibly dedicating itself to the enfranchisement of Irish voters. In 1854, just as American nativism was on the cusp of decline, the Tammany-Catholic alliance neared the zenith of its power when it managed to elect former congressman Fernando Wood mayor. The campaign was nakedly Identitarian. Wood and his allies pandered remorselessly to Irish voters, often by demonizing New York City's free blacks and appealing to Irish prejudices against their primary source of competition for work. Wood tacitly aligned himself with some of New York's worst Irish gangs of the period, to say nothing of the Municipal Police, who amounted to little more than an organized crime syndicate themselves.

Wood's election was a jarring demonstration of the political power wielded by urban political machines aligned with the immigrant masses. It was such a shock, in fact, that the Republicans in control of the legislature in Albany went to work shortening Wood's term in office and establishing a competing police force that would enjoy supremacy over the one loyal to the city's mayor.

Despite the controversy, Tammany had demonstrated that the future of urban politics lay in the forgotten ethnic ghettos. By organizing, registering, and pandering to ethnic interests—the Irish in New York, the Germans in St. Louis, the Polish in Chicago—the machines of the mid-nineteenth and early twentieth centuries came to dominate urban politics.

Samuel Johnson is said to have called patriotism the last refuge of a scoundrel. There was an old Tammany saying that Johnson had "underestimated the possibilities of compassion." It was in the name of compassion and Catholic doctrine, to which Tammany's new constituents were already amenable, that Identitarian social justice as we know it today was first practiced.

Payback for the Planter Class

In the eyes of some of its advocates, social justice is a way of addressing grievances that can't be adjudicated by a legal system that is blind, by design, to historical injustices suffered by groups. A system that ignores the intangible factors of historical and institutional discrimination, they say, does not deliver justice. In the case of present-day America, this is fatuous nonsense.

The United States is not a broken society in which the justice system has become an instrument of a vindictive, unrepresentative government. Any assertion to the contrary is a fairy tale invented by activists looking to justify their radical program as a moral imperative. But there are occasions in history when a state's justice system is incapable of bringing about restitution and reconciliation, usually following massive social upheaval. That is when a nation must appeal to restorative or transitional justice.

After a civil war or when institutional abuses have been wrought by a repressive government, a nation must occasionally abandon the Anglo-American model of depoliticized justice to reestablish social cohesion. Pádraig McAuliffe has studied the many forms that justice may take, including sectional, non-state, or even extrajudicial institutions established to address extraordinary circumstances. "[T]raditional justice mechanisms present a 'clash of two goods,'" he writes. "Respect for local customs and practices, on the one hand, and the goals of sustainable, rights-based, non-discriminatory state-building on the other."[11] In other words, a post-conflict society is occasionally obliged to mete out retribution that would be gravely unjust in any other context. In the early years after the Civil War, the American South was just such a society. Near the end of the war, the country engaged in fractious debate over how conciliatory the victorious North should be and what kind of justice the vanquished rebels deserved.

Abraham Lincoln's view, shared by many in the North, was that it was in the best interests of the country to reunite with the South on generous terms, though his Radical Republican critics bitterly disagreed. James Russell Lowell, the editor of the *Atlantic Monthly*, was particularly scornful of those who believed that the rebellious states deserved special treatment. Those who favored reconciliation, he believed, fell into three groups, none of which he held in much esteem: those who sympathized with slavery outright, those who hoped to recouple "slavery and a party calling itself Democratic," and, largest among these factions, those "who seem to confuse their minds with some fancied distinction between civil and foreign war."[12]

"The public mind should be made up as to what are the essential conditions of real and lasting peace, before it is subjected to the sentimental delusions of the inevitable era of good feelings in which the stronger brother is so apt to play the part of Esau," Lowell wrote. His argument, though a veiled one, was for retribution against the planter classes lest they ever restore the repressive conditions that once made their lives so comfortable.

Radical Republicans like Thaddeus Stevens, Ben Wade, and Charles Sumner were bolder still in their recommendations. "Clemency has its limitations," Sumner wrote. "And when it transcends these, it ceases to be a virtue and only has a mischievous indulgence." He argued not for frenzied vengeance but proportionality, as he saw it. "Be just before you are generous," he counseled. To sleepwalk into another endless cycle of "concession and compromise, which from the beginning of our history has been a constant peril," would be to regress to the dynamic that typified North-South relations before the war. "In trusting them, we give them political power, including the license to oppress loyal persons, whether white or black."[13]

The essayist Edwin Percy Whipple joined in heaping condemnation upon those, including Lincoln, who, having secured so costly a victory, sought to reconstitute Southern governments quickly to shield their elites from the wrath of Radical Republicanism: "We are therefore expected to act like the savage, who after thrashing his Fetich for disappointing his prayers, falls down again and worships it."[14]

In making a compelling and complex argument for extending
universal suffrage to all the nation's four million blacks, Whipple
abandoned the abolitionist tactic of seeking to persuade Northern
whites by appealing to their self-interest. This was a tactic that even
righteous anti-slavery crusaders like Fredrick Douglass eventually
adopted, though he did not always favor moderation over the moral
force of his convictions. In his oration on July 4, 1852, for example,
Douglass declared that those arguing against black humanity primarily deserved "blasting reproach, withering sarcasm, and stern rebuke,"
though he conceded that this satisfying style of argument didn't do
much to persuade the opposition.

By the end of the Civil War, Radical Republicans, exemplified by
Whipple, had shed any doubt that the vengence they intended to mete
out was of a righteous sort:

> The white inhabitants who occupy [the South's] old geo-
> graphical limits are defeated Rebels. They are all born again
> into citizens by Federal fiat; they are "pardoned" into voters;
> they derive their rights, not from their old charters, but from
> an act of amnesty.

> Having converted the loyal blacks from slaves into the con-
> dition of citizens of the United States, there can be no reason
> or justice or policy in allowing them to be made, in localities
> recently Rebel, the subjects of whites who have but just
> purged themselves from the guilt of treason.

> If negro suffrage is not granted in the election of members
> to the present conventions, the power will pass permanently
> into the hands of the whites, and the only opportunity for a
> peaceful settlement of the question will be lost. At the very

time when, abstractly, no party has legal rights, and only one party has claims, we propose to deliberately sacrifice the party that has claims to the party which will soon acquire legal rights to oppress the claimants. For disguise it as we may, the United States government really holds and exercises the power which gives vitality to the preliminaries of reconstruction, and it is therefore responsible for all evils in the future which shall spring from its neglect or injustice in the present.[15]

And those evils did spring, but not at first.

The postwar constitutions adopted by the Southern states and the actions of the federal government eventually allowed for the passage of pioneering civil rights legislation, the establishment of public school systems for former slaves, and the enfranchisement of millions of black voters. By some estimates, two thousand Americans of African descent served in elected office between the surrender at Appomattox Courthouse and the collapse of the Reconstruction in 1877.

In Virginia, the debate over how to fund prewar debts held by Northern banks spawned the birth of a political party dedicated to its renegotiation and readjustment. Having set out "to break the power of wealth and established privilege" of the land-owning antebellum elite, the "re-adjusters" briefly won a legislative majority and the governor's mansion. Led by former Confederate brass, this party was hardly opposed to white supremacy, but they also favored laws that would cap hours worked, place restrictions on child labor, fund public education, ensure fair ballot counting, and provide government aid for the black population, and they fielded African-American candidates for office.[16]

But what began as an experiment in transitional justice fast dissolved into corruption and violence, well before the federal government simply washed its hands of the thing. Andrew Johnson, a Union

Democrat, quickly abandoned the notion that the South's white landed class deserved retribution, and he soon allowed the antebellum political order to reassert itself. Johnson and the Republican-controlled Congress did battle over the extent to which the planter class should be checked and the rights of black Americans preserved. In the end, though Johnson's vetoes of retributive legislation were occasionally overridden and his efforts to subvert anti-racist federal initiatives resulted in his impeachment and political impotence, reactionary forces won the day.

Socialist Justice

It's one of the underappreciated ironies of American history that the novel that gave its name to an era of unprecedented wealth and excess, Mark Twain's and Charles Dudley Warner's *The Gilded Age*, was published just as the country sank into a crippling depression in 1873. The hardship that followed occurred at a time of heightened social consciousness in the United States. The boom-and-bust economic cycles caused by mid-nineteenth-century populist antipathy toward central banking soon gave way to the Progressive Era and the industrial and financial reforms that accompanied it. It was during this period that Identitarian social justice began to develop an economic program and to see the state as the chief instrument for administering reparative justice.

The Progressive Era was a time of significant public sector activity. Utility commissions sought to impose uniformity on rail and streetcar fares. The management of municipal gas and water supplies was taken out of the hands of corrupt political machines and handed over to experts. New regulations mandated quality standards for food manufacturers. Health and safety guidelines were established for previously unregulated small factories, occasionally following unspeakable tragedies like the Triangle Shirtwaist Factory fire. This was also a time in which traditions of racial discrimination were codified into law. The imposition of hardship on rural Southern blacks resulted in an exodus northward, mostly into the cities, which would have profound consequences for the generation of urban reformers who came of age in the 1910s and came to power in the 1920s and '30s.

Meanwhile, a great experiment in the reversal of social fortunes was ongoing in the nascent Union of Soviet Socialist Republics. The Soviet Union frequently pioneered misguided and ultimately counterproductive attempts to achieve retributive justice consistent with the Bolsheviks' central operating theory: namely, that the owners of capital represented an oppressive class and were due their comeuppance. Despite their equalitarian rhetoric, the Soviets had their own problems with identity politics, to say nothing of ethnic and religious discrimination. It was the USSR that first experimented with ethnic discrimination in service to the goals of affirmative action by robbing ethnic Russians, who governed the empire's territories in the Tsarist period like viceroys, of their favor.

When the Bolshevik Party came to power, Vladimir Lenin inherited a vast Russian empire. Convinced that Russia was plagued by the ethnic chauvinism that so often accompanies great power and that tribal sentiments are inimical to an extroverted socialist state, he decided that "Russian chauvinism" had to go. To achieve this, the young Soviet Union adopted a policy of embracing, albeit tentatively, local nationalism. Only ethnic Russians would be denied nationalism as a source of pride and social cohesion. Ultimately, the Soviets believed, nationalism would be undone by these Potemkin ethnostates. Semi-autonomous zones of local control would buy Moscow time to dissolve the people's backward attachments to nationhood and replace that lost nationalist fervor with class consciousness. In sum, the Soviet Union discriminated against the majority ethnic group while conferring advantages on previously marginalized minorities. It did not go well.

This policy made a substantial number of ethnic Russians, now subjected to discrimination by their new state, resentful. The idea that the Soviets could inculcate in their citizens a self-sacrificing social consciousness that would allow them stoically to endure this kind of soft oppression was a profound misreading of human nature. Joseph Stalin went out of his way to undermine the Soviet system's embrace of what he contemptuously referred to as a "concession." He called it "positive affirmative action of the bourgeoisie," invoking Lenin's attack on the ethnic discrimination that once favored ethnic Russians in the Tsarist period as a feature of capitalist corruption. "Positive action on behalf of one nationality implies negative action toward others," the historian Terry Martin writes. "In the Soviet case, where all non-Russians were to be favored, Russians alone bore the brunt of positive discrimination."[17]

"Such policies are common internationally and go by various names: compensatory discrimination, preferential policies, positive action, affirmative discrimination," Martin continues. "They often accompany de-colonialization."[18] In fact, they are a feature of the kind of transitional and reparative justice that complements extrajudicial reconciliation efforts. The Bolsheviks believed that their movement—indeed, the cause of international socialism itself—was an effort to achieve justice for those who were denied it by the corrupt institutions that governed them. Only the socialist program could deliver true justice for the subjugated and abused working class, they believed. But the Soviets were not colorblind. Providing the Russian empire's far-flung peoples a national identity, even at the expense of Russian sovereignty, also served a utilitarian purpose by making the Soviet government feel less remote and giving it an indigenous face. "Indigenization" was not to last.

A combination of Soviet xenophobia and the unique incompetence of the apparatchiks who benefited from affirmative action in the republics soon provoked a backlash. By the mid-1930s, indigenization gave way to its mirror image: Russification. The kind of "ethnic particularization" that typified the socialist republics and autonomous zones in the USSR before 1935 gave way to the concept of "enemy nations." No fewer than nine major Soviet nationalities (Finns, Baltic peoples, Koreans and Chinese, Poles and Germans, Kurds, Persians, and Tartars) were subject to forced migrations and ethnic cleansing. Local languages were suppressed and non-Russian speakers were forced to adopt a Cyrillic script. Local nationalism suddenly represented a greater threat to the Soviet project than Russian chauvinism.

A mentality in Moscow that saw distinct individuals as members of a cohesive hive encouraged the psychology that facilitated these crimes. To illustrate this mindset, Martin quotes a September 1937 dispatch from V. V. Chernyshev, the assistant head of the NKVD (the organization that would become the KGB), requesting permission to deport every last ethnic Korean from the Far East:

> "To leave these few thousand Koreans in the Far Eastern *krai* (territory), when the majority have been deported will be dangerous, since the family ties of all Koreans are very strong. The territorial restrictions on those remaining in the Far East will undoubtedly affect their mood and these groups will become rich soil for the Japanese to work on."

"In other words," Martin writes, "we have injured some Koreans, therefore we can assume all Koreans are now our enemies. This psychology is extremely important not just for the spread of ethnic cleansing, but for the ratcheting up of all Soviet terror."[19]

Of course, the rehabilitation of ethnic Russians and the Russification of the republics did not usher in an era of unparalleled competence. This was not a merit-based initiative. Both Russification and indigenization failed to undermine nationalism's appeal. Eventually, a substantial number of those who benefited from both practices were liquidated in Stalin's purges, but that did not prevent ethnic affirmative action and other socialist programs from gaining purchase among Westerners, especially those who fancied themselves "progressives."

We're from the Government, and We're Here to Help.

Though progressive activists who are devoted to the memory of the sainted Franklin Delano Roosevelt might deny it today, Soviet thinking on social and economic issues was considered radically forward-thinking when FDR took office in 1933. In the depths of the Great Depression, many influential people dismissed capitalist social structures as a discredited relic of the past. There was no shortage of Westerners who admired the Bolsheviks' uncompromising ways. Among them was Stuart Chase, the author of the 1932 book *A New Deal*.

"[M]odern industrialism," Chase wrote, "because of its delicate specialization and interdependence, increasingly demands the collectivism of social control to keep its several parts from jamming. We find a government meeting that demand by continually widening the collective sector through direct ownership, operation and regulation of economic functions." The book is replete with condemnations of both capitalism's excesses and its essential characteristics, like competition, and it is laden with unqualified praise of Stalin, whom Chase interviewed in person on a trip to the Soviet Union in 1927. The book famously concludes: "Why should the Soviets have all the fun remaking a world?"[20]

A Soviet sympathizer and an outspoken proponent of government planning, Chase was one of the more discreet members of FDR's inner circle of advisors. Along with a handful of other fellow travelers, they were the authors of some of the New Deal's most overreaching programs, many of which did not survive scrutiny in the courts. The New Deal's sweeping effort to *stabilize* the economy encompassed provisions designed to *remake* it. The Roosevelt administration's pursuit of policies ostensibly designed to help disadvantaged Americans reverberates to this day. One of those efforts is illustrative of the social justice movement's blind spots and the laws of unforeseen consequences that its devotees so recklessly flout.

Amid the Depression-era collapse of the property market, the pliant Seventy-Third Congress passed the Homeowners Refinancing Act of 1933, establishing the Home Owners' Loan Corporation (HOLC), which subsidized the cost of mortgages and halted the rash of foreclosures.

This program kept millions of Americans in their homes, but it also compelled the HOLC to mitigate investment risk by labeling some neighborhoods better investments than others. The criteria for determining what areas were and were not good investments included race. In this way, and with the best of intentions, the small ethnic enclaves that peppered American cities were consolidated into vast, segregated urban ghettos.

The process worked like this: an appraiser would be dispatched to a neighborhood to summarize for banks the area's prospects on a single-page document. The appraiser might find some blighted areas, some rundown buildings, some immigrant communities, and, as was the case in many cities following the mass migration of Southern blacks northward, majority-black enclaves. "Colored infiltration a definitely averse influence on neighborhood desirability," read one appraiser's assessment of the Bedford-Stuyvesant neighborhood of Brooklyn.

Thus, the HOLC would draw a red line around this neighborhood and mark it with a "D," the worst grade, and the point at which banks would not underwrite a mortgage for prospective white residents.[21]

"These maps became self-fulfilling prophecies," the *New York Times* reports, "as 'hazardous' neighborhoods—'redlined' ones—were starved of investment and deteriorated further in ways that most likely also fed white flight and rising racial segregation."[22] Eventually, "redlining" became a de facto way to segregate and marginalize minorities, particularly blacks. In 2017, the Federal Reserve Bank of Chicago found that the effect of HOLC border-drawing lingers today and exerts downward pressure on home values, credit scores, and homeownership in the areas once afflicted with the scarlet "D."

The top-down segregation of American cities ramped up following the 1949 American Housing Act and the "slum clearance" programs it mandated. In the name of providing fairly-priced housing for the poor and relieving the pressure on "distressed" urban neighborhoods, the American government and its technocratic elites destroyed vibrant minority communities and the organic social networks that allowed them to function.

"Why is there a black ghetto in every city in the United States?" the historian Craig Steven Wilder asks mournfully. "The answer is public policy."[23]

The Dream Declined

By the 1960s, the identity consciousness that developed in the early 1900s had matured into a political force. So much so, in fact, that it came to define the period: the civil rights era.

In the mid-twentieth century, identity consciousness gave rise to political crusades including black empowerment, feminism, the gay rights movement, and many others. Today's Black Lives Matter movement is one of those convention-challenging phenomena. It arose naturally around high-profile episodes of over-policing in African-American neighborhoods and is, in many ways, the progeny of the identity politics movements of the twentieth century that unquestionably moved America closer to the ideals of its founding. It continues to challenge the conscience of the United States and compel us to ask discomfiting questions about our society.

What has led to disproportionate rates of incarceration and wrongful conviction among African-Americans? Studies suggest that education levels are strong predictors of whether someone will be incarcerated in his lifetime. So what factors are preventing some from reaching the educational level at which incarceration rates decline? Is this entirely about individual responsibility, or are there environmental factors? What are the effects of economic inequality on social mobility? Of discrimination? Can those discriminated against also be discriminatory themselves? Can identity ever be divorced from the pursuit of true equality?

These are important questions, and Black Lives Matter deserves credit for raising them. But Black Lives Matter is not immune to the conditions that transform civil libertarian movements into illiberal movements.

In October 2017, for example, students affiliated with Black Lives Matter at the College of William and Mary in Virginia crashed an event headlined by the ACLU's Claire Guthrie Gastañaga. They were not interested in a dialogue. "ACLU, you would protect Hitler too," the demonstrators yelled. "The revolution will not uphold the Constitution," others added. "Liberalism is white supremacy."[24] When illiberal activists tell you exactly who they are in no uncertain terms, it is wise to believe them.

The demonstrators carried on for twenty minutes before one of them was finally handed a microphone, into which a student disgorged a list of demands. Following that, the demonstrators surrounded Gastañaga. They shouted over both her and her inquiring audience members and eventually forced the event to disband.

For most of the history of the United States, social justice—even the branch of it tinged with paranoia and identity obsession—was focused on ensuring that minorities were able to achieve the American dream. At some point in the progression of American scholarship, a toxic idea sank its hooks into the minds of the intelligentsia. Suddenly, the activist class went from fighting for the American dream to determining that it was unattainable—at least by minorities. Non-white Americans, devotees of a non-Western religion, women, gays and lesbians, the transgendered, and anyone else who is neither male, white, nor straight cannot reach their full potential—not in a nation as deviously bigoted as the United States. Those who don't agree are only improperly educated.

In his 2012 book *The Victims' Revolution*, Bruce Bawer describes the philosophy of Eden Torres, a professor of gender and Chicano studies at the University of Minnesota, for whom the success of her students is an obstacle to instilling in them a revolutionary consciousness. "As far as she's concerned, the American dream was, and is, an illusion. The problem, she explains, is that they simply don't recognize 'Western cultural imperialism' when they see it."

"She tells us about one of her Latino students who lamented—yes, lamented—that he'd never experienced racism," he continued. "She makes it clear that she finds this preposterous: of *course* he'd experienced racism; he just hadn't recognized it as such."[25]

Hostility toward the notion that a better life is attainable insofar as one's talents and determination allow is not limited to the identity-fixated activist left. It also extends to left-leaning policymakers. "To a large extent, the American Dream is a myth," Joseph Stiglitz has insisted. The Nobel prize–winning economist, former World Bank chief, and Columbia University professor clearly wasn't speaking from experience.

In 2015, at the height of the Democratic Party's fixation with the scourge of "income inequality," as though income *equality* had ever existed or would have been desirable, Stiglitz's dreary assertion was warmly welcomed by the usual suspects. "America is no longer the land of opportunity that it (and others) like to think it is," he wrote. "In terms of income inequality, American lags behind any country in the old, ossified Europe that President George W. Bush used to deride."[26]

Explore the universe of liberal opinion, and you will find plenty of provocative assertions that, in essence, the United States is a fetid sewer of corruption, racism, and economic stagnation. The only thing keeping Americans from recognizing and rebelling against their abhorrent conditions is their naïve refusal to accept that social mobility is unattainable in an exploitative, prejudiced, ruthlessly capitalistic society like ours.

The pervasive notion that the American Dream is at best a zero-sum game and at worst a fantasy has extended to those who occupy the other end of the social justice spectrum. Following Donald Trump's presidential election victory, an industry sprouted up around the notion that impoverished white residents of the Rust Belt and Appalachia are the victims of some cosmic injustice. They are not masters of their own destinies; something horrible has been *done* to them. Whether Trump-supporting denizens of the American interior believe that themselves is immaterial. They have been told that they believe it by the sociological taxonomists who parachuted into their towns to classify this strange new species: the Trump voter.

In her book on conservatives in the American heartland, Arlie Russell Hochschild insists that "the shifting moral qualifications for the American Dream" transformed what we once called Tea Partiers into "strangers in their own land." These Americans were "afraid, resentful, displaced, and dismissed by the very people who were, they felt, cutting in line," and they wanted revenge.[27] Even J. D. Vance's wildly successful memoir, *Hillbilly Elegy*, is often described as an autopsy on upward social mobility in Middle America. The Aspen Institute has described Vance's book as "an urgent and troubling meditation on the loss of the American dream for a large segment of this country." Never mind that Vance himself—a man born into poverty who enlisted in the Marine Corps, graduated from an Ivy League law school, and became a bestselling author—is the embodiment of that dream.

"The Dream thrives on generalizations, on limiting the number of possible questions, on privileging immediate answers," the celebrated liberal essayist Ta-Nehisi Coates writes in his 2015 bestseller, *Between the World and Me*. "The Dream is the enemy of all art, courageous thinking, and honest writing." Framed as a series of letters to his teenage son imparting the author's experiences as a black man in America, his book is an expansive rumination on the untold history of the United States from the Civil War to the present day, and it arrives at a sour verdict on the nation.

"The Dream," Coates concludes contemptuously, is a mirage that compels minorities to look past the structures of oppression that surround them. "The problem with the police is not that they are fascist pigs," he wrote, "but that our country is ruled by majoritarian pigs. And so to challenge the police is to challenge the American people who send them into the ghettos armed with the same self-generated fears that compelled people who think they are white to flee the cities and into the Dream."[28]

Coates is seeking to inculcate in his son the apprehension that "'White America' is a syndicate arrayed to protect its exclusive power to dominate and control our bodies." And if anyone who is not a member of this oppressive, white-led power structure achieves anything in his life, that becomes an impediment to reaching the liberating consciousness that comes with accepting that his successes are not truly his own. "This is the foundation of the Dream," Coates asserts, "its adherents must not just believe in it but believe that it is just, believe that their possession of the Dream is the natural result of grit, honor, and good works."

Born in Baltimore in 1975 to a Vietnam War veteran and a teacher, Coates was by no means destined for success. Despite their suspicion toward the United States, his parents instilled in Coates values and a work ethic that served him well in his career as a journalist and, eventually, a celebrated writer. By the age of forty-two, Coates was the author of several books and graphic novels, which he wrote when he wasn't working as *The Atlantic*'s national correspondent. Coates received a 2015 MacArthur Fellowship grant and the 2014 George Polk Award for Commentary, among other accolades. He also preaches that the American dream is a fraud.

The Engine of Equality

Democratic analysts are not mistaken when they identify a recent decline in upward economic mobility. There are several reasons for this decline, notably among them the erosion of the nuclear family.

In 2012, the poverty rate among families with children headed by single mothers was more than 40 percent.[29] As the Brookings Institution's Aparna Mathur writes, single parenthood is "highly correlated with children's high school dropout rates, teen pregnancy rates and men's labor force participation rates."[30] This is an instinctive truth that you don't need to be especially perceptive to deduce yourself. Anyone who has seen in person what life is like in both two- and single-parent households wouldn't argue with that conclusion. It is, though, strangely controversial among a certain class of activists. This is not the only unassailable truth from which tragically earnest social justice advocates recoil.

Economic mobility in the United States has slowed since the collapse of the mortgage market in 2008, which was itself the result of a misguided public sector effort to legislate economic equality. When Bill Clinton unveiled the National Homeownership Strategy in 1995, he dedicated it to those who "were trying to build their own personal version of the American dream."[31] By underwriting loans to families who could not afford or "were excluded" from homeownership, the government under Clinton and later George W. Bush inflated a bubble. When it burst, it ushered in the longest-lived recession in modern times.

Amid all the associated benefits, globalization and the end of the Cold War posed fiscal as well as geopolitical challenges to the United States. The Great Recession only made those ordeals worse. To assume, however, that hardship and privation are the permanent state of affairs in America is to ignore the nation's character and history.

A fair reading of the American story must concede that this nation has struggled and often failed to live up to the lofty ideals expressed so eloquently in the Declaration of Independence, the Constitution, and the Federalist Papers. But that same fairness would lead most to acknowledge that the United States has made remarkable strides toward racial, social, and economic equality in the space of 240 years— strides that are unrivaled by any other culturally heterogeneous nation in any similar span of human history.

This is good news, but good news is often regarded as a display of profound ignorance by the arbiters of political discourse. Those who have endured discrimination (and reverse discrimination) contend not infrequently that these and other empirical observations are dangerous, not because they're untrue but because they fail to advance a particular narrative. Imperfect as it is, America remains the most potent force for achieving social and economic equality that man has ever devised. Often, that reality is denied by those who fancy themselves equality's fiercest advocates. This is hardly the only indisputable fact that irritates the social justice movement to no end.

CHAPTER 3

Truths and Transgressions

Perhaps the simplest method for distinguishing classical liberals from militant social justice advocates is the extent to which the latter are threatened by the articulation of challenging ideas. The members of this movement tend to share a suspicion of certain forms of expression, exposure to which they believe is dangerous. Specifically, the expression of some empirical observations that refute their most cherished assumptions.

Increasingly, social justice advocates on the left and the right believe their counterparts are prone to genetic stereotyping. And they're both right. Purporting to protect vulnerable people from dangerous ideas—ideas that may be deeply offensive, threatening, or, even worse, alluring—social justice advocates have adopted a set of dogmas that bear a suspicious resemblance to the biological determinism they supposedly abhor.

Often, the developments that most agitate social justice advocates are entirely beneficial, particularly those that suggest progress toward racial and economic equality. Even making note of progress is evidence of ignorance or, worse, some malign effort to undercut the logic that reinforces their shared conclusions about America's fundamentally repressive nature. From improving race relations to the march toward equality of the sexes to the success of the melting pot, the United States is making headway every day. That truth is undeniable, and for some reason social justice activists passionately resent it.

Dangerous Speech

Some, like Howard Dean, the former chairman of the Democratic National Committee and governor of Vermont, have endorsed the notion that the First Amendment does not protect "hate speech." Unfortunately for Dean and his hypercritical compatriots, the entire Supreme Court disagrees.

In 2011, Simon Tam—the Asian-American leader of an Asian-American rock band—tried to register the name of his group, The Slants, with the U.S. Patent and Trademark Office. Tam contended that his band's name neutralizes a common racial epithet for Asians. It was an attempt to "reclaim" the hurtful stereotype. That reclamation would have to wait.

Registration was denied under the Lanham Act, which excludes from trademark protection "matter which may disparage...persons, living or dead, institutions, beliefs, or national symbols, or bring them into contempt, or disrepute." Tam sued and won. "Whatever our personal feelings about the mark at issue here," the federal court of appeals ruled, "the First Amendment forbids government regulators to deny registration because they find the speech likely to offend others."[1]

The case went to the nation's highest court, which came to the same conclusion. "Speech that demeans on the basis of race, ethnicity, gender, religion, age, disability, or any other similar ground is hateful," wrote Justice Samuel Alito in the majority opinion, "but the proudest boast of our free speech jurisprudence is that we protect the freedom to express 'the thought that we hate,'"[2] quoting Justice Oliver Wendell

Holmes Jr., who observed that, even in tumultuous times, America's commitment to the belief that free expression serves as a bulwark against tyranny was absolute.

Justice Anthony Kennedy wrote in concurrence, "A law that can be directed against speech found offensive to some portion of the public can be turned against minority and dissenting views to the detriment of all. The First Amendment does not entrust that power to the government's benevolence."

The decision in *Matal v. Tam* had sweeping implications, the most immediate of which was the federal government's decision to abandon its campaign to compel the National Football League's Washington Redskins to surrender their trademark and change their name. A fight that began in 1999, when a federal court found that a 1992 complaint against the team's name had merit, ended in June 2017. "There's the legal case, and then there's the cause," declared Jesse Witten, the attorney representing five Native Americans who brought the suit over the Redskins' trademark. "It was a galvanizing force that caused people to pay attention to the cause."[3]

Though the federal government is prohibited from imposing speech codes on private individuals or associations, those private individuals and associations are still perfectly free to police one another. And they do so liberally—at times, even recklessly.

Gender Roles

In August 2017, political media were shaken by the release of an internal memorandum disseminated among Google employees concerning a problem that preoccupies progressives: "gender inclusivity," particularly in the sciences and technology.

The author of the memo observed that there are many more men than women at every level of the technology industry, an imbalance that, in Silicon Valley, is universally attributed to prejudice against women. The only remedy for that implicit discrimination against women, therefore, must be explicit discrimination against men. Such a policy, the memo argued, isn't just immoral; it is conceptually flawed and doomed to fail.[4]

"Google has several biases, and honest discussion about these biases is being silenced by the dominant ideology," the memo's author, James Damore, wrote. Like the media and the social sciences, he contended, Google and its employees "lean left"—a conclusion that Mark Zuckerberg, the founder of Facebook, later reinforced when he testified before Congress that Silicon Valley is "an extremely left-leaning place."[5] "We should critically examine these prejudices," Damore urged.

His memo outlined how Google might address the "gender gap" in ways that do not discriminate against qualified applicants—an effort, Damore contended, that could succeed only if Google acknowledged some inviolable truths. Among them is the fact that women and men are different. The sexes respond differently to social pressures and incentives, he noted. Though it is hardly a universal determinant, biology is an indication of how men and women navigate the world and how they make choices in their individual pursuits of happiness.

Damore's most heretical charge was that the fealty the left displays toward the ideal of ethnic and sexual diversity blinds it to the detrimental effects of ideological homogeneity. He argued against segregating by sex and race in "safe spaces." The company's employees and principals, he wrote, should confront their own political biases and "treat people as individuals, not as just another member of their group."

"I value diversity and inclusion, am not denying that sexism exists, and don't endorse using stereotypes," Damore concluded. "If we can't have an honest discussion about this, then we can never truly solve the problem."

Within forty-eight hours of the memo's publication in the press, Damore had been terminated.

He was hardly a perfect messenger. When describing the traits associated with women that may dissuade them from pursuing a career in science and engineering, he used indelicate words like "anxiety" and "neuroticism." He described men in similarly unflattering ways, calling them "biologically disposable" and ambitious to the point of mania. These are the same stereotypes that Damore was allegedly railing against.

Furthermore, once Damore had become a public figure, his posts on social media became grating and deliberately provocative. Perhaps he became addicted to the attention he received and craved more of it, even if that attention was unfavorable. But keeping disreputable company, behaving contemptibly, and appearing to take pleasure in gratuitously antagonizing his critics does not negate the truth of Damore's observations.

In 2016, women earned only 35 percent of undergraduate degrees in the United States in science, technology, engineering, and mathematics, though that rate varies considerably among the different fields.[6] For example, while women received more than 40 percent of undergraduate degrees in mathematics, they earned only 18 percent of the degrees in computer science. A study published in 2016 attributes the underrepresentation of women in technology fields to a variety of factors, among them a lack of pre-college experience, a self-confidence deficit, and a culture of intimidating masculinity. According to the study's lead author, associate professor of psychology Sapna Cheryan, sex discrimination in hiring and other opportunities could not entirely account for the lack of women in this particular field. In other words, the discrepancy must in part be attributed to women's *choices*—some of which may be attributable to conditions we find undesirable and should seek to change—but choices nonetheless.[7]

Damore contended that his company's habit of "protecting women" from their environment is ruthlessly paternalistic. "Nearly every difference between men and women is interpreted as a form of women's oppression," he declared, and Silicon Valley's sexual disparity was the result not of sex discrimination but of fewer women seeking careers in computer science. Women do not need to be treated like infants who cannot achieve their life's goals without help. Damore's true crime was pointing out the patronizing principle at the heart of the social justice movement: the assumption that accidents of birth prevent certain classes from achieving their aspirations without the aid of enlightened liberal Sherpas.

As a wave of online fury over the transgressive memo crested, outrage-cultivating media outlets brazenly mischaracterized its recommendations. It was an "anti-diversity screed," the tech blog Gizmodo declared.[8] CNN called it an "anti-diversity manifesto" in which one of the firm's "male engineers" said "women aren't suited for tech jobs for 'biological' reasons."[9] Social media, which rewards uncompromising hysteria, exploded with ever more emphatic denunciations. Google employees took to the web to demand Damore's firing. Sources at the company told National Public Radio that some women were all but boycotting their workplace because the memo had made them feel "uncomfortable going back to work."[10]

Damore violated no explicit company rule. "We encourage an environment in which people can do this," said Google's chief executive, Sundar Pichai, "and it remains our policy to not take action against anyone for prompting these discussions."[11] But the mob demanded a head, and it usually gets what it wants. A fastidious parsing of Google's employee guidelines yielded the required violation: "perpetuating gender stereotypes." By making a martyr of their nonconformist engineer, Google eloquently, if unintentionally, confirmed his depiction of Silicon Valley's ideologically conformist culture.[12]

Inconvenient Truths

Some who advocate silencing speech with which they disagree are admirably honest about their goal: neutralizing dissent. Others are more bashful about stating their intentions plainly.

Simple decency, some contend, should compel those who are inclined to be gratuitously offensive to think twice. Others make the "fire in a crowded theater" argument, insisting that some inflammatory speech has the power to incite violence or result in physical harm and, therefore, should be curtailed by the state. The Supreme Court defined incitement in *Brandenburg v. Ohio*, and this loose definition doesn't pass the "Brandenburg test." It's hard enough to prove that someone's speech was an incitement to "imminent lawless action," but that's not enough. A prosecutor must also demonstrate that the incitement was intended. There's a reason you rarely see prosecutions for incitement, though it is not technically protected speech.

The most compelling (relatively speaking) argument in favor of censorship has nothing to do with the law or decency but with the idea that the reckless exercise of the right to free speech by some might prevent others from enjoying that same right. New York University's vice provost and professor of comparative literature, Ulrich Baer, has attempted to make this case.

Writing in the *New York Times*, Baer contends that certain inflammatory speakers, particularly those who offend members of marginalized communities, should be able to say whatever they want—just not on campus. Those speakers should be denied the "platform" of the campus to air their views, a denial that does not infringe upon their constitutional rights and respects the sensibilities of those whom they seek to offend. According to this view, students who engage in tactics ranging from protest to violence designed to shut down speakers with whom they disagree are combatants in a morally righteous crusade.

So what views deserve Baer's "no-platforming" treatment? Racism, of course, but that isn't explicit. Relative power dynamics, he writes, should be considered before anyone opens his mouth. By way of example, he invokes the Holocaust. Since the Nazis denied the humanity of Jews and sought their extermination, pro-Nazi sympathies should be considered "unmentionable and undebatable" in certain venues—particularly those where their victims might be exposed to potentially traumatizing sentiments. This principle could and should be extended to American minorities, he adds. Baer has convinced himself that the right of "minorities to participate in public discourse" is under attack, even on—of all places—American college campuses. The asymmetry between students and speakers—particularly conservative speakers— is so glaring that authority figures are obliged to step in to protect their powerless charges.

"Liberal free-speech advocates rush to point out that the views of these individuals must be heard first to be rejected," Baer writes. "But this is not the case." Views that "invalidate the humanity" of some do not deserve a hearing.[13] Presumably, he's referring to noxious expressions of unalloyed white supremacy. Yet reasonable people who never entertained the alt-right have also been chased off campuses by hypersensitive leftists who believe, like Baer, that certain forms of expression do not deserve a hearing. Former Secretary of State Condoleezza Rice, *Wall Street Journal* opinion writer Jason Riley, the activist Ayaan Hirsi Ali, IMF chief Christine Lagarde, and conservative commentator Ben Shapiro have all been "no-platformed" by censorious students across the country.[14]

Baer and his young acolytes have a bizarre view of what constitutes power disparity. When Bernie Sanders visited the overtly conservative Liberty University to make an appeal for universal health care to young evangelicals, he was not shouted down or denied a platform. Do these students benefit from a power structure in America that a sitting

United States senator does not? Baer and other social justice advocates might say yes, but they should ask an evangelical how he feels about the matter. A 2017 Public Religion Institute survey found that 57 percent of evangelical Protestants believe Christians face discrimination in America. Only 44 percent said the same for Muslims.[15] Is their perception in error? Would Baer and others like him presume to speak for them and their experiences even though they do not share them? They might, but they would also passionately reject that rationale if it were applied to any other "marginalized" demographic.

It often seems that nothing is more frustrating to social justice advocates than humble truths which, though undeniable, are regarded as oppressive. Those truths are usually so intuitively understood that they can be boiled down to a single sentence.

For example:

Race: "Racism is not the force in American life that it once was."

In June 2015, Dylann Roof walked into a black church in Charleston, South Carolina, sat and listened to a Bible study, and then killed nine parishioners.

By any objective assessment, he was a grotesque aberration. Draping himself in the banners of defunct regimes like those of the Confederate States of America, Apartheid South Africa, and Rhodesia, he was proudly anachronistic and overtly racist. His was an act of racial terrorism. But it soon became clear that, contrary to the claims of a small but influential cast of agitators, Roof was not the vanguard of a forthcoming wave of racist violence. In fact, the American response to this gunman's horrible actions demonstrated how far the United States had come on the issue of race.

In the aftermath, Americans groped desperately for some renewed sense of agency in the face of helplessness. Though all agreed

removing the Confederate battle flag from public spaces would do
nothing to prevent another shooting, the atrocity gave rise to an
organic campaign to do so. The furling of that symbol of Southern
defiance provided a sense of control over events. This activity was
undertaken enthusiastically by those for whom forgiving the killer,
as the infinitely graceful parishioners of the church he targeted had
done, was out of the question.

But while the nation's initial response to that attack was in many
ways productive, the demands of our all-consuming politics soon
became inescapable. The drive to "do something" soon led the hysterical to flail wildly at innocuous cultural symbols. For example, the
network TV Land pledged to remove the 1970s sitcom *Dukes of Haz-
zard* from syndication. The celebrity golfer Bubba Watson, who owns
the Dodge Charger featured on that program, its rooftop adorned with
the Confederate battle flag, promised that he would paint over that
hateful symbol.[16]

The notion that America had begun backsliding on race in the
second decade of the twenty-first century gained new converts in 2016.
Donald Trump's ascension to the presidency after a primary campaign
tinged with racial antipathy was enough to test the faith of any egalitarian. "[They're] bringing drugs. They're bringing crime. They're rapists,"
Trump said of undocumented migrants from Mexico at the start of
his presidential bid. "And some, I assume, are good people." As he
prepared to claim the Republican presidential nomination, he continued the agitation, questioning the impartiality of the judge adjudicat-
ing a fraud suit against him because "he's Mexican."[17]

As the American right's concerns over security at the border shifted
to concerns over security in Europe and the Middle East following a
bloody terrorist attack in Paris in 2015, Trump seamlessly transitioned
from agitating against Latin Americans to stoking a fear of Muslims.
It was then that he concocted the constitutionally dubious and

impossibly impracticable plan for a "total and complete shutdown" of Muslims entering the United States—a proposal enforced by the establishment of a "database" of Muslims designed to register and surveil suspect elements, including U.S. citizens.[18]

When asked to renounce the support of David Duke, a man whom Trump had denounced in earlier years, the future president suddenly pretended he had never heard of him. When asked to denounce the KKK, Trump also declined. "You wouldn't want me to condemn a group that I know nothing about," he told CNN's Jake Tapper.[19] With just a few months to go in the 2016 race, Trump hired as his campaign chairman Breitbart chief Stephen Bannon, who had once said his blog provided a "platform for the alt-right."[20]

When people who are sensitive to racial intolerance confessed that they feared the worst from a Trump presidency, they had plenty of evidence to justify their apprehensions. A careful analysis of the 2016 election suggests, however, that Trump won the presidency in spite of these comments, not as a result of them.

At a time when the Democratic Party appeared to have been brought low by its commitment to Balkanizing the electorate, Jacob T. Levy, a political theorist at Canada's McGill University, insisted that social justice and identity politics were not political tactics but integral elements of any successful defense of liberty. In a scholarly post-2016 pep talk for depressed liberals, he noted that Trump won a lower share of the white vote than Mitt Romney. Moreover, the episodes in which Trump thrilled the members of his coalition who reject "political correctness" were also moments in which his standing in the polls collapsed, and Republican elected officials felt compelled to denounce him.

Levy showed that Trump's attacks on a judge's "Mexican heritage," a Muslim Gold Star family, and a former beauty contestant whom the future president decided had put on too much weight did not advance his political prospects. Just the opposite: Trump succeeded despite, not because of, his habit of stoking animosities. "Ultimately Trump's racism, misogyny, Islamophobia, and willingness to give a platform to online anti-Semitism didn't stop a normal level of white voters from voting for him," he wrote. "But the poll evidence suggests that they were most reluctant to support him at the moments when these things were most vividly on their minds."[21]

Many believe that the Trump campaign was evidence that white racism remains a potent cultural force, but the Trump presidency has shown that it is not a dominant political force. The courts have checked the Trump administration when shown compelling evidence that his policies verged on racial or religious intolerance, and the president's Justice Department has not turned a blind eye to negative discrimination in public or private organizations. American institutions are far less tolerant of overtly prejudiced policies that unfairly encumber or disenfranchise minorities than they have been historically. That is not to say that individual and structural prejudice does not exist. It does. The Department of Justice still uncovers discriminatory policies on an institutional level, but they are exceptions that prove what is increasingly becoming the rule. For the social justice left, that truth is unacceptable. The assertion that race relations in the United States have improved is regarded as a display of ignorance or malice or both.

Racial progress in America is measured in fits and starts. It is not a straight line, but the arc of the moral universe bends inexorably toward justice, as the abolitionist minister Theodore Parker said. In 2008, the United States became the first Western country to elect a man of African descent to serve as the head of government. On the eve of his reelection in 2012, 89 percent of poll respondents told Gallup that race relations in America were either "greatly" or "somewhat" improved. In that year, 76 percent said "new civil rights laws" were not necessary. Just 21 percent disagreed, down from 38 percent as recently as 1993.

These numbers reflect more than the hope that a black president would usher in a new era of racial harmony. A half-century earlier, interracial marriage was illegal in some states, the desegregation of schools required the deployment of the 101st Airborne Division on U.S. soil, and some college basketball conferences were segregated even if the colleges were not.

In 2014 and 2015, the nation's urban centers were paralyzed by a spontaneous series of grassroots protests against police violence targeting African-American communities. They were fueled by a series of highly publicized incidents in which it appeared that police were too quick to pull the trigger on blacks.

And yet, the notion that the United States is plagued by endemic and racially discriminatory police violence is not supported by the data. A 2016 study conducted by Harvard University's Rolando G. Fryer Jr., an African-American economist, found that the Black Lives Matter movement's central animating grievance was based on deficient statistics. His study of 1,332 police shootings in ten major American cities found that blacks are more likely than whites to be touched or handcuffed in an encounter with police but not more likely to be shot. "In officer-involved shootings in these ten cities, officers were more likely to fire their weapons without having first been attacked when the suspects were white," Fryer's study concluded. "Black and white civilians involved in police shootings were equally likely to have been carrying a weapon."[22]

Before the onset of the Great Recession, the income gap between blacks, Hispanics, and whites was shrinking steadily. Those gaps exploded after 2008, but they are slowly narrowing again as home values recover and home equity accounts for more household wealth.[23] In 1940, 60 percent of employed black women worked as household servants; today that figure is 2.2 percent. From 1940 to 1970, "black men cut the income gap by about a third," the scholars Abigail and

Stephan Thernstrom wrote for the Brookings Institution. Indeed, the number of African-Americans entering the white-collar professional class exploded in the latter half of the twentieth century, as did the number of black homeowners.[24]

According to a Census Bureau report in 2015, 87 percent of African-Americans have a high school diploma, nearly 53 percent have attended some college, and 22.5 percent have earned a bachelor's degree. Those numbers can and should be improved upon, but they are markedly improved from fifteen years earlier, when only 72 percent of blacks earned a high school diploma, 42 percent had earned some college credits, and just 14 percent secured a bachelor's degree.

Graduation rates among blacks still trail those of whites, but the average graduation rate for African-Americans at four-year public institutions increased by 4.4 percent from 2003 to 2013. For whites, the rate of graduation improved by a comparable 5.6 percent. An experimental program at Ohio State University that includes pre-college outreach and support for first-generation, low-income black students produced a 31 percent increase in African-American graduation rates and shrank the racial graduation gap by 11 points.[25]

This is progress. You might call it unacceptably slow progress, but it is indisputable. Marking these milestones does not constitute a denial of racism's existence. Social justice activists would surely agree that racial progress in America cannot be accurately measured without historical perspective, yet that perspective is so often spurned by those who have the gall to call themselves "woke."

Biology: "Gender is binary. Race exists on a spectrum."

For the social justice left, it's the other way around. Gender is a fluid concept. It isn't biological but sociological and cultural. Race, by contrast, is static and absolute. Racially distinct character traits cannot be transferred through cultural osmosis. This is tantamount to theft. To contend otherwise is an expression of social and intersectional illiteracy.

The social justice left's war on gender identity began with and is still focused on typical gender roles, as opposed to gender stereotypes, a distinction too many decline to make. Popular culture is devoted to destigmatizing behavior in children that is atypical of their sex. We're no longer talking about inculcating an interest in science and engineering in young girls or allowing boys to experiment with toys and costumes marketed toward girls, though both themes are prevalent in popular culture and advertising. What began as an effort to combat sexism and bigotry has reached the point that rejecting transgenderism even in grade-school children is seen by many on the social justice left as narrow-mindedness.

In an op-ed for the *New York Times*, Lisa Selin Davis politely informs her well-meaning peers who keep asking if her daughter is really a man deep down inside that she is, in fact, a tomboy. "She is not gender nonconforming. She is gender *role* nonconforming," Davis writes. "She does not fit into the mold that we adults—who have increasingly eschewed millenniums-old gender roles ourselves, as women work outside the home and men participate in the domestic sphere—still impose upon our children."[26] This seems obvious, but it isn't; not to the identity-obsessed left.

The study of how accidents of birth shape our gender role preferences later in life is a nuanced and evolving discipline. "[G]endered interests are predicted by exposure to prenatal testosterone," writes Debra Soh, a columnist with a doctorate in sexual neuroscience. Writing in defense of the author of the infamous Google memo, Soh observes that testosterone exposure in utero can affect a person's affinity for mechanically-oriented activities, whereas the absence of testosterone is linked to an interest in social occupations. In other words, the behavior we associate with a tomboy may be partly preprogrammed by our hormones.

"We see evidence for this in girls with a genetic condition called congenital adrenal hyperplasia, who are exposed to unusually high levels of testosterone in the womb," Soh notes. "When they are born, these girls prefer male-typical, wheeled toys, such as trucks, even if their parents offer more positive feedback when they play with female-typical toys, such as dolls. Similarly, men who are interested in female-typical activities were likely exposed to lower levels of testosterone."[27] Of course, Soh adds, our environments and experiences shape who we become as we mature, but biology is a fundamental factor.

The incoherence of the social justice left on this issue is illustrated by its intolerance toward arguments in favor of biological determinism, unless we're talking about transgenderism—even in children. In that case, biological determinism isn't prejudiced. It's enlightened! Even to countenance the perfectly debatable notion that grade-school kids are not old enough to determine their own gender identity—much less to pursue hormonal treatments that induce a transition—is to invite the scorn of the social justice left.

In September 2016, it was announced that a four-year-old Australian child had become the youngest person ever to undergo a sexual transition.[28] A few months later, an American couple announced that their daughter had broken that record, becoming a boy at the age of three and supposedly making everyone's life better.[29] Perhaps. But researchers at the VU University Medical Center in Amsterdam have warned that indulging gender dysphoria in pre-adolescents can be warping and traumatic, especially if they "grow out" of their dysphoria and choose to return to the sex of their birth, as happens not infrequently.[30] Treating these children with puberty-blocking drugs is a step into the unknown; they are not FDA approved, and researchers know that they slow the growth of bone density and may inhibit brain development.

Gender identity is complicated, and non-Western concepts of gender roles can be wildly unfamiliar, even threatening, to Westerners. Certainly, there are adults, adolescents, and even pre-teens who feel more comfortable and secure living as members of the opposite sex. The debate over how to help people with this inclination to seek and find fulfillment won't be settled here, but it is also beside the point. What deserves more attention is the often under-emphasized key word in this paragraph: "opposite."

With the rarest of exceptions, there are only two genders. Chromosomal conditions like hermaphroditism and Androgen Insensitivity Syndrome are quite rare. Klinefelter Syndrome, a condition in which a boy inherits an extra X chromosome from his mother, as well as XXX females and XYY males are only slightly more common (one in five hundred to a thousand births), but these chromosomal conditions do not render a person any less one gender or the other. In one village in the Dominican Republic, so-called "Guevedoce" boys spend their childhood living as girls because they fail to develop external genitalia until puberty.[31] Deficient in the enzyme that spurs the growth of the penis and testicles before birth, these boys endure the world's most disorienting awkward phase. But they were never females, and their sex does not fall along a spectrum. Their fates are sealed by their genetics. No one can pass to the next generation anything other than the genes he inherited at birth. Though that may seem like an obvious truth, it is enough to send those committed to Identitarian social justice into fits of incoherent rage.

Those who believe that fluidity is a gender in itself reject these facts, in part because they can be used by intolerant people to deny the preferred identity of those who transition or are transitioning from one gender to another. The lamentable fact of life that some people are jerks does not negate genetic realities. The idea that society would be better off if we let everyone choose his sex is not a universal value, even on the social justice left. A broad current of feminist thought rejects transgenderism for reinforcing the gender binary.[32] Again, the key word is "opposite."

Biology is hardly the only sex-related truth that irritates the social justice left. A study published in 2016 by *Pediatrics*, the journal of the American Academy of Pediatrics, concluded that it was "ethically inappropriate" to describe the process of breastfeeding infants as "natural" because doing so reinforces gender roles. "Coupling nature with motherhood," the report reads, "can inadvertently support biologically deterministic arguments about the roles of men and women in the family (for example, that women should be the primary caretaker)."[33]

The New York City Commission on Human Rights warns employers that they can be fined if their employees report being called by something other than the pronoun of their choice. Princeton University staffers were ordered to stop using gendered pronouns altogether, preferring the plural "they" even if referring to a single person. The Oxford University Student Union recommended that the invented pronoun "ze" replace "he" or "she" as "part of a drive to make the union intersectional."[34] The University of Tennessee tried to follow suit but backed off the proposal following a backlash.[35]

Even the Associated Press is getting in on the action. In late 2017, the AP introduced a new set of style guidelines that represent not just a surrender to anti-pronoun activists but an assault on the meaning of language itself. Advising journalists to "avoid references to being a boy or a girl" because "gender refers to a person's identity, while sex refers to biological characteristics," AP's editors endorsed referring to single individuals by plural pronouns—"they" or "their"—and pointedly refused to limit the usage of invented pronouns that are supposedly stripped of gender. Finally, the AP introduced a new rule: Writers are no longer to refer to a "sex change" or even a "transition." Instead, they're to call it "gender confirmation."[36]

"This was a deep kowtow to the transgender movement, which believes that physicians don't alter anything essential or fundamental when they perform a sex-change operation," *Commentary*'s Sohrab Ahmari explains. For social justice activists with a grudge against the English language, the process of undergoing a transition from one gender to another is not a transition at all but a sacrament conferred on those who have achieved enlightened discretion.

This is not science. It's an ideological crusade. As Simon Baron-Cohen, a professor of developmental psychology at Cambridge, writes, gender is not solely a product of socialization or environmental conditions. There are real distinctions baked into those one thousand genes populating a single X chromosome. "Genes on the X chromosome are responsible for why 1 in 20 men but only 1 in 400 women have red-green color blindness," he writes. "Genes on the X chromosome are also responsible for why 1 in 5,000 men, but hardly any women, have hemophilia type A." As Baron-Cohen notes, using determinist theories to justify sexism is detestable, but pretending biological distinctions between the sexes do not exist is deluded.[37]

People who feel trapped in bodies they do not recognize as their own experience real psychological trauma, which can lead to higher rates of suicide, addiction, and homelessness. A virtuous society will dedicate itself to combatting all forms of unjust discrimination, including that which targets those who are struggling with gender or transitioning to their preferred identity. Too many on the right confuse "political correctness" with simply not being a quarrelsome jackass. Sympathy and understanding are noble traits. The triumph of gentility over rudeness isn't something to mourn, and combatting stereotypes is an honorable enterprise. But those who would confuse psychology

with physiology are seeking a mock scientific justification for a political program, not an explanation for a sociological phenomenon.

As we've seen, social justice activists are not as unfriendly to genetic
determinism as they make themselves out to be. Though ostensibly
dedicated to combatting hurtful labeling, the social justice left loves
another kind of genetic determinism: racial determinism. The notion
that race is indissoluble, non-transferable, and informs how a person
navigates every daily social interaction is increasingly prevalent on the
social justice left, and it is as toxic as any other kind of bigotry.

In 1950, the United Nations Educational, Scientific, and Cultural
Organization issued a statement on a consensus anthropological conclusion: There is no such thing as race.[38] That is to say, there are no
biological realities that contribute to supposed "racial characteristics."
In 1942, Ashley Morgenthau, a student of the famous anthropologist
Franz Boas, determined that what we commonly associate with racial
traits are, in fact, clines—micro-evolutionary gradients in the gene
pool.

"For example, skin color is related to the amount of solar radia-
tion, and dark skin is found in Africa, India, and Australia," writes
Robert Wald Sussman in *The Myth of Race*. "However, many other
genetic traits in peoples of these areas are not similar. Furthermore,
similar traits such as skin color are convergent; different genes can
cause similar morphological and behavioral characteristics."[39] The
science of genetic testing and genome mapping has proved that
human genetic diversity does not reach the threshold required to
classify racial gradation as speciation. Humanity just interbreeds too
much.

The idea that race doesn't exist is a hard sell. It undercuts not just
liberal preconceptions but almost everyone's daily experience. Of
course, there are distinctions among races, and those distinctions have
fueled discrimination and conflict, exacerbating tribal divisions and

social tensions throughout the centuries. But observing that race is a cultural reality and not a scientific one is, for the social justice left, an expression of poisonous "race denialism," and it cannot be tolerated. Racial distinctions are absolute, and those who seek to transcend or blur them meet with aggressive pushback. Maybe the most famous of those transgressors is the former head of the Spokane, Washington, chapter of the National Association for the Advancement of Colored People (NAACP), Rachel Dolezal.

Socialized in African-American communities and feeling more kinship with her black neighbors than with her white family, Dolezal shed her identity as a white person, fabricated an "authentic" backstory, and changed her appearance so that she could pass for a person of African descent. For this, Dolezal was attacked as a "mentally ill" person who "reduced [African-American] humanity and perpetuated centuries of cultural appropriation."[40] Long after she lost her NAACP position and abandoned her adopted identity, there was no forgiveness. "The woman formerly known as Dolezal is still a white lady with fussy hair and a bad tan, trying to make fetch happen," Denene Millner wrote in an op-ed for National Public Radio.[41]

Many of those who took offense at Dolezal's impersonation of African-Americans made a rational and persuasive case that her impersonation cheapened their reality. The African-American experience in the United States is unique, and it cannot simply be adopted. Those who protested Dolezal's actions reveal, though, that the distinctions they cherish are cultural, not biological.

The research and experience of Rebecca Tuvel, an assistant professor of philosophy at Rhodes College in Memphis, illustrates the double standard. In a more academically structured manner, Tuvel asked why Dolezal's "transracialism" prompted such outrage when "transgenderism" is seen as courageous. It was an intentionally provocative argument, but not an illogical or unreasonable one. The responses—not just from political agitators and bloggers but also from fellow academics—revealed a terrifyingly censorious new trend.

More than eight hundred professors signed an open letter demanding that *Hypatia*, the feminist journal that published Tuvel's article, retract it. Much of the condemnation of Tuvel was steeped in ideology. "Tuvel enacts violence and perpetuates harm in numerous ways throughout her essay," declared Nora Berenstain. Violence! Many of *Hypatia*'s own editors lambasted the work as "a product of white and cisgender privilege."[42]

There are a lot of words that describe this behavior, but "scholarship" isn't among them.

Immigration: "Immigrants to America are assimilating as they always have."

So far, we have focused on the empirical realities that irritate the social justice left, but the right's Identitarians are just as susceptible to comforting myths. It is a commonly-held belief among those on the identity-conscious right that major immigrant groups in America today are not assimilating into the mainstream as quickly as their predecessors did. That's a popular misperception, but a misperception nonetheless.

The United States is today experiencing an influx of legal immigration, perhaps accounting for the increased sensitivity to the perception that new immigrants are not acclimating to their adopted homeland. In the 1960s, less than 10 percent of the population of the United States was a first-generation immigrant. Today, more than 25 percent of the population is either a first- or second-generation immigrant.[43]

Immigration skeptics on the right cite studies that purport to show that rates of assimilation, measured by education levels, household earnings, and English language fluency, have trailed off among Hispanic immigrants. They're not entirely wrong. "In what some scholars have described as a pattern of negative assimilation," according to the Pew Research Center in 2013, "41 percent of second-generation [immigrant] women who recently gave birth were unmarried, compared with 23 percent of immigrant women who recently gave birth. The higher share of non-marital childbearing among the second generation has been driven mostly by second-generation Hispanic women (52 percent of these women with a recent birth were unmarried).["44] Though these statistics paint a disturbing picture, it's an incomplete one.

Some immigration skeptics on the right have blamed an "anti-assimilation" culture prevalent among left-leaning identity studies scholars for this condition. "These cultural orientations are not only incompatible with what an advanced free-market economy and a viable democracy require, they are also destructive of a sense of solidarity and reciprocity among Americans," observe Amy Wax and Larry Alexander, professors of law at the University of Pennsylvania and the University of San Diego, respectively.[45] Wax and Alexander aren't imagining things; anti-assimilation advocacy has a constituency. Social justice advocates who promote racial separatism under the guise of cultural sympathy do appear to resent assimilation into American society and the adoption of American culture by immigrant groups. But Wax and Alexander are overstating the extent to which those ideas have purchase among the broader Hispanic-American population.

In 2007 (incidentally, the year in which illegal immigration from Mexico peaked), four political scientists set out to test the late Samuel Huntington's famous proposition that "the sheer number, concentration, linguistic homogeneity, and other characteristics of Hispanic immigrants" will dilute what it means to be American. They found that second-generation Mexican immigrants were learning English—the chief metric for gauging assimilation—as fast as their Asian and European predecessors, though their first-generation parents were, in fact, slower to adapt than previous immigrant groups.

"Hispanics acquire English and lose Spanish rapidly beginning with the second generation," the political scientists found. "Moreover, a clear majority of Hispanics reject a purely ethnic identification, and patriotism grows from one generation to the next. At present, a traditional pattern of political assimilation appears to prevail."[46]

A 2015 report from the National Academies of Sciences, Engineering, and Medicine revealed that integration into society by first-generation Mexican and Central American immigrants was hindered by the undocumented status of more than eleven million of them. Most of their children do not, however, have that impediment to overcome. "Immigrants are healthier than the native-born, have longer life expectancies, and have lower crime rates, the academics concluded," read a *Washington Times* summary of the report. "And more than a quarter of immigrants have a college education, giving them a head start, and their children 'do exceptionally well' in integrating."[47]

One reason that some of these trends might not be showing up in survey data is that more and more Hispanics identify as white. A 2014 study of the 2000 and 2010 census data revealed that approximately 2.5 million Hispanic-Americans who identified as "some other race" in 2000 checked off "white" in 2010. "The data provide new evidence consistent with the theory that Hispanics may assimilate as white Americans, like the Italians or Irish, who were not universally considered to be white," observes the *New York Times* reporter Nate Cohn.[48] Research has indicated that Hispanics who experience racial discrimination in their lives are less likely to identify as white than those who have not. This suggests that not only is assimilation proceeding apace but also that millions of Hispanic-Americans are facing less discrimination.

Lately, though, fears involving Hispanic integration, or the lack thereof, into the mainstream of the United States have taken a back seat to the concern that America is incubating homegrown terrorism in its unassimilated Muslim communities. These fears are not entirely irrational. The United States, Canada, and Europe have suffered deadly attacks by naturalized immigrants or Muslim residents who became radicalized. On the whole, however, the kind of alienation experienced by Muslim migrants in European ghettos is unknown in the United States. Indeed, Muslims are among the most well-integrated immigrant groups in America.

In quadrennial surveys of Muslim Americans taken since 2007, the Pew Research Center found that, while geographically varied and diverse, they remain a predominantly first-generation immigrant group. You might, therefore, think they'd experience the same troubles integrating into society that first-generation Hispanics encounter. Not quite.

A majority of Muslim Americans rate the communities in which they live "good" or "excellent" and describe themselves as middle-class. In 2007, seven out of ten Muslims believed in "the American dream," which Pew defines as the conviction that "people who want to get ahead in the United States can make it if they are willing to work hard."[49] American Muslims were far more likely than their European counterparts to reject extremism and violence as a feature of Islam.

"U.S. Muslims are about as likely as other Americans to report household incomes of $100,000 or more (14 percent of Muslims, compared with 16 percent of all adults), and they express similar levels of satisfaction with their personal financial situation," Pew reported four years later.[50] Because they are on average a younger population, Muslim Americans are more likely to attend college than their native-born counterparts, and fewer than half of all respondents said "all" or "most" of their friends are also Muslim.

Pew's 2011 study found that a plurality of American Muslims do not think their community's leaders have done enough to "speak out against extremists." By 2015, even amid the rise of ISIS and a resurgence of radical Islamic terrorism abroad, Pew's data had not reflected any substantial shift in opinion among Muslim-American respondents.[51] Pew found that just one-quarter of American Muslims—quite unlike Muslim communities in Europe—were native born (meaning third-generation immigrants or older), but that the vast majority of Muslims living in America—82 percent—are American citizens. Sixty-nine percent of all foreign-born Muslims elect to go through the naturalization process. [52]

For every Nidal Hasan, the U.S. Army psychiatrist who murdered thirteen of his fellow soldiers at Fort Hood in 2009, there are nearly six thousand active-duty Muslims serving in the U.S. armed forces (as of 2015). Anwar al-Awlaki, a propagandist for al-Qaeda who was killed in Yemen in 2011, was born in America, but a majority of American Muslims, Pew found, believe that their faith is open to multiple interpretations. Those who persist in believing that there is no distinction between American Muslims and European Muslims—both first-generation and native-born—are taking refuge in a category error. By alienating and stereotyping the American-Muslims who are intent on assimilation, they risk encouraging the development of dangerous and isolated communities.

Lies We Tell Ourselves

These are only a handful of the unquestioned myths that animate Identitarians and fill the sails of social justice activists. Anyone who honestly seeks a just society should be glad that they are only myths.

The reality is that race relations in America have improved, sex-specific life choices are often mistaken for sexism, and immigrants are integrating into American society at a pace consistent with their predecessors. That is obviously not to say that race relations in the United States are perfect or that women and minorities do not face discrimination.

Similarly, the left's antipathy toward the assimilation of immigrants into American culture is not a figment of conservative imaginations.

And yet, the idea that the United States is in the midst of a terrible societal regression is the height of sophistry. Identitarians are wallowing in a self-serving ideology that confirms unhealthy biases. That should be greeted as good news. But for an influential contingent of identity-obsessed activists, it is a threat to their very reason for being.

CHAPTER 4

Lifting the Veil

How did a set of principles ostensibly devoted to achieving a fair and just society bring about an acrimonious movement dedicated not to justice but to retribution? So far, we've examined the people and ideas that are typical of the social justice movement's excesses. To understand its core beliefs, though, we need to explore social justice's philosophical roots.

Modern social justice activism owes its origins to ageless philosophical speculation about the nature of justice itself. Some of history's greatest thinkers devoted their lives to studying justice at a conceptual level. From Aristotle to David Hume, philosophers have tried to pin down mankind's true nature to determine whether we are even capable of such high-mindedness.

While an embryonic conception of social justice had taken hold in the public imagination by the mid-nineteenth century, it was more or less indistinguishable from charity. In the mid-twentieth century, the idea of social justice as we understand it today became a defined line of philosophical thought, though it was subsequently abused and disfigured by the activists who adopted it as their lodestar.

Perhaps the best description of the Identitarian activist class's ethos is a collective antipathy to fortune and the fortunate. Not a very lofty ethos, perhaps, but it is not without philosophical and ideological precedents. A variety of philosophers and theoreticians throughout history dedicated their careers to polishing envy and class-consciousness until they shine with a bogus academic luster.

Rewriting History

Sadly, many of today's students of philosophy have little use for those who laid the foundations of their disciplines simply because of the philosophers' demographic backgrounds.

In 2018, Arizona State University became the subject of an adversarial *New York Times* profile as a result of the school's decision to establish a program for the study of "political economy and moral science." Designed to focus on under-taught works like Adam Smith's economic theories and the supremely valuable Federalist Papers—all eighty-five of them—the program came under fire because it was "too heavily focused on white male thinkers from the United States and Europe."[1]

This kind of racial reductionism is common in academia. In 2017, for example, students at the University of London's School of Oriental and African Studies, bent on "decolonizing" the syllabus and "address[ing] the structural and epistemological legacy of colonialism," demanded that thinkers such as Plato, Descartes, and Kant give way, for the most part, to non-Western philosophers. If white European philosophers *must* be studied, let it be from "a critical standpoint."[2]

At first glance, it is not unreasonable for students who want to immerse themselves in non-Western cultures to maximize every opportunity to do precisely that, even if it means relegating the giants of European philosophical thought to the footnotes. But that is not how philosophy works. Its thinkers are interdependent, each relating to the others. There is no comprehensive study of Kant without the study of his contemporary David Hume. Nor can Descartes be comprehended without understanding Aristotle, Plato, and Socrates.

The idea that Western and non-Western philosophy can be entirely compartmentalized is a product of ignorance. Some of the most influential works of medieval Islamic philosophy, for example, were composed in Spain—a nation that engaged in a fair bit of colonizing long after its Islamic influences had been integrated into Iberian society. Those Islamic philosophers, heavily influenced by their classical predecessors, in turn had a profound effect on the philosophical minds that came after them. The Dutch philosopher Baruch Spinoza set Europe on a course toward the Enlightenment, but he was also a dark-skinned Sephardic Jew from Portugal. Spinoza's works are, however, unlikely to appear on the preferred reading list of London's irate anti-colonial student activists. Their objections are less a matter of geography or ethnicity than a self-referential preconception about what they believe *ought* to constitute white European thought.

Minna Salami is among many on the left who insist that a racially correct philosophy curriculum is long overdue. History's female philosophers, she charges, were persecuted or killed, and the Aztec world was purged of its deep thinkers by murderous colonialists. African philosophy, like that of the seventeenth-century Ethiopian Zera Yacob, whose criticism of organized religion and deism long predates Nietzsche, is not found on many syllabi.[3]

These are valuable critiques of philosophy's core curriculum, and Salami is arguing in favor of inclusivity in good faith. But she is not making the same argument as the students for whom she presumes to speak. Salami is not calling for intellectual partitioning in pursuit of historical justice, but her comrades in the grassroots most certainly are. Down that road lies illiteracy, not enlightenment.

For instance, an item posted on the website Accredited Times praising the anti-white philosophy campaign asserts that our own age, graced by the philosophy of the great hip-hop artists, is "far superior" to that of the ancient Greeks. "When modern geniuses like Kanye West and Dr. Dre are still very much alive," writes a self-described "transpecies activist, new age spiritual guru, and chief diversity coordinator," "it is nothing short of perverse that our youth are forced to study philosophy from over two thousand years ago."[4]

These activists don't know what they don't know, but they also don't seem to care that they don't know it. They are not familiar with the Western philosophy they claim to resent. They don't appear to know much about philosophy in general—neither the philosophy of others nor even their own. The pursuit of pure justice is rich with history. It's a satisfying irony that since the philosophical minds who gave birth to the concept of social justice were, by and large, white males, they would be spurned by their disciples.

Justice in Antiquity

Aristotle was among the first Western philosophers to examine the nature of justice—who should enjoy its benefits and how inequality results in or exacerbates injustices. Aristotle believed in objectivity and absolutes, but for the Sophists who preceded him, morality was relative. That's a pretty cynical way to go through life. A society operating on this principle would quickly descend into sloth, venality, and intemperance. Abandoning this self-obsession masquerading as high-mindedness was a great leap forward.

If justice is viewed as a commodity, Aristotle thought, it should be equitably distributed across a population. Because all commodities are finite, a happy medium lies somewhere between getting more than your fair share and not getting enough.

Aristotle saw justice in terms familiar to future generations of redistributionists, even Karl Marx himself. If a society is possessed of only a handful of unique musical instruments, for example, Aristotle thought that they should be distributed to those who can play them best, giving society the maximum benefit from their use.[5] This might seem a reasonable judgment if you don't consider some of the more intangible virtues we prize today, like dignity, property rights, and enfranchisement.

Aristotle endorsed equality, but not as we understand it today. He took for granted slavery and the inferiority of women. In fact, Aristotle saw the human condition as suited to social stratification. His concept of justice exemplifies a problem with which all of his successors would struggle. If justice is a virtue, it's a strange one. It is not doled out by the charitable, and its recipients are not obliged to be grateful upon its delivery. If justice is giving each man his "due," then those who are owed justice may seize it—by force, if necessary. But who determines what is "due" to someone? That's a moving target.

Enlightened Justice

Fortunately, Aristotle's descendants were not as comfortable as he was with a stratified society. Subsequent thinkers like Rousseau, Hegel, and eventually Marx all took a stab at understanding and addressing the causes of social inequality. Many philosophers of justice during this period focused on the establishment of just institutions. With the right social mechanisms, they reasoned, inequality will take care of itself.

Luigi Taparelli's acolytes disagreed. "[L]et it be laid down in the first place that in civil society, the lowest cannot be made equal with the highest," declared Pope Leo XIII in *Rerum novarum*.[6] This is hardly a theory of retributive justice—indeed, in its contemporary political context, this encyclical "on the condition of the working classes" was distinctly anti-socialist. But it also advocated activist government and articulated a progressive view of how governments might mollify potential revolutionaries before they rose up to demand Marxist reforms.

"Social and public life can only be maintained by means of various kinds of capacity for business and the playing of many parts," Leo declared. "There are truly very great and very many natural differences among men. Neither the talents, nor the skill, nor the health, nor the capacities of all are the same, and unequal fortune follows of itself upon necessary inequality in respect to these endowments." In other words, the virtue of an unequal society is that all can find fulfillment simply in the pursuit of their individual interests and abilities.

This is beginning to sound like a pretty conservative, even Lockean, articulation of the theories that resulted in free market economics as we understand it today. And, indeed, *Rerum novarum* reiterated that the ownership of property is a natural right. But it also contained the seeds of an idea that would blossom into the governing vision of today's social democrats.

Leo warned that "riches do not bring freedom from sorrow." Asserting that the Church's mission is to bring "the rich and the working class together," he railed against the exploitation of the working class and advocated, albeit in veiled terms, a regulated living wage. "[S]ince wage workers are numbered among the great mass of the needy," he concluded, "the State must include them under its special care and foresight." *Rerum novarum* is therefore considered one of the foundational philosophical arguments for the modern welfare state. Because Leo's philosophy accepts inequality as the natural state of man, we might not recognize its connection to "social justice" in its present incarnation. The ideological scaffolding that would later be used to construct the modern definition of social justice was nevertheless evident in the encyclical.

Upon this foundation, Harvard's John Rawls built a theory of social justice that animates its activists today, many of whom have probably never read a word he wrote.

The Contemptible Veil

Over the course of several decades, Rawls secured his status as the preeminent philosopher of social justice. More critically, he established a universal definition for the concept in practice that endures today.

A virtuous distribution of justice doesn't mean perfect equality, Rawls postulates. Inequality among individuals isn't inherently unjust as long as that inequality makes society, on balance, better off. "The basic structure is perfectly just when the prospects of the least fortunate are as great as they can be," he wrote in 1969. And unequal outcomes are themselves just, but only as long as they are the result of decisions by just institutions.[7] So how do you create a just institution? Rawls prescribes what he calls the "veil of ignorance," according to which justice is "redistributed" by those who have no idea who the lucky and unlucky recipients will be. The veil ensures that the distributors of justice cannot know the class, abilities, tastes, physical characteristics, or morality of the people who will benefit from their actions. Justice (a Rawlsian definition of which has very little to do with courtroom proceedings) would therefore be dispensed without consideration for any of the individuals involved, so those doing the distributing are more likely to be fair about it.

As much as these distributors of justice might want to bestow advantages upon themselves or their particular tribe, they are blinded by the veil. Their adversaries might end up being the beneficiaries of their unfair distribution of social goods as much as their allies.

Therefore, the operator behind the veil will choose the fairest distribution possible.

No one should enjoy an unearned advantage in a just society, Rawls theorizes, and the veil eliminates that temptation. Rawls contends that this is the place from which any just society must begin.

"Activists, social workers, and policymakers may have absorbed only secondhand versions of Rawls," Carl Bankston writes. "Nevertheless, social justice advocates in general sound quite Rawlsian."[8] He notes, however, that "seeing people as positions rather than as individuals implicitly reduces them to categories." Bankston observes that Rawlsian thought leads to the division of society based on perceived levels of "victimization or oppression."

Here is where Rawls's veil becomes a source of consternation for today's social justice advocates. Supreme Court decisions like *Brown v. Board of Education*, which desegregated public schools, and *Loving v. Virginia*, which struck down bans on interracial marriage, could not ignore the identities of those who suffered discrimination and disenfranchisement. The policymakers who crafted the Civil Rights and Voting Rights Acts knew full well which groups were being persecuted and who was doing the persecuting. In these cases, applying the veil to the redistribution of justice, both social and economic, would have been both counterproductive and morally obtuse. They have a point.

To achieve real social justice, the activists have determined that Lady Justice needs to lose her blindfold.

The Libertarian Counterattack

There wasn't much righteousness in Rawls's conception of the ideal just society, argued his Harvard colleague Robert Nozick in 1974.

Resources are not the product of divine intervention. All goods that exist today were crafted, produced, extracted, or designed by the hands of man. Insofar as someone has secured his resources legitimately, he has every right to them. The Rawlsian idea that resources—both tangible and intangible—should be distributed independently of the personal investment that brought them into existence has been tried in the communist world. Nozick observed that conditions in Marxist societies were not only objectively unjust but also wildly economically inefficient.[9]

While Nozick criticized Rawlsian philosophy for its impracticality, the economist Friedrich A. Hayek savaged its immorality in *The Mirage of Social Justice*, the second volume of his three-volume philosophical work, *Law, Legislation, and Liberty*. As the volume's title suggests, Hayek had no use for the concept of social justice. A passionate critic of redistributionism, he had no use for "social" anything. Calling it "a weasel word" that "wholly destroys" the meaning of whatever it happens to modify, Hayek deemed social justice among the worst of the lot of 160-odd "social" somethings.[10]

"Everybody talks about social justice, but if you press people to explain to you what they mean by social justice...nobody knows," Hayek told William F. Buckley on *Firing Line* in 1977.[11] He dismissed the expression as "empty and meaningless," "a quasi-religious belief with no content whatsoever," having the potential to lead to "the destruction of the indispensable environment in which the traditional moral values alone can flourish, namely personal freedom." It is an "intellectually disreputable" idea, which carries with it "the mark of demagoguery and cheap journalism, which responsible thinkers ought to be ashamed to use because, once its vacuity is recognized, its use is dishonest." He was not a fan.

Hayek's principal objection to social justice was that it distorts the marketplace, which he viewed as the most powerful engine of human potential and happiness. "[F]ew circumstances will do more to make a person energetic and efficient than the belief that it depends chiefly on him whether he will reach the goals he has set himself," Hayek contended.[12] He reasoned, therefore, that social justice is an illusion.

Rawls's idea of a just institution is a fallacy, Hayek declared. The minute that an institution starts redistributing society's goods, it becomes unjust. The more a set of institutions commits itself to addressing inequalities, the more inequalities it causes. "This would go on until government literally controlled every circumstance which could affect any person's well-being."[13] No one can depend on anyone but himself to secure his maximum economic benefit. To give in to the temptations of distributive justice is to empower the state, invite collectivism, socialism, and ultimately tyranny.

Social justice is "a demand that the state should treat different people differently in order to place them in the same position," Hayek told Buckley. "Making people equal—a goal of governmental policy— would force government to treat people very unequally, indeed."

Hayek was no absolutist. He did not see the state as a purely oppressive institution, nor did he resent basic welfare programs like social safety nets or public education. The libertarian dogmatist Ayn Rand described him as "an example of our most pernicious enemy" because of his willingness to compromise with the demands of the modern liberal state and its voters. Hayek did, however, understand that Rawlsian ideals break down when they are applied in the real world. Men are fallible, advantage-seeking political animals, a truth that cannot be theorized away. The veil as Rawls envisioned it is an entirely theoretical construct that denies essential human nature.

The Paradox of Equality

Though they may be loath to admit it, social justice advocates agree with Hayek on one core point: perfect equality isn't just unattainable, it's undesirable. This is the contradiction inherent in the modern conception of social justice with which we should most forcefully contend.

Like society's tangible goods, intangible goods such as justice simply cannot be doled out from behind a veil of ignorance without perpetuating the very injustices we are trying to rectify. True justice, social justice advocates would argue, requires a social reversal. Oppressors must be subjugated and the subjugated must be lifted up. The veil prevents a just society from achieving that objective and is therefore morally reprehensible.

Modern social justice advocates have no interest in a colorblind society. Nor would they accept the notion that just institutions can be trusted to maximize collective benefit. They are suspicious of institutions in general, in fact, since those institutions are invariably the flawed inventions of corruptible men. They are unconvinced that perfect equality is desirable, as we've seen, because such a naïve ideal ignores historical injustices. We must all bear burdens that are passed on to us at birth by our parents. These are obligations we cannot shrug off, no matter how hard we try.

In truth, social justice advocates aren't pure Rawlsian theorists, but they are not doctrinal Marxists either. They're certainly not libertarians. So what are they? Their theory of justice is rooted in a more subjective notion—a hatred of luck.

Brute Luck

Can institutions be made morally perfect? Can mankind? The answer is, alas, no. So the social justice movement's intellectual class has largely concluded that the pursuit of pure equality is not just a waste of time, it's ethically flawed.

These theorists are content to use the noble idea of equality as a starting point, but they veer off the paths forged by Aristotle, Hume, and Rawls when individual actions or circumstances should preclude one person from receiving the same justice as another who is more deserving. How can it be just for people to enjoy the benefits or suffer the burdens associated with the conditions into which they were born? Are the less fortunate and the historically "privileged" truly equivalent? If we treated them equally, is that justice? Or does justice require confiscating benefits, perceived to be unearned, from some to give to others?

Andrew Lister, a lecturer at Oxford University's Centre for the Study of Social Justice, expands on the notion that true distributive justice may have to account for the luck of the draw:

> The rationale for focusing on social positions is that people will be born into different starting points in life, which make it more or less likely that they will be able to succeed. People are born with different levels of innate talent. And assuming that liberty must permit private childrearing in some form, we will never have perfect equality of opportunity. Moreover, even if there were perfectly fair equality of opportunity and no differences in levels of innate talent, any economic system involving the market will involve a substantial element of luck. People who are willing to play by the rules will suffer unmerited failure; others less meritorious will win success.... Since everyone depends on the cooperation of others, we ought to take advantage of this morally arbitrary luck to claim a greater share of what we produce together— not unless this inequality will make everyone better off.[14]

This is an opinion that can be arrived at only by those with a powerful aversion to internalizing the lessons of history. Eliminating hereditary claims to title and nobility is one thing; neutralizing less tangible benefits based upon a subjective assessment of "privilege" is something else. Social leveling is predicated on the sacrifice of individual liberty and potential, which is why Hayek was so suspicious of the practice. Indeed, as Lister concedes, "Maximizing expected opportunity means being willing to accept that some may have very small chances in life in order that others who have already greater chances can have greater chances still."[15]

For the social justice left, that is an unacceptable concession. Theirs is a crusade against "brute luck." Those who believe in this philosophy and are familiar with the literature on the matter call themselves "luck egalitarians." Natural talent, opportunity, or even personal tastes— these are disparate circumstances that must be corrected through social leveling. This is the dismal future Kurt Vonnegut envisioned.

"The aim of justice as equality is to eliminate so far as it is possible the impact on people's lives of bad luck that falls on them through no fault or choice of their own," writes Richard Arneson.[16] As he and other critics of luck egalitarianism point out, this kind of forced leveling only makes people bitter, ungovernable, and unproductive. These circumspect critics of luck egalitarianism call themselves "rational egalitarians."

Anca Gheaus tries to smooth over these divisions by identifying how social goods can be distributed in a way that doesn't make the public want to rise up in violent revolution: "To promote equality of status, we could eliminate (especially early) school selection based on merit and de-emphasize quantitative evaluation of pupils and exams. To promote equality of power and inclusion we can, for instance, plan towns having in mind the goal of racial integration or introduce workplace democracy."[17] This is the fatal conceit of the haughty technocrat.

Gheaus has inadvertently allowed the social justice advocates' mask to fall. Believers in her particular form of social justice see society not as an infinitely complex set of interactions and traditions shaped by trial and error over generations but as one big problem to fix. What's more, they think they are sharp enough to fix it. If only they had the power to remake the world in their own image, this would be a just society at long last. This kind of hubris inevitably gives way to power hunger.

It is often overlooked that racial and sexual segregation on the scale America witnessed in the nineteenth and twentieth centuries was a result of social engineering that had to be enforced from the top down. The fad of "urban planning," typified by a mid-twentieth-century love affair with the idea of the "radiant city" promoted by, among others, architectural theorist Le Corbusier, did not result in radiant cities. It yielded stark, soulless towers punctuated by what Jane Jacobs famously dubbed "promenades that go from no place to nowhere and have no promenaders."[18]

In the process of deconstructing centuries of organic, incremental social evolution, the central planners empower government to engage in what government does best: boondoggles. Even the history of the practically sanctified national highway system has been whitewashed. "Haste, waste, mismanagement, and outright graft are making a multibillion-dollar rat-hole out of the Federal Highway Program," wrote Karl Detzer in 1960.[19] At least that project had a necessary military dimension. The people who were displaced, the lives that were ruined, the inefficiently allocated labor, and the millions of wasted dollars are the forgotten costs of indulging those prideful enough to consider themselves the enlightened distributors of society's goods.

Taking Social Justice Back

Some conservatives have tried to appropriate both the term "social justice" and its equalitarian message by advocating positive social leveling based on a more circumspect understanding of what the public sector can achieve.

Arthur Brooks of the American Enterprise Institute asserted in 2014 that conservatives should seek social justice not by instituting top-down solutions that tell the disadvantaged what they should want but by asking them what they would prefer. He defined "marginalized communities" in a much more expansive way than the Identitarian left does by describing one of its members—a man, "single with no kids and no religion," who is "professionally and socially disengaged."[20] Perhaps this man is white, perhaps not; Brooks doesn't say. But by expanding the definition of marginalization to include not only race and sex but also lower-income persons with no attachment to local mediating institutions and a lack of opportunities for economic advancement, Brooks was ahead of the curve. The persons and communities he described would become a preoccupation of political analysts when they united to form the backbone of Donald Trump's winning coalition of voters.

Brooks and other reformers argue that the conservative fear of public sector intervention into private affairs turns off voters who would otherwise find conservative policy prescriptions attractive. "As even the libertarian economist Friedrich Hayek argued, guaranteeing 'some minimum food, shelter, and clothing' is an appropriate task for government." Brooks advocates the reformation of the public education system, a program for economic growth that focuses on the lowest rungs of the social ladder, and a renewed emphasis on free enterprise. "Drop the materialistic fight against spending and take up a moral fight for people," he later argued. "Empathy doesn't contradict fiscal conservatism; it actually requires it."

This is social justice divorced from Identitarianism. For Identitarians, there is no true justice without tribal consciousness and a full understanding of who the presumably marginalized and disadvantaged really are. Unreservedly embracing Rawls's veil, Brooks insists that any virtuous program of social justice must be blind to the identity of its beneficiaries. That's why his prescription was doomed to be ignored and eventually abandoned.

By describing "marginalized communities" as those who are estranged from society whatever their sex or race, Brooks has attacked a sclerotic liberal paradigm that needs to be challenged. But because he refuses to endorse racial and demographic hierarchies, no social justice activist will take his prescriptions seriously. He is more likely to be shunned as a beneficiary of "white privilege," unaware of his true station in life or the unfair advantages he has enjoyed.

In 2015, the Supreme Court was asked to rule on the University of Texas's use of racial preferences in admissions. In a four-to-three decision the following year,[21] the Court upheld the constitutionality of a university's use of race as a criterion for admissions. The oral arguments in the case revealed how hotly the issue was debated. "There are those who contend that it does not benefit African-Americans to get them into the University of Texas, where they do not do well, as opposed to having them go to a less-advanced school, a less—a slower-track school where they do well," remarked Justice Antonin Scalia, who would die before the case was decided.[22] "One of the briefs pointed out that most of the black scientists in this country don't come from schools like the University of Texas. They come from lesser schools, where they do not feel that they're being pushed ahead in classes that are too fast for them. I'm just not impressed by the fact that the University of Texas may have fewer. Maybe it ought to have fewer."

The usual suspects howled in outrage, proclaiming Scalia's comments racist, but his statement was simply a sympathetic reference to an amicus brief. It was an argument for racially blind justice and maximum equality of opportunity, albeit one that is not easy to state inoffensively for those who consider meritocracy to be inherently discriminatory.

Social justice in today's America is bound up with race. Perhaps a capable reformer will one day decouple Identitarianism from social justice, but that task has so far confounded all who have tried.

The Veil Falls

The pursuit of a purely just, rational, and equal society has preoccupied philosophical minds for millennia despite the impossibility of ever achieving such a thing. By defining justice as a tangible and therefore finite good, social justice advocates are trapping themselves in a constricting paradigm that is intrinsically flawed.

The veil of ignorance is supposed to blind society's enlightened distributors to the identities of those who would receive their judgments—a utopian goal that modern-day social justice advocates resent. So they've simply let the veil drop.

Neither the alt-right nor the social justice left believes that blindness to traits acquired at birth can produce optimal justice. The alt-right is wholly suspicious of any distribution of social goods that does not account for America's uniquely deserving white majority. The social justice left is generally hostile toward any distribution of social goods that does not disadvantage that majority, if only to make up for the centuries of unfair advantages from which its members benefit even today, whether they know it or not. The fractiousness of Identitarianism ensures that pure equality, even if it were attainable, will never be seen by all as justice.

In the end, conservatives who are attracted to the idea of appropriating social justice for the cause of individual liberty and equality of opportunity will find themselves frustrated by Identitarians both to their left and right.

CHAPTER 5

Entry-Level Politics

D o not be misled by the preceding chapters; rank-and-file
social justice activists are not consumed with life's big questions. Far from it. Grand, cosmic notions of social equality
and reparative justice are deliberated by only a handful of this movement's most thoughtful members. Today's most vociferous social
justice activists are preoccupied with small things.

Hyperventilating over piddling controversies, fixating on fleeting
scandals resulting from the latest celebrity's artless comment, and
ostentatious displays of sanctimony—these are the forms that so much
"social justice" activism takes today. The Identitarian left, in particular,
goes in for dramatic displays. As this movement has become more
doctrinaire, it has attracted fewer new recruits. So their targets have
become smaller and softer.

More often than not, the people who face retribution for offending
the social justice activists of the left are social justice enthusiasts themselves—producers of popular mass media, progressives in finance or
the law, writers, artists, chefs, and scientists. This movement draws its
power from its ability to torment even inadvertent trespassers, though
a measure of complicity is required from the tormented.

As the social justice left has grown angry, insular, and radical, it has become devoted not to persuading the country but to imposing a rigid code of behavior on those who already agree with them. Doing so is easy and gives the appearance of efficacy. That facade is particularly valuable for millions of "woke" activists because where there is perceived value, there is profit to be made.

Entry-level activism is a scourge that dumbs down American political discourse, but transforming the public into a nasty and civically illiterate mob can be a lucrative enterprise.

Idolatry

On March 8, 2017—International Women's Day—New Yorkers awoke to find a new bronze idol erected in lower Manhattan. Face to face with the famous Wall Street *Charging Bull* stood a statue of a young girl, chin out, hands on hips, defying the snarling symbol of American capitalist energy. *Fearless Girl* practically demands that Fortune 500 boards add more women to their ranks. Yet for all the talk about its bold challenge to the dominant business culture, it is almost impossible to find anyone in the dominant business culture arguing against the ideals it supposedly represents. The diminutive statue achieved overnight fame, enhanced by the political media's obsession with the supposedly transgressive ornament. Its erection, gushed the *New York Times*, was one of the most courageous acts of defiance since the 1854 protest that led to the end of the segregation of the sexes on New York's trolleys.

When the sculptor of *Charging Bull* protested that the intrusion of *Fearless Girl* completely changed the meaning conveyed by his own work, New York Mayor Bill de Blasio taunted him on Twitter: "Men who don't like women taking up space are exactly why we need the Fearless Girl." It seems that the only other person who did not respond to the statue with due veneration was a (likely inebriated) young man photographed thrusting his hips lewdly at *Fearless Girl*. The photo was the occasion for ginned-up outrage on myriad traffic-starved click-farm blogs from Kansas City to India, each write-up more outraged than the last. In fact, demonstrating one's outrage over this photo became something of a competitive online sport.

This supposed attack on bourgeois commercialism was, in fact, part of a public relations campaign by an investment firm. State Street Global Advisors commissioned the work ostensibly to raise awareness of the lack of women in its industry, and its president, Ronald O'Hanley, took advantage of the attendant publicity to call for an increase in "gender diversity." The statue's message dovetailed with the firm's "Gender Diversity Index" fund, which invests in companies heavy on female leadership—an objective that rewards diversity over other traits like, say, profitability. No one seemed to notice that women occupied only 17 percent of State Street's leadership positions or that no woman had ever held O'Hanley's position.

Because identity comes before everything else, the American left fell head over heels for a commercial—a commercial for a bunch of Wall Street fat cats, no less. This spectacle culminated in the pilgrimage of Senator Elizabeth Warren of Massachusetts to New York City, where she was photographed standing alongside the sculpture over the caption "Fight like a girl." The irony of a politician who cannot draw two breaths without attacking "Wall Street greed" endorsing an advertisement for a Wall Street investment firm was entirely lost on both Warren and her fan base.

The statue did receive an analytical once-over from some earnest progressives, but only those already on the margins of American politics. Because their arguments deteriorated rather quickly into Marxist nattering, they were easily dismissed. "Woke, bougie liberalism coexists, and is to some extent dependent on, economic exploitation," wrote one critic, *Paste* magazine's Jason Rhode. "It is methadone for progressives, who tell themselves they are doing righteous work to buy socially-aware brands." This sensible observation was subsequently obscured by the author's prattling on about "late-stage capitalism," "the liberation of women," and, for some reason, the plight of indigenous peoples all around the world.[1]

This critique of *Fearless Girl* through the lens of socialist realism exposed what should discomfit the left: there were no hair-on-fire denunciations of this statue from those on the left who can reliably be counted on to deconstruct art and distill it into its most problematic elements. The dog that didn't bark was even more conspicuous here, since this statue practically begged for an Identitarian deconstruction.

"Stop infantilizing women," wrote the Breitbart News reporter Frances Martel. "Stop using the genitalia of a plurality of human beings to build a social class." It was, indeed, eye-catching that it took a conservative writer to highlight the subtext associated with depicting female potency in the form of a child. It didn't seem to occur to anyone on the left that the image of a preadolescent girl exposed to the rampaging bull of capitalism contained culturally mixed messages. Martel's was a sentiment that any student of feminist theory would accept at face value if it were offered by a member of the tribe. But this statue escaped such scrutiny, because its politics was the right kind of politics.

Amid all the adoration, the social justice left somehow forgot to apply to State Street Global Advisors the standards it applies to other heretics. For example, a review of this supposedly socially responsible firm's recommendations for attracting "alpha female" investors is full of what more discerning critics might consider old-fashioned gender stereotyping.

"Genetic factors like levels of testosterone and how the brain deals with stress can skew female investors into being more risk adverse [sic]," reads the promotional pamphlet for the Gender Diversity Index fund. "Unlike their male counterparts women also have more vivid memories of negative experiences—the female brain is hardwired for less-selective memory, which can further deter risk-taking." The document adds that women tend to be "risk and loss-averse" and relate "investing to emotional constructs, such as security and independence." And you men out there should avoid "excessive rumination" while advising your "alpha female" on an investment strategy, which is a fancy way of saying don't think too hard.[2]

These thoughts could ignite a multi-day social media furor if they were expressed by—to pick a hypothetical at random—a Google engineer. But because State Street paid proper, albeit superficial, homage to the tenets of social justice, the mob provided them with a special dispensation.

We soon learned why State Street's executives were so eager to project themselves as sophisticated feminist crusaders amid a sea of unevolved dinosaurs. In October 2017, State Street agreed to settle a lawsuit that followed an audit by the Department of Labor finding that the firm had systematically discriminated against its female and black employees in favor of white men. State Street disbursed five million dollars to the 305 women and fifteen African-Americans who were due compensatory damages.[3] Suddenly, all the feting of this statue disappeared, along with the dignity of those who had fawned over it.

Yet one should not take *Fearless Girl* and its fifteen minutes of fame too seriously. The love affair with this statute isn't about politics. It's about conformity. This statue attracted attention because of the emotional response it provoked. Stimulating that emotional response and simulating the experiences associated with real and effective political activism has become the social justice business model.

Fearless Girl is a perfect example of the modern plague of entry-level political opinion. This statue isn't politics. It has nothing to do with any policy proposal, but it touches on a vaguely political theme—sex discrimination—and the intensity of the emotion around that issue makes it feel like politics. This process is self-perpetuating. Political media outlets seek out controversy where it is a barely glowing ember, fanning it into a conflagration with the potential to go viral online. It is no coincidence that this phenomenon tends to occur around Identitarian issues.

From movies to comic books, from monuments to the faces that grace American currency, social justice crusades only mimic politics. They require little expertise or background knowledge. All that is required to weigh in on them and to be taken seriously by the self-appointed gatekeepers of elevated political discourse is a "marginalized" identity.

Reducing the barriers to entry into political discourse has helped the bottom lines of some revenue-starved media outlets, but it hasn't done much for the standards of public dialogue. So many of the issues that consume social media, traveling from there up the chain to cable news and into the mouths of America's political and business elite, are pitifully trivial. These are small people occupying themselves with small things, but their influence can be considerable.

Getting Art Right

The nearly religious fervor that social justice inspires among its faithful would be justified if the issues that animated its adherents were serious. Instead, they are objectively trite. More often than its proponents will admit, identity politics is dumbed-down politics.

At some point in the recent past, the social justice left resolved to focus its rage on soft targets. Art and its producers are of particular concern to activists, but not just any art. It is often the sort created and developed by people who share liberal political and cultural sensitivities and are, therefore, most likely to capitulate to the demands of their like-minded critics. Because Identitarian activists take the media they consume so seriously, so must we. And so, with a heavy sigh, we begin with comic books.

When the hero of the *Captain America* series joined the Nazi-inspired organization Hydra in a provocative attempt to generate sales, a disturbingly large number of "anti-fascist" demonstrators attacked the comic for "normalizing" National Socialism. "There's a rise of anti-Semitic behavior in this world right now," Greg Gage, proprietor of Black Cat Comics in Utah, told the *Guardian*'s Kieran Shiach. "The last thing I want to do is force my queer, Jewish employee to wear a Hail Hydra shirt."[4]

In protest, fascism's showiest opponents sent videos of themselves burning copies of the heretical comic book to its creator. "When you burn books you're not taking a stand against fascism, you're taking a stand against irony," wrote the graphic novel's author, Nick Spencer.[5] In response to this deluge of outrage, Marvel comics felt compelled to "politely ask you to allow the story to unfold before coming to any conclusion."[6] But the company had already reached its own conclusions about the ill-informed tirade from their most energetic readers: the customer is always right.

This controversy occurred at a difficult time for this purveyor of superhero titles. A sequel to the *Avengers: Civil War* comic, released to tie in with the movie by the same name, met with disappointing sales and lackluster reviews. In February 2017, the only Marvel properties to break the top ten in units sold were *Star Wars* titles. In response to this adversity, the company concluded that taking risks just wasn't worth it. "What we heard was that people didn't want any more diversity," Marvel's senior vice president of sales and marketing, David Gabriel, told an interviewer at a March 2017 marketing summit. "We saw the sales of any character that was diverse, any character that was new, our female characters, anything that was not a core Marvel character, people were turning their nose up against."[7]

The uproar was as predictable as it was potent. A co-creator of *Ms. Marvel*, G. Willow Wilson, insisted that Gabriel's remark was simply ignorant. Her fans, she added, appreciated how her graphic novels dealt with "the role of traditionalist faith in the context of social justice."[8] Maybe that's true for devoted readers of Wilson's franchise, but Gabriel's observation wasn't groundless. Marvel had been experimenting with the gimmicky reimagining of its characters, and the core audience of readers rejected these reboots.

"Over the past few years just some of the character shifts have brought about a female Thor, Ms. Marvel becoming a Pakistani Muslim, Captain America becoming an African-American, Spider-Man a black-Hispanic teen, and Iron Man is currently a black female college co-ed," wrote The Federalist's Brad Slager.[9] The assumption by Marvel executives seemed to be that tweaks to their creations' accidents of birth would yield entirely different characters with radically changed personalities. This is not how character development works in the real world, and it's no surprise that this tiresome ploy resulted in stilted characters and stale plotlines. If only there were a word that described the assumption that people are defined entirely by their physical features.

Marvel isn't the only entertainment company obsessed with identity. We are "in the midst of a great cultural identity migration," writes the *New York Times* critic Wesley Morris.[10] "Gender roles are merging. Races are being shed.... [W]e've been made to see how trans and bi and poly-ambi-omni- we are." In 2015, the year Hollywood discovered Identitarianism, Neil Patrick Harris joked at the Academy Awards ceremony about how the event was a celebration of "Hollywood's best and whitest." It was the year that birthed the hashtag #OscarsSoWhite, a banner under which activists united in opposition to the Academy of Motion Picture Arts and Sciences' habit of nominating white actors and actresses.

From 2007 to 2014, between 73 and 77 percent of speaking characters in major motion pictures were white, according to a University of Southern California study.[11] These figures might have been reflected in the pool of Academy Award nominees. While those figures were similar to those of the broader American population, the ratio of women to men in speaking roles was not. "Along gender lines, 30.2 percent of the 30,835 speaking characters evaluated were female across the 700 top-grossing films, and only 11 percent of the films had gender-balanced casts or featured girls/women in roughly half (45–54.9 percent) of the speaking roles," *Variety* reported.[12]

Hollywood's brightest stars dismissed the notion that this disparity was anything other than a sign of the latent misogyny and bigotry typical of the still male, straight, and white film and television industry. "The nominations reflect the Academy. The Academy reflects the industry, and then the industry reflects America," said actor Will Smith. "There is a regressive slide towards separatism, towards racial and religious disharmony, and that's not the Hollywood that I want to leave behind."[13] Say what you will of Smith's complaint, he was not venting about the frustrating bigotries of red-state America. Like Marvel's travails, the clash over the extent to which Hollywood has pursued the mandates of social justice is primarily an intramural debate on the left. And yet, even amid all this introspection, Hollywood was incubating monsters.

In October 2017, it was finally proved that the famous producer and tastemaker Harvey Weinstein had engaged in long-rumored violent abuse, verbal assault, and sexual harassment of scores of women. After those allegations were printed in the *New York Times*, the dam burst. Dozens of female entertainment industry professionals began telling their stories, not only about Weinstein but also about men up and down the hierarchy of the entertainment industry. For Weinstein and his fellow abusers, time was up, but he wasn't going to go down without a fight.

Weinstein hired Lisa Bloom, the daughter of the feminist attorney Gloria Allred, to represent him. Entirely unrelated, of course, Bloom's book on the killing of the Florida teenager Trayvon Martin was slated to be made into a television miniseries by the rapper Jay-Z in conjunction with the Weinstein Company. Barack Obama's former communications director, Anita Dunn, provided him pro bono public relations advice. The famous producer had donated vast sums to liberal candidates, including Hillary Clinton, and to causes like Planned Parenthood, as his surrogates were quick to remind his detractors. Weinstein spent a lifetime building up his credibility among liberal politicians and activists, and he called in every favor he was owed.[14]

Weinstein's tone-deaf attempt to mitigate the damage to his reputation was perhaps understandable. His liberal bona fides, which once earned him so much indulgence, no longer had the same purchase. In a last desperate effort to salvage his career, Weinstein released a letter pledging to sue the *New York Times* and donate the proceeds to "women's organizations" and to devote his time to combating the National Rifle Association. All these tawdry appeals to solidarity by tickling liberal erogenous zones had worked in the past. It makes sense that he thought he could emotionally manipulate the Democratic political culture into letting him off easy.

The deforming influence of social justice dogma on art affects the young as well, as the case of Laurie Forest's young-adult novel *The Black Witch* demonstrates. This much-anticipated book received favorable reviews prior to its release, until its publicity train was derailed by a bookstore employee and blogger, Shauna Sinyard. "The *Black Witch* is the most dangerous, offensive book I have ever read," Sinyard wrote. "It was ultimately written for white people. It was written for the type of white person who considers themselves to be not-racist and thinks that they deserve recognition and praise for treating POC [people of color] like they are actually human."

She went on to savage the thematic elements in the book as "racist, ableist, homophobic," and "written with no marginalized people in mind." What were these insensitive thematic elements? For one, *The Black Witch* is set in a fantasy world in which human beings live alongside other fantastical races of lore, some of which are more suspicious of miscegenation than others. This construct compelled Sinyard to write a traumatized nine-thousand-word review of the not-yet-released book.

"That made me interested in exploring this particular controversy because it's a remarkable example of how one person's interpretation of a book as offensive, even if it's not particularly intelligent, can become almost gospel in the community," the young-adult novelist and journalist Kat Rosenfield told me. She spent several months investigating and chronicling this episode in a widely-read column for the website Vulture. "The novel became the object of sustained, aggressive opposition in the weeks leading up to its release," she writes. Forest's publisher received reams of hate mail. Online mobs methodically drove down the book's online ratings. Prospective reviewers were targeted with harassment, and presales were no doubt hurt by the controversy and negative publicity.

Sinyard "politely declined" Rosenfield's request for an interview but then tweeted that she had been "scared" by her interaction with the young reporter; soon Rosenfield stood accused of harassing and threatening Sinyard. Vulture came under intense pressure to abandon the reporter and her story. "I was expecting to get dragged," Rosenfield reflects. "I was not anticipating how quickly or intensely it would happen and take the form of outright fabrications designed to torpedo my credibility in personal ways."

A young-adult novelist herself, Rosenfield notes sadly that the community that reviews books like hers was once engaged in a "real, robust conversation surrounding diversity and wanting to improve diversity" in an industry dominated by white women. No longer. That community has spawned a subculture of self-appointed "woke" overseers who exercise undue influence. "Instead of pushing books by minority authors," she observed, "it was dedicated to singling out and dragging out books that were perceived to have done something wrong."

E. E. Charlton-Trujillo's young-adult novel *When We Was Fierce* was subjected to a similar ordeal. Praised by *Publishers Weekly* as a "heartbreaking and powerful modern American story," it features a fifteen-year-old African-American protagonist who witnesses the beating of a disabled teenager. Charlton-Trujillo, who is not black herself, had become controversial among a small but disproportionately influential set of social justice minders for adapting and exploring cultural traits predominately shared by African-Americans. *When We Was Fierce* was pulled from the shelves on the eve of its publication with the consent of both its publisher and author, because it violated the fluctuating standards of social justice advocates.

As Rosenfield concludes in her powerful Vulture column, the crusade to impose social justice realism on art has become so widespread that it is almost indistinguishable from the suppression of free expression:

> In recent months, the community was bubbling with a dozen different controversies of varying reach—over Nicola Yoon's *Everything Everything* (for ableism), Stephanie Elliot's *Sad Perfect* (for being potentially triggering to ED survivors), *A Court of Wings and Ruin* by Sarah J. Maas (for heterocentrism), *The Traitor's Kiss* by Erin Beaty (for misusing the

story of Mulan), and *All the Crooked Saints* by Maggie Sti-efvater (in a peculiar example of publishing pre-crime, people had decided that Stiefvater's book was racist before she'd even finished the manuscript.)[15]

Rosenfield's challenge prompted a brief bout of introspection within the community of young adult novelists and critics, but it didn't last long. Within weeks, a rabble of vicious censors targeted another author and her reviewers for failing to properly reinforce their conception of the United States as a Hobbesian morass of racism and bigotry. In Laura Moriarty's novel *American Heart*, a fear of Muslims has led the government to establish vast internment zones in the Western desert. The protagonist initially supports this policy but changes her mind when she meets a Muslim seeking freedom in the United States.

An online review in the trade journal *Kirkus Reviews* was almost entirely positive, describing the work as a "moving portrait of an American girl discovering her society in crisis, desperate to show a disillusioned immigrant the true spirit of America." Those proved to be fighting words, and a horde of bitter scolds descended on *Kirkus* for publishing a review that upheld "oppressive power structures." The vast majority of the critics had never read the book, but because it dealt with the internment of Muslims—even though with obvious disapproval—the work and its favorable review were savaged.

After a few days of this manufactured outrage, *Kirkus* pulled the review. "[W]hile we believe our reviewer's opinion is worthy and valid, some of the wording fell short of meeting our standards for clarity and sensitivity, and we failed to make the thoughtful edits our readers deserve," the editor's letter read. And so a review of a book condemning mob mentalities became the victim of one, an irony that escaped *Kirkus* and its critics.[16]

More disturbingly, though, *Kirkus* revealed that its reviewer was herself an "observant Muslim person of color" who was "well-versed in the dangers of white savior narratives." You see, this particular review was consistent with *Kirkus*'s "Own Voices" policy, which holds that a literary opinion is only as valuable as the identity of the person who holds it. When "evaluating texts," *Kirkus* reviewers must be able to "draw upon lived experience."[17] That is to say, a book about Muslims can be faithfully reviewed only by a Muslim, just as a book about African-Americans can be reviewed only by an African-American, and so on.

This sorry story is the fruit of Identitarianism, an ideology that insists that the key to a person's mind and heart is the stereotypes associated with his culture and external features. We used to call that prejudice.

An Age of Idiocy

For some, engaging in these campaigns against figures of prominence is its own reward. It's exciting and provocative, and it feels like political activism. Perhaps because the stakes are so low and the consequences of failure virtually nonexistent, this kind of "activism" is popular among social justice advocates. But this is not politics; it's playing at politics.

Trifling cultural disputes have become even more important in an era of dumbed-down, identity-obsessed discourse. Trivialities like the allegedly monochromatic Oscars or the gender identity of Marvel's latest super hero would be dismissed as peculiarities were they not indicative of a more militant strain of political engagement that has splintered off from the pursuit of social justice.

Judging one's forebears by the moral standards of one's own time rather than seeking to understand theirs is an exercise for the arrogant and the ignorant. The objective of those who engage in this practice is usually not a fuller understanding of their predecessors but confirmation of their own sense of moral superiority. This spreading folly is deforming the American left's otherwise noble desire to communicate the unequivocal sins of America's past, such as slavery, and fueling a trend among Democrats to repudiate the two founders of their party—Thomas Jefferson and Andrew Jackson.

Following Dylann Roof's racist attack on a black church in South Carolina, annual Democratic "Jefferson-Jackson" fundraising dinners—a decades-old tradition—were renamed or abandoned entirely. Activists and commentators wondered aloud whether the Jefferson Memorial in Washington, D.C., ought to be dismantled. Lost in this moral panic was any appreciation of the complexities of the lives and times of these great but flawed men.[18]

Jefferson was both a populist and one of the most enlightened men to attain high office. His declaration that "all men are created equal" was a radical sentiment at the time of its adoption by the Continental Congress. And while Jefferson was himself a slaveholder, his views on the institution were conflicted. The first anti-slave law in the United States, the Northwest Ordinance of 1787, which paved the way for the territories of the Upper Midwest to enter the Union as free states, was based on a law drafted by Jefferson in 1784. In a message to Congress as president, Jefferson wrote that "the morality, the reputation, and the best of our country have long been eager to proscribe" slavery.[19]

Andrew Jackson, the founder of the modern Democratic Party, was a terrible president. His refusal to reauthorize the charter of the Second Bank of the United States set off the most turbulent century in America's financial history. But Identitarians do not condemn Jackson for his economic illiteracy. Their focus is on his execution of the Indian Removal Act, which led to what came to be known as the Trail of Tears. This was a great crime by any standard, but it was not long ago that

Jackson was revered by his fellow Democrats for his commitment to populism. What Jackson's critics derided as the "Reign of King Mob" saw the expansion of voting rights to all white males, not just those of property. But Jackson's populism knew prudent ends. At a time of great evangelical fervor, the seventh president was unmoved by the petitions of powerful religious leaders who sought to weaken the separation of church and state.

These confounding contradictions have been forgotten amid the new moral necessity to blanch our history of the memory of all those who tolerated, actively or passively, the practice of human bondage in the United States. And following a national tragedy in the spring of 2015, an old campaign to banish Jackson from the twenty-dollar bill received new life. This campaign quickly became more preoccupied with not just jettisoning Jackson but ensuring that his visage would be replaced by that of a woman.

Six hundred thousand votes later, the informal contest arranged by the group "Women on 20s" found that online voters wanted to see the antislavery activist Harriet Tubman replace Jackson on the twenty. Within weeks, President Barack Obama's Treasury Department revealed that Alexander Hamilton was to be banished from the ten-dollar bill. After all, Treasury had determined as far back as 2013 that the sawbuck was the next note slated for a redesign, and a little online fury wasn't going to scuttle the plan. But such was the Obama administration's commitment to the demands of identity politics that they didn't want to argue with the crowd, so long as it was their crowd.

So who was to replace Hamilton, the visionary co-author of the Federalist Papers, the architect of the modern financial system, the immigrant and Revolutionary War veteran whose rise from poverty made him the epitome of the new democratic man? Treasury's only criteria were that it be a woman and that she be remembered as "a champion for our inclusive democracy." Suddenly, those on the left who had been so deeply haunted by the memory of Jackson's slaves and the Native Americans who perished on the forced exile he ordered forgot about the man on the twenty-dollar bill.

Hamilton eventually received a reprieve, not because he championed the federal banking system, the assumption of a national debt and the foreign credit that sprang from it, and the country's industrial evolution. No, Hamilton's reputation was restored by the hit Broadway musical *Hamilton*. The coastal elites who fell in love with the show joined with the musical's lead actor, Lin-Manuel Miranda, in successfully pressing the secretary of the treasury, Jack Lew, to abandon his plan to relegate Hamilton to a modest position on the back of the bill he has graced since 1928.[20]

The key to that musical's popularity wasn't just its script, score, and message but the creative decision to cast non-white actors as the white historical figures. Indeed, only after the show received effusive acclaim did its casting directive, which explicitly excluded white actors, come under scrutiny by New York City for violating its nondiscrimination laws. The city has, of course, looked the other way, if only to avoid antagonizing the influential artists and politicians who gushed over the musical and its bravely transgressive casting choices.

This Identitarian principle—celebrating a race-bending musical—soon ran headlong into another: the need to give women their due by putting a female face on a Federal Reserve note. "With this decision, Secretary Lew is proving, once again, that in America it's still a man's world," read a press release from the deeply wounded organizers of the Women on 20s campaign. "It was a chorus of mostly men who implored him to keep Hamilton on the $10, and he listened."[21]

This is a truly stupid time to be alive.

It would be comforting to write all this off as the mania of a class of politically active young people who will mature with age into something more reasonable, but it's becoming harder every year to distinguish between hyperventilating youth and radicalized—or cowed—adults.

So far, the national effort to expel historical figures with complicated legacies from the public square has been rooted in some understanding of history, though it is often a shallow one. Removing monuments dedicated to the Confederacy is, for example, an effort to confront historical realities. Those monuments were never designed to provide clarity about America's past but to whitewash it. It did not take long, however, before the campaign that targeted Confederate statuary began zeroing in on history's towering figures not because of what they did but because of how they made people feel. The most asinine example of this crusade comes to us courtesy of Pennsylvania's Lebanon Valley College, where a new villain, Claude A. Lynch, haunts the imaginations of the school's social justice devotees.

Lynch was not a slave owner. He was born decades after Emancipation. In fact, he was, by all accounts, a humanitarian. Lynch served as the school's president during the Great Depression and World War II, and he helped resettle refugees displaced by conflict abroad. So what was the offense so grave that his name should be scrubbed from the school's façade? "I think it has to do with the historical association of it. The word as a verb, not as a name of a person," the college's executive director of marketing, Marty Parkes, told The Daily Beast. "I think it creates feelings of discomfort in some quarters."[22]

That's right. In 2015, students demonstrating for a "more diverse curriculum and faculty recognizing varied gender identities and disabilities," as PennLive reported, also included in their list of demands the renaming of a memorial hall at Lebanon Valley College. They were undeterred by the fact that the African-American attorney general of the United States at the time shared the same discomfiting name.

Lynch Memorial Hall was ultimately spared the whitewash, but other institutions named for a "Lynch" weren't so lucky. Two years later, the Centennial School Board in Southeast Portland, Oregon, voted to rename two of their elementary schools named for a local Lynch family, who donated the land upon which they sit. The board reasoned that these schools might invoke the memory of violent, racist hangings. This is not even akin to the historical revisionism of totalitarian ideologies like those practiced by Soviet Bolsheviks or the Afghan Taliban, which erased from public memory their country's inconvenient histories to achieve a coherent political objective. This is the eradication of that which could *erroneously* invoke the memory of America's flawed racial past.

This is paranoia, not enlightenment. It is indicative of a savior complex in many social justice advocates, and it's how the nonintellectual fad of "cultural appropriation" became weaponized.

Cultural Appropriation

Cultural appropriation isn't just the social justice left's obsession du jour; it's a contradiction in terms.

Cultural appropriation is ostensibly the study of how one culture adopts elements of another, but this definition refutes the very thing it sets out to define. Culture is not property and cultural transmission is not a zero-sum game. The adoption of some elements of one culture by another is not theft because no one has lost anything in this transaction. Since culture can be transmitted, adapted, and disseminated, it defies both legal and colloquial definitions of ownership.

But we're missing the point. Cultural appropriation isn't about sovereignty, dignity, or integrity; it's about establishing boundaries. Susan Scafidi, a professor at Fordham University's law school and the author of *Who Owns Culture? Appropriation and Authenticity in American Law*, defines appropriation as "taking—from a culture that is not one's own—intellectual property, cultural expressions or artifacts, history, and ways of knowledge."[23]

"This can include unauthorized use of another culture's dance, dress, music, language, folklore, cuisine, traditional medicine, religious symbols, etc.," Scafidi tells an interviewer. "It's most likely to be harmful when the source community is a minority group that has been oppressed or exploited in other ways or when the object of appropriation is particularly sensitive."[24] There's the rub. In theory, this is a well-meaning effort to preserve cultural heritage from perversion or commercialization by those who neither understand it nor cherish it. In practice, it is yet another method by which the social justice left wields power.

Like so many aspects of the social justice movement, this concern about "cultural appropriation" springs from an otherwise admirable sensitivity to the feelings of others. But then activists blow it out of proportion and it becomes a celebrity cause, to be exploited by the supposed victims of appropriation and by those who would play the redeemer.

On October 30, 2015, Yale University students received an email from Erika Christakis, an early education professor and the associate master of Silliman College, about the urgent matter of Halloween costumes. She had taken it upon herself to respond to a directive from Yale's Intercultural Affairs Committee setting guidelines for appropriate garb. The directive noted that Halloween is a time when many students' ethnicity, religion, or class is lampooned in costume form. "In many cases, the student wearing the costume has not *intended* to offend," the memo concluded, "but their actions or lack of forethought have sent a far greater message than any apology could after the fact."[25]

This did not sit well with Christakis. In a letter distinguished by the saintly patience typical of an early education instructor, Christakis noted that the essential nature of Halloween is that it is a time when individuals can lose themselves in characters that are wildly different from themselves. "[I]f you don't like a costume someone is wearing, look away, or tell them you are offended," she suggested. "Talk to each other. Free speech and the ability to tolerate offense are the hallmarks of a free and open society."

Professor Nicholas Christakis, Erika's husband and the co-master of Silliman College, echoed his wife's sentiments in a follow-up email: "[W]e believe strongly that our job is to help students to speak for themselves, rather than to speak for them. We want students of all stripes and ideologies to talk to each other, and we will try to foster an environment in which students can debate any issue with their peers."

Shortly after this email was sent, students began organizing to have the Christakises fired. "Students gathered Thursday outside Yale's main library to draw in chalk their response to recent events they say have confirmed that Yale is inhospitable to black students and to black women in particular," the *Washington Post* reported. "There was so much coded language in that e-mail that is just disrespectful," one student told the *Post*. Others were allegedly so traumatized that they contemplated withdrawing from Yale altogether. "They can't stay in the master's house," said one student, who thus trivialized and appropriated the experience of American slaves.[26]

Determined to confront his accusers, Nicholas Christakis appeared before this irritated group of young students, a scene that was captured on video. One particularly agitated young woman berated Christakis and demanded that he remain silent through her emotional lecture. "It is your job to create a place of comfort and home for the students that live in Silliman," she screamed. "By sending out that email, that goes against your position as master."

"No," Christakis replied calmly, "I don't agree with that."

"Then why the f—k did you accept the position!" his accuser yelled. "It is not about creating an intellectual space. Do you understand that? It is about creating a home here."[27]

Six months later, both Nicholas and Erika Christakis resigned their posts.

The hysteria over appropriative Halloween costumes is not limited to adults who think they are still children. It's being inflicted on actual children. In October 2017, the women's magazine *Cosmopolitan* advised parents to teach their children about "the importance of cultural sensitivity." Specifically, parents should tell their white daughters that it is inappropriate for them to dress as the Polynesian Disney character Moana. "If your kid wears a racist costume," the piece read, "you're kind of wearing it, too."[28] Steeping children in racial consciousness and teaching them that they are allowed to appreciate only one culture—their own—seems like a counterproductive way to combat racism.

The fabricated scourge of cultural appropriation extends beyond the college campus. In the spring of 2017, the artist Dana Schutz revealed her latest work in the Whitney Museum, part of a collection of paintings aimed at combating racism and poverty in America. Her portrait, titled *Open Casket*, features the likeness of the body of Emmett Till—the fourteen-year-old African-American who was falsely accused of offending a white woman and lynched in Mississippi in 1955, an atrocity that catalyzed the civil rights movement. Art critics liked it, but the social justice mob panned it. "This painting should not be acceptable to anyone who cares or pretends to care about Black people because it is not acceptable for a white person to transmute Black suffering into profit and fun," wrote the British critic Hannah Black in an open letter co-signed by forty-seven other artists. "White free speech and white creative freedom have been founded on the constraint of others, and are not natural rights." Black and her co-signers demanded that the painting be taken down.[29]

The artist Parker Bright, calling the painting "an injustice to the black community," accused Schutz of perpetrating "the same kind of violence that was enacted on Till." Bright then displayed his own art at the Whitney—of the performance variety—when he allowed himself to be photographed standing in front of Schutz's painting wearing a T-shirt that read "black death spectacle."

The protesters charged that Schutz's painting represents the "appropriation of Black culture by non-Black artists"—specifically, according to one blogger for The Root, "a white woman from Brooklyn."[30] Soon, the social justice league insisted that Schutz's career be discredited along with her painting. Protesters called for the cancellation of a showing of her work in Boston's Institute of Contemporary Art, even though the offending painting of Till would not be present.

To be fair, not everyone on the left thought this lashing out was a productive exercise. The *New York Times* critic Roberta Smith objected, as did the artist Clifford Owens. "I don't know anything about Hannah Black, or the artists who've co-signed her breezy and bitter letter," Owens wrote, "but I'm not down with artists who censor artists."[31] The social justice left had overreached, and the painting remained on display, but this movement's demands for scalps are not always so unsuccessful.

For what may be the sorriest tale of misery resulting from the fanatical policing of cultural appropriation, we must journey to Portland, Oregon, to the little taco truck Kooks Burritos. This trendy pop-up brasserie was owned by two women who built a popular and profitable business from scratch. The business's success would be its downfall.

The proprietors, Kali Wilgus and Liz Connelly, confessed to a reporter that they came up with the idea for their business while on a trip to Mexico. They fell in love with the food, asked local chefs for their recipes and techniques, and replicated them in the Pacific

Northwest to wild acclaim. The outrage that followed their success was hysterical even by the standards of the social justice left.

The media company Mic attacked Kooks and its proprietors as "white cooks bragging about stealing recipes from Mexico." The *Port-land Mercury* included Kooks on a short list of "white-owned appro-priative restaurants," adding that it was just one of many problematic restaurants "birthed as a result of curious white people going to a foreign country."[32] The restaurant's reviews went south, so to speak, and the customers stopped coming. When the death threats started, Wilgus and Connelly shut down their business.

"Because of Portland's underlying racism, the people who rightly owned these traditions and cultures that exist are already treated poorly," read a triumphant column that ran in both the *Mercury* and on Mic's website. "These appropriating businesses are erasing and exploiting their already marginalized identities for the purpose of profit and praise."[33]

Just a week after this story's publication, the *Mercury* scrubbed this final attack on Kooks Burritos from its website: "It was not factually supported, and we regret the original publication of this story," read the apologetic editorial note. Sure, a few lives were ruined and a jour-nalistic outlet lost its credibility, but those clicks must have been pretty sweet.[34]

An Unethical Business Model

Anyone examining the modern social justice movement quickly encounters a chicken-and-egg conundrum. Which came first, a move-ment that is so myopically obsessed with identity that it can't distin-guish a legitimate case of discrimination from a ginned-up contre-temps, or the media culture that exploits that obsession for profit? For clarity on this question, consider the rise and decline of Mic.com.

PolicyMic, a website targeting a burgeoning audience of news-consuming millennials, launched in 2010. Like many sites of that period, it cast a wide a net by publishing a lot of material, often with the help of "aggregation"—scraping content from other sites with bigger budgets and real reporters and writing some original opinion around it, thereby avoiding the legal mess associated with the outright theft of material. Many aggregators paid their staffers poorly, if at all, but they gave young writers a valuable platform. Their potential in the early age of social media—and it was often just potential—led to speculative ten-figure valuations and venture funding in the tens of millions of dollars.

PolicyMic was one of the more successful such sites. By 2013, it had found its niche as a left-leaning outlet catering to the growing obsession with identity, launching a section dedicated exclusively to Identitarianism and the traffic generated by that special brand of narcissism.

"At PolicyMic Identities, we aim to feature articles as thoughtful, complex, and unique as the stories of our generation," read a job listing for that site. "We examine what it's like to be a white woman of color, explore what it means to be a male feminist, talk back to the Pope as a young gay man, and reflect on how Abercrombie & Fitch failed you and other homeless youth."[35] Vital stuff.

The site expanded rapidly. By the end of 2013, it published almost a hundred posts per day, generating tens of millions of unique visitors and boasting a network of thousands of writers. That success was reduced to a formula, and that formula was built around the idea that social justice activism was fueled by anxiety, a preoccupation with oneself, and the need for a constant stream of new enemies.

In 2014, PolicyMic rebranded itself "Mic" and dedicated its staff to chasing whatever traffic Facebook had sent its way the day prior. "I think a lot of people in today's day and age want to know, 'What are we supposed to be outraged about?'" a former Mic staffer told the liberal website The Outline. "Mic realized earlier than most places that they could commodify people's feelings about race and gender."[36]

Mic relied on rote efforts to stoke anger—anything that encouraged the perception that the Anglo-American West, in particular, is steeped in racial injustice. "'Minority Report' Is Real—And It's Really Reporting Minorities," read one typical headline. In another, a description in Britain's *Sunday Telegraph* of the first female head of the BBC as a "mother of three" was described by one no doubt childless Mic reporter as "sexism at its worst." When the comedian Sasheer Zamata left NBC's *Saturday Night Live*, Mic described the departure as a sign that "TV's race and gender problems are more systemic than ever." Viewing race through the prism of a late-night comedy program, Mic brought the complex history of racial tensions and disparities in America down to a level that it believed young readers could grasp—and, more importantly, share on social media.

In 2017, Mic began to shed disillusioned staffers and shifted from text to the production of video content, which was more likely to generate a return on investment. Among the new ventures was a comedy along the lines of *Chappelle's Show*, "except it's hosted by a trans woman of color." Presumably, this comedy host with a challenging identity would possess a modicum of talent. But that consideration seemed to be, at best, an afterthought.

The effort to shoehorn identity politics into every facet of modern life extends beyond click-farms on the internet. "Why is science so straight," the *New York Times* asked in September 2015.[37] "Why are our parks so white?" the paper of record queried three months earlier.[38] The following year, the *Washington Post* explored "Discomfort food: Using dinners to talk about race, violence, and America."[39] Some of this kind of baiting is provocative, challenging, and valuable. Most of it is not.

Corporate Social Justice

There was a time within living memory when corporations were obliged to avoid politics. Given the relatively even divide in America between liberal Democrats and conservative Republicans, taking a side meant alienating half your potential clientele. Your job is to sell widgets, not change the world. That maxim is dead and gone. The pressure on corporate America to comply with the shifting dictates of social justice orthodoxy is immense, and corporate identity now includes—indeed, is often incomplete without—the appropriate politics. Usually, it is the politics of the left.

In 2016, the state of North Carolina passed a controversial law requiring people to use the public restroom corresponding to their sex, regardless of their "gender identity." Many people viewed the law as discriminatory—including the future Republican president, Donald Trump. "There have been very few complaints," Trump told NBC's *Today* when asked if he preferred the status quo ante to post-transgender bathroom law. "North Carolina did something—it was very strong—and they're paying a big price. And there's a lot of problems," he added.[40]

Trump was right. Immediately after the law was passed, the film and television production studio Lionsgate canceled a project scheduled to film in the Tar Heel State. PayPal followed suit by withdrawing from a deal that would have produced four hundred new jobs. A few days later, Germany's Deutsche Bank dropped its plan to open a technology development center that would have brought 250 new jobs to North Carolina. The NBA and the NCAA announced that games scheduled to take place in North Carolina would be played elsewhere. Two months later, sixty-eight companies—including Apple, Nike, and American Airlines—filed a court brief along with the Human Rights Campaign seeking to block the implementation of the "Bathroom Bill."

In the end, North Carolina lost more than $630 million to the backlash.[41]

The law was not only financially costly but also a mess for the local Republican Party. Even though Trump beat Hillary Clinton by nearly 4 percentage points in North Carolina, the incumbent Republican governor was run out of office. Within three months of his inauguration, North Carolina's new Democratic governor signed a repeal of the Bathroom Bill.

Anyone who thought North Carolina's bill was unjust would have a favorable view of the pressure applied by corporate America. This is, however, hardly the only instance in which corporate America hopped off the referee's chair and got into the game.

In 2016, the pharmaceutical company Pfizer announced efforts to ensure its drugs would not be used in executions in states that impose capital punishment by lethal injection.[42] Marc Benioff, the chief executive of the cloud-computing giant Salesforce, mounted a crusade to compel Indiana and Georgia to abandon plans to pass state versions of the Religious Freedom Restoration Act—a law that allows individuals and the owners of closely-held companies to avoid violating their religious principles.[43] In 2015, Apple spent enormous sums lobbying in favor of the international Paris Agreement on emissions. Those expenditures, to which Amazon and Google added in 2017, spiked after Donald Trump's election to the presidency. The three tech giants spent more than ten million dollars in the first three months of the Trump administration lobbying against efforts to scale back environmental regulations and in favor of relaxed immigration policies and "government funding of science" (the wording as it appeared on Google's lobbying disclosure).[44]

Corporations and brands used to resist even vaguely political messaging. They assumed that endorsing any kind of political message would alienate someone, and losing even one potential client or consumer was bad for business. Not anymore. Consumers across the political spectrum now specifically seek out brands associated with an explicit social or political "stance."[45] In this way, they can appear to be engaging in civic and political culture without devoting any time to learning about civic or political culture.

Furthermore, the bread of most major American firms is no longer buttered at home. Writing in 2016 for the *Los Angeles Times*, Daniel Gross observed that coastal enterprises, particularly large firms, are less sensitive to their consumers than to the sensibilities of influencers and policy makers—especially when an ever-increasing share of sales is generated overseas. That's why American business culture has become less sensitive to the U.S. electorate and more responsive to political elites and opinion-makers on the coasts and in Europe.[46]

These firms rarely respond to pressure from below and are all but impervious to boycotts. They are situated in elite liberal enclaves and are largely staffed with people who share the same political sensibilities. As a result, fewer and fewer C-suite executives see associating with social justice activism's "call-out culture" as a threat to their bottom lines. Indeed, failing to adopt a socially responsible mission statement is a far greater risk than appearing neutral and maintaining a politically diverse clientele. That's not courage or conviction. It's just best practices.

Perhaps the impulse to go along with progressive crusades is why representatives from more than one hundred businesses packed into the East Room of the White House in April 2014 to sign Barack Obama's "equal pay pledge." Rooting out pervasive, unspoken prejudices in the workplace that result in the systematic oppression of women was this campaign's ostensible purpose. In truth, however, it was an effort to mobilize a coalition of social justice advocates to vote Democratic in the upcoming midterm elections.

The pledge compelled businesses to acknowledge the existence of the alleged "national pay gap," the ever-shifting chasm between what men and women make for the same work. Among other non-binding and symbolic measures, the pledge committed employers to review "personnel process to reduce unconscious bias and structural barriers." If this sounds to you less like a policy initiative and more like politics, you are astute. Ahead of the 2014 midterms, Obama's political operation pushed all their chips in on the "wage gap."

"Oh, hi. I'm Sarah Silverman, writer, comedian, and vagina owner," Ms. Silverman said in a pro-Obama radio spot that aired in 2014. "Women make up almost half the working population, yet we typically earn just 78 cents for every dollar a man makes in almost every profession." Silverman also released a viral video alleging that being a woman costs approximately eleven thousand dollars per year in lost earnings. This amounts to approximately five hundred thousand dollars in lost wages for women. Silverman demurely called it the "vagina tax."[47] In his State of the Union address that year, the president himself made the same assertion, minus the references to female anatomy: "Today, women make up about half our workforce. But they still make 77 cents for every dollar a man earns. That is wrong. And in 2014, it's an embarrassment."

"Did you know that women are still paid less than men," the Obama White House's website asked its credulous readers. "On average, full-time working women earn just 78 cents for every dollar a man earns." Upon learning of this tremendous injustice, WhiteHouse.gov visitors were prompted to print out a selection of greeting cards featuring their favorite agitprop illustration. The White House's example featured a happy man enjoying his whole dollar while a miserable looking woman is forced to make due with three quarters and two pennies. "The wage gap is not a myth," the greeting card read.[48]

The greeting card lied.

The data the president and his allies used to buttress the "pay gap" claim came from his Bureau of Labor Statistics (BLS), which found that women working a full-time job in 2012 made 81 percent of the median earnings of their male counterparts. The problem with this statistic is that, as Obama's BLS acknowledged, men were twice as likely to work more than forty hours per week. This little detail, when factored in, substantially shrinks the "pay gap." When lifestyle choices are taken into account, the "gap" shrinks again. For example, single women who have never married are more likely to work longer hours, shrinking the pay gap on average to the point of negligibility. "Among women and men with similar 'human capital' characteristics," the BLS economist Lawrence H. Leith wrote in 2012, "the earnings gap narrows substantially and in some cases nearly disappears."[49]

"If women were paid 77 cents on the dollar, a profit-oriented firm could dramatically cut labor costs by replacing male employees with females," the American Enterprise Institute's Mark Perry and Andrew Biggs have observed.[50] Of course, even if an unscrupulous firm were inclined to do that, it would be violating the law. President Kennedy signed the Equal Pay Act in 1963, making sex-based discrimination illegal. Title VII of the 1964 Civil Rights Act allows employees to sue their employers over such a claim. Finally, in 2009, Barack Obama signed the Lilly Ledbetter Act, extending the period in which an employee can sue for discrimination beyond the 180 days after the initial offense.

Women who have children often seek occupations that have flexible hours or allow for telecommuting, jobs that might pay less than their full-time, on-site counterparts and do not offer overtime. Because men are statistically more likely to pursue a formal education in finance, accounting, and the sciences, they are more likely to enter the workforce with a higher starting salary. Riskier occupations are also more likely to be occupied by a man. That includes both physical risk and financial risk, such as working in a job in which compensation is made up largely of commissions and bonuses. Such a job can yield a good year as easily as a bad one. Compensation rates in these occupations reflect an employee's higher relative jeopardy. BLS was not saying that all employers pay women less, but that women often make less in the aggregate as a result of their liberty to pursue convenience and personal satisfaction.

The dogma that American employers are conspiring to make women second-class citizens has so far been impervious to these facts. For political activists, April 4 is now a holiday, but it's not a happy one. On "Equal Pay Day," feminist activists remind one another of their systematic oppression and go about pressuring businesses to give them special discounts.[51] Facebook COO Sheryl Sandberg and devotees of her book *Lean In* have taken to leaning *on* businesses to provide their female patrons with a 20 percent discount on that day's purchases, thereby attracting more customers.[52] On April 4, bars and coffee shops in the hipster parts of town have been known to offer their female customers a 23 percent discount on drinks. In the process, they provide the men they're allegedly punishing with environments replete with women, filling the establishment to capacity.

These are truly affecting sacrifices on everyone's part.

Social Justice and the Sciences

Identity politics and social justice have given rise to a new cultural litmus test that is, on its face, a contradiction in terms: Everyone is supposed to "believe in science."

"I believe in science!" Hillary Clinton declared on the stage at the Democratic Party's 2016 nominating convention. "I believe climate change is real, and that we can save our planet while creating millions of good paying clean energy jobs."

She didn't invent this construction. Political journalists and activists (often a distinction without a difference) have commended or condemned public figures for the extent to which they "believe in science" for years. Almost anyone can be judged a heretic depending on whether he accepts global warming as an existential threat to mankind, the efficacy of vaccines or pseudoscientific holistic medicines, or the risk associated with consuming genetically-modified foods. But this label is reserved primarily for Republicans. Writing for both *Mother Jones* magazine and Think Progress, Chris Mooney, the author of *The Republican War on Science*, attributes the GOP's skepticism of things like fluid climate models to "motivated reasoning." He adds that "conservative white males in particular" appear to be uniquely hostile toward science.[53]

Of course, scientists do not *believe* in a dynamic climate; they know it to be a fact. It has been changing since the planet formed, as we have observed in the fossil record and through glacial ice core samples. Moreover, the climate has been warming for the past eleven thousand years, ever since the glaciers started to subside. What climate change dogmatists mean when they refer to "science" is actually "consensus" around the idea of anthropogenic global warming.

Clinton's use of the phrase "believe in science" prompted a modest backlash among empiricists for whom faith-based constructs like "belief" are anathema. "Science is not a philosophy or a religion," *Wired* magazine's Katie Palmer observed.[54] "It is a method—imperfect, yet powerful—of testing and accumulating knowledge." A genuine researcher will always allow for the prospect that a consensus is wrong. That's the logical basis for experimentation.

"Settled science" is rarely scientific. As we've seen, though, this kind of simplistic absolutism has the potential to generate real income for anyone willing to monetize ignorance. Couple a pseudo-scientific secular religion with social justice, and the thing sells itself.

"The term social justice tends to get people hackled up, but social justice issues tie into science," proclaimed Caroline Weinberg, a science writer and one of the organizers of the March for Science—one of several anti-Trump rallies that proliferated in the early days of the administration. That demonstration was officially dedicated to advocating "evidence-based policymaking." As you can infer from Weinberg's tendentious statement, the march quickly descended into Identitarian gobbledygook.

The organizers made a fateful decision to appeal to social justice activists with intersectional buzzwords. "Colonization, racism, immigration, native rights, sexism, ableism, queer, trans-, intersex-phobia, and econ justice are scientific issues," read one of the March for Science's tweets, punctuated by a fist and a rainbow emoji. When Jerry Coyne, a cognitive scientist at Harvard, criticized this "hard-left rhetoric," BuzzFeed's Summer Anne Burton accused him of possessing the false consciousness associated with "a white man threatened by the end of patriarchy and white supremacy."[55]

Identitarianism began infecting pop science before the Trump era. In 2003, Dr. Michael Bailey, a psychologist at Northwestern University, published *The Man Who Would Be Queen* with the goal of explaining the biology of sexual orientation for a general audience. "The next two years were the hardest of my life," Bailey told the *New York Times*.[56]

Bailey's offense was to argue that some men's desire to live as the opposite sex is not the result of the biological accident of having been born into the "wrong" body but of erotic fascination. The Lambda Literary Foundation, the self-described "leader in LGBT book reviews," nominated Bailey's study for an award. But it wasn't long before transgender activists began attacking the author, his motives, and his methodology. Over the course of several months, his character was besmirched and his work deemed unethical. He barely made it out with his career intact.

"What happened to Bailey is important, because the harassment was so extraordinarily bad and because it could happen to any researcher in the field," warns Alice Dreger, an advocate for people born with ambiguous sexuality and a researcher whom Northwestern University assigned to investigate the allegations made against Bailey. "The bottom line is that they tried to ruin this guy, and they almost succeeded." Coming to Bailey's defense was the worst career move Dreger could have made.

"The online story soon morphed into 'Alice Dreger versus the rights of sexual minorities,' and no matter how hard I tried to point people back to documentation of the truth, facts just didn't seem to matter," she wrote seven years later. Even while recalling her abuse at the hands of a band of militant activists, Dreger did not express any ill will toward social justice as an organizing principle. And yet, she remained troubled. "[I]t seems that, especially where questions of human identity are concerned, we've built up a system in which scientists and social justice advocates are fighting in ways that poison the soil on which both depend," she wrote. "It's high time we think about this mess we've created, about what we're doing to each other, and to democracy itself."[57]

Indrek Wichman, a professor of engineering with thirty years of experience, shares Dreger's concerns. His field—the study of structure, architecture, and mathematics—has become obsessed with diversity. "Instead of calculating engine horsepower or microchip power/size ratios or aerodynamic lift and drag, the engineering educationists focus on group representation, hurt feelings, and 'microaggressions,'" he writes with palpable exasperation. He cites the biography of a fellow engineering professor who focuses on "professional ethics and social responsibility" and "de-centering Western civilization."[58] One has to ask, what does any of that have to do with making sure the roof doesn't collapse?

This combination of idiocy and belligerence can only end in tragedy, and that tragedy has a name: Bill Nye the Science Guy.

Once a children's television host on a mission to popularize the
scientific method, Nye now cashes checks from Netflix for promoting
leftist clichés. In one standout moment on *Bill Nye Saves the World*, the
actress Rachel Bloom performs a song about the glories of sodomy,
celebrating her talking vagina (figuratively speaking, one would imagine) and rejoicing in the virtues of gender fluidity. "Versatile love may
have some butt stuff," she raps in a program aimed at children. "Sexuality's a spectrum. Everyone is on it. Even you might like it if you sit up
on it."[59] Weeks after its release, this episode's writers were nominated
for an Emmy Award.

In another episode, Travis Rieder of Johns Hopkins University
contended that, because climate change is an existential threat and the
developing world does not consume as much energy as the developed
world (an assertion that is incorrect), wealthier countries should be
subjected to government-mandated population controls. "So should
we have policies that penalize people for having extra kids in the developed world?" Nye asked. "I do think that we should at least consider
it," Rieder replied.[60]

In between segments advocating eugenics and pansexual promis-
cuity and denying the genetics of sex, Nye issues bromides about how
American income taxes should be raised to pay for perennial European
welfare state priorities. *Bill Nye Saves the World* is the dumbing down
of science in microcosm—a dumbing down largely attributable to the
modern dogmas of Identitarian social justice.

Ignorance and Arrogance

Racial and cultural awareness are perfectly valid subjects of study.
Some of America's most profound thinkers have advanced the sum of

human knowledge by dedicating themselves to the exploration of identity issues. But venerating the wisdom and experience supposedly conferred by skin color and external genitalia is as prejudicial as despising someone for the same traits.

The application of social justice standards to the conduct of law, politics, and science does not produce a healthy civic culture. There is, though, money to be made in stoking division. The steady stream of inane Identitarian agitation emanating from the centers of American cultural literacy is not a directionless expression of angst. It has a purpose: commercial accessibility.

Geopolitics, economic theory, political dynamics, and history are complex topics. Speaking to these subjects with any authority requires years of dedicated study. Gender, race, and sexual preference are easy. Blogs and newspapers need readers; television programs need eyeballs. Reducing political discourse to the lowest common denominator can attract a large audience. Political discourse suddenly becomes accessible, readership and ratings increase, click-through rates improve, and advertising dollars flow.

From art to the sciences; from business culture to the academy; we've seen how dumbed-down discourse is profitable discourse. But when a jealous rabble weaponize the rhetoric of social justice to attack people more successful than themselves, that rhetoric becomes a threat to meritocracy.

CHAPTER 6

Victimocracy

A thriving industry has grown up around servicing Identitarian self-obsession, but that industry didn't create the demand it is addressing. It originated with America's elites—celebrities, intellectuals, opinion-makers, and political leaders—and the rank-and-file activists followed. The most important credential for Identitarians, one that yields tangible rewards, is being a victim. It does not take long for an ideology that is convinced of its victimhood to become fixated on its alleged victimizers. From there, it is a short leap to conspiratorial paranoia.

One of America's founding ideals is the individual's freedom to rise as far as industry and talent will take him or her. Today that ideal is becoming unrecognizable, as victimhood is mistaken for agency and worth.

You've Got to Be Carefully Taught

American individualism gives us a seemingly hereditary aversion to the socialist creed. Rooted in Rawlsian and Marxist soil, social justice arouses the suspicion of a generation of Americans who remember socialism in practice. That resistance had to be broken down somehow. How better to achieve that than through education?

You'll find many a nouveau Marxist text in the syllabus of just about every humanities course in every liberal arts college in America, but few are as influential as *Pedagogy of the Oppressed* by the Brazilian lecturer Paulo Freire.

More than a recitation of Marxist dogma, *Pedagogy* is a terrible read. Freire's style is surely more oppressive than the capitalist structures he rails against. "Reflection and action become imperative when one does not erroneously attempt to dichotomize the content of humanity from its historical forms," reads one typically impenetrable sentence.[1] Amid a typhoon of multisyllabic jargon, the reader is presumably supposed to forget that nothing much has been said and be satisfied instead with the secret handshake offered to those who pretend the time spent reading this book has been well spent.

"Since the publication of the English edition in 1970, *Pedagogy of the Oppressed* has achieved near-iconic status in America's teacher-training programs," Sol Stern wrote in his review of the book for *City Journal* in 2009, savaging the ur-text of modern educational theory as a one-dimensional manuscript notable only for the novel ways in which it aggravates class tensions and apologizes for murderers like Mao Zedong and Che Guevara. Stern saw little value in "proselytizing for America-hating causes in the college classroom." Indeed, that is the book's whole purpose.[2]

Freire does, however, give his readers a window into a formative worldview that has shaped the lives of many an educator and molded many minds over the past fifty years. He contends that, like the peasantry of Tsarist Russia, today's students are hobbled by a false consciousness: "[T]heir perception of themselves as oppressed is impaired by their submersion in the reality of oppression.... Their vision of the new man or woman is individualistic; because of their identification with the oppressor, they have no consciousness of themselves as persons or as members of an oppressed class."[3]

In other words, students need to be told that they are victims first. It's a tough sell, particularly in the United States, where reverence for what Freire derisively calls "individualistic" identity is celebrated. This Marxist doctrine is today a typical feature of social justice movements. Identitarians see not only traditionally marginalized communities as persecuted but also themselves.

Oppression according to American Identitarian movements is a funny thing. It should not be mistaken for hopeless subjugation. It is, in fact, a ladder to the upper strata of society. Why else would so many people be so eager to claim it?

Railing against a "victimhood mentality" has become a conservative cliché, but clichés become clichés for a reason. The pursuit of victimhood long ago moved beyond the ivied confines of the academy to become the national pastime. The rewards for acquiring this coveted status are real enough, but the cult of victimhood is robbing Americans of that individualism and agency of which Freire was so disdainful, turning us into wounded, hostile animals.

Blameless

Few things rouse American passions as much as blame. We cast it about as passionately as we avoid it. To be blameless is, after all, to have been a prisoner of exigent circumstances. In buck-passing, there is freedom. Our failures are not our own; they're someone else's. This ugly practice seems to have an ever-broadening appeal, but the average citizens who take it up are only following their leaders.

A survey conducted by YouGov for the *Economist* in May 2017 demonstrated the power of blame by testing the American electorate's receptiveness to "conspiracy theories." When we hear the phrase, we think of Oliver Stone movies and disreputable online message boards. But the "conspiracy theories" YouGov tested are not the fevered dreams of paranoiacs but the myths that the highest echelons of American society have endorsed, if only to liberate themselves from the prospect of suffering even mild embarrassment.

According to YouGov's poll, 52 percent of self-described Republicans (and 46 percent of self-identified independent voters) believe that "millions of illegal votes were cast in the election," even though such a notion is entirely unsupported. Indeed, a scheme of that magnitude would represent a substantial logistical challenge, involving hundreds of people, probably including some high-ranking state officials. It's a baseless lie concocted for one reason: explaining Donald Trump's loss of the popular vote to Hillary Clinton.[4]

For the sake of appearances, Democrats can often be found dishonestly insisting that voter fraud does not exist. However, fraud is a documented fact. The regular prosecution and conviction of people guilty of this crime puts the lie to the left's false posture. Trump's contention, however, that "millions" of illegal immigrants stole a moral victory from him was inspired by twin evils: Identitarianism and bias confirmation.

To validate his assertion, Trump's supporters cited a 2014 study by political scientists at Old Dominion University purporting to show that 14 percent of America's non-citizen population was registered to vote. According to the study's authors, Trump and his supporters got the study wrong.[5] They mistook the uppermost end of the study's confidence interval for the paper's conclusion, and they disregarded peer criticism of the research as flawed by its hopelessly unrepresentative sample size.

Of course, this was ignored by the study's partisan boosters. The paper's methodology was irrelevant. Its conclusion had the invaluable potential to expunge from Donald Trump's political record a relatively trivial blemish. You see, he was really the victim in all this. That was what mattered most.

The pro-Trump right's belief in hordes of illegal voters should have been dispelled by the series of comic errors that typified President Trump's Commission on Election Integrity. For the purpose of rooting out voter fraud while also providing the president with an excuse for losing the popular vote to Hillary Clinton, the commission's chairman, Kris Kobach, the Kansas secretary of state, requested from the states an unreasonable trove of information on registered voters. Within one month of the request, forty-four states had turned down all or some of the commission's requests.

Some states were legally obliged to resist the violation of their citizens' privacy rights, but many Republican-dominated states issued objections with more than the perfunctory level of gusto. "They can go jump in the Gulf of Mexico," scoffed Governor Phil Bryant of Mississippi. Even Kobach's own office declined to provide all the materials requested by the commission he chaired.

This was a heartening moment for conservatives who regarded the voter fraud commission as an example of executive overreach. It showed that Identitarian faith and the demands of tribal fealty could yet be overcome. The same cannot be said for the Democrats. The left is arguably in worse shape when it comes to wallowing in comforting myths of its own faultlessness.

That same YouGov poll found that 52 percent of self-described Democrats (and 39 percent of independents) believed that "Russia tampered with vote tallies in order to get Donald Trump elected president."[6] Though Moscow's intervention in the 2016 election was expansive and flagrant—and included efforts to tamper with voting systems and voter registration databases—no Obama or Trump administration officials would corroborate this conspiracy theory.

How can you blame rank-and-file Democrats for indulging in some magical thinking? The champion of their movement lost the presidency to one of the most unpopular persons ever to win it—a political neophyte whose most recent professional engagement was as a reality show host. Hillary Clinton and her supporters are mortified, as they deserve to be. Whereas an earlier generation might have responded to such a humiliation by falling on its sword, today's political leaders opt instead to tilt at windmills.

Pity the Fallen

After a period of exile literally in the wilderness (the former secretary of state was often captured on camera shuffling around secluded hiking trails in those bleak winter months following her unexpected 2016 loss), Hillary Clinton emerged determined to rehabilitate herself. "I was the candidate. I take absolute personal responsibility," she affirmed in a televised interview with Christiane Amanpour. This cursory display of graciousness was, however, fleeting, for she immediately launched into an elaborate exposition on why she neither accepts nor deserves blame for her failure.[7]

Clinton blamed her loss on former director of the FBI, James Comey: "If the election had been on October 17, I would be your president," she told Amanpour. "I was on the way to winning until a combination of Jim Comey's letter on October 28 and Russian WikiLeaks raised doubts in the minds of people who were inclined to vote for me and got scared off." Indeed, voters can be forgiven for being a tiny bit concerned when the FBI revealed that State Department emails, which should have been housed on a secure government server, found their way onto the personal computer of a lascivious former congressman who was being investigated (and later convicted

and jailed) for having improper contacts with a minor. That sort of thing tends to raise eyebrows.

Clinton also blamed her loss on political media—specifically, debate moderators who expected more of her than of her novice opponent. "I kept waiting for the moment," she reflected. "I've watched a million presidential debates in my life, and I was waiting for the moment when one of the people asking the questions would have said, well, so exactly how are you going to create more jobs? Right?" In fact, that was the very first question of the very first debate. "Beginning with you, Secretary Clinton," said the moderator, NBC News's Lester Holt, "why are you a better choice than your opponent to create the kinds of jobs that will put more money into the pockets of American workers?"[8] Clinton responded with a promise to increase the minimum wage, impose profit-sharing on private enterprises, and, of course, raise income taxes. Perhaps the voting public thought this was an unsatisfactory response to a question about job creation. Inveterately resistant to introspection, Clinton may never know for sure.

Finally, the former secretary of state indulged in some Identitarianism of her own, partly blaming her loss on America's latent hostility toward women. Here Clinton enjoyed a big assist from her host. "Were you a victim of misogyny, and why do you think you lost the majority of the white female vote?" Amanpour asked. "Yes," Clinton replied. "I do think it played a role." Somehow, a nation that Clinton claimed was poised to elect her president on October 28 had become irredeemably bigoted twelve days later.

This is hardly the first time in Clinton's career that she has blamed her own failures on the prejudices of those less enlightened than she. "I often feel like there's the Hillary standard and then there's the standard for everybody else," she complained in the summer of 2016. The year prior, when asked by a Turkish reporter if a man would face similar questions over her decision to use a private server exclusively as secretary of state, she deferred: "I will leave that to others to answer."

These appeals to the sympathy of Democrats were only slightly less effective than those she employed in 2008. Clinton's expressions of self-pity have ranged from tearful reflections on her struggle as a woman to bitter expressions of frustration with media ("If anybody saw *Saturday Night Live*, maybe we should ask Barack if he's comfortable and needs another pillow," she said in an especially vinegary debate performance in 2008).[9] And the former first lady has found playing the victim card to be amply rewarding.

She made it abundantly clear over the course of the 2016 Democratic primaries that her candidacy was the ultimate expression of social justice, and that the most compelling rationale for her presidency was the satisfaction such a reversal of patriarchal fortunes would presumably yield.

When Bernie Sanders's primary challenge caught fire, Clinton tried to reignite passion for her campaign by promising to appoint "a cabinet that looks like America, and 50 percent of America is women, right?" For a precedent, Clinton looked to Canada, where the new prime minister, Justin Trudeau, had staffed his cabinet not with the meritorious but with those who had the preferred chromosomes. Why, a reporter asked? "Because it's 2015," Trudeau blithely replied.[10]

The former secretary of state never missed an opportunity to remind voters about her sex. When she appeared alongside Sanders at a PBS debate moderated by Judy Woodruff and Gwen Ifill, Clinton made a ham-fisted attempt to highlight the lack of men on the stage. "I would note, just for a historic aside, somebody told me earlier today we've had like two hundred presidential primary debates, and this is the first time there have been a majority of women on stage," she said. "So, you know, we'll take progress wherever we can find it." The audience applauded dutifully but not enthusiastically.[11]

Even Clinton's choice of venue for her expected election-night victory party was calculated to symbolize her triumph over misogyny. Gathered in New York City's Javits Center, which features an all-glass façade, the celebrants would mark Clinton's victory with the firing of confetti cannons that would simulate the "shattering of the glass ceiling."[12] In the end, of course, the "ceiling" remained intact.

The Power of the Terse

Who would want to be a victim? Victimization, after all, is a consequence of suffering some trauma. To be victimized is to be denied control, and that is a terrible feeling.

Real victims do not relish coming forward. They're often afraid of what they might suffer at the hands of their abusers, or even their family and friends. Victims of genuine discrimination face an uphill battle in proving their claims, and the threat of social ostracism or the legal repercussions of making poorly substantiated accusations keep many real victims hidden in the shadows. Even confirmed and vindicated victims of discrimination and abuse suffer a stigma, often for the rest of their lives. Someone who says he is a victim of criminal discrimination deserves sympathy but not reflexive deference—not until his claims are fairly and impartially adjudicated.

A just society stands up for victims and provides redress to those who prove the harm they have suffered. This noble obligation is occasionally abused by the unscrupulous and fraudulent, but the risks of being discovered as a fraud used to outweigh the rewards. That risk was once a powerful deterrent. Not anymore.

The dangers of fraudulent victimhood were on display at the University of Missouri in 2015 and 2016. Racial tensions on campus had risen by September 2015, when the president of the African-American student association alleged that passengers in a pickup truck driving through campus had hurled racial slurs at him. "I had experience with racism before, like microaggressions," the student confessed, "but that was the first time I'd experienced in-your-face racism."[13] Three weeks later, the Legion of Black Collegians announced that its members, too, encountered racism when a "young man" approached the group and responded with slurs when he was asked to leave. "There was a silence that fell over us all, almost in disbelief that a racial slur, in particular, was used in our vicinity," one of the students who was privy to the remark told reporters.[14]

The trauma these students experienced in their confrontation with genuine racial resentment is palpable, and only the most callous would dismiss that pain. But their honest shock betrays how rare episodes of racial hatred are in their lives. The sting was so acute because the experience was new. If someone's only frame of reference is "macroaggressions," that suggests the only overt bigotry he has previously encountered is so subtle that it requires subjective analysis to divine.

Maybe it was the novelty of these alleged slurs that turned them into such a potent organizing force. The allegations swept across campus like wildfire. Just days after the second alleged incident was reported, the school's chancellor announced a mandatory online diversity training seminar for faculty, staff, and students. "Not enough," one graduate student told the *Columbia Missourian*.[15] Amid outrage over what many perceived to be the administration's deliberate effort to slow-walk the investigation into these claims, a group of students began harassing the president of the University of Missouri System, Tim Wolfe.

Student demonstrators issued a list of demands, including a formal apology from the president accompanied by his resignation. After meeting with those calling for his removal, Wolfe confessed that he was "not completely aware of systemic racism, sexism, and patriarchy on campus."[16] His refusal to resign prompted at least one student to go

on a hunger strike, which evolved into a broad-based protest movement. Protesters erected a tent city and resolved to boycott their
school's services until Wolfe was gone.

Wolfe eventually apologized for appearing callous toward allegations of racism. Maybe these students acted impetuously, demanding
scalps even as investigations into their allegations were ongoing. Maybe
Wolfe did respond lackadaisically to the unnerving notion that a band
of overt racists had infiltrated campus and was spreading slurs. But
that was in the past. Surely the dialogue this event sparked had defused
racial tensions, right? Wrong.

Two days after Wolfe's apology, student activists hijacked a university fundraiser in Kansas City. "Tim Wolfe," one student demonstrator
demanded, "what do you think systemic oppression is?"

"It's—systemic oppression is because you don't believe that you
have the equal opportunity for success," he replied. Boos erupted from
the angry crowd.

"Did you just blame us for systemic oppression?" an irate protester
shouted. "Did you just blame black students?"[17]

National conservative media turned their attention to Mizzou
when the students, who felt entitled to a "safe space" for themselves on
state-owned land, became aggressive with the video journalist who
was attempting to film the scene. The self-appointed "safe space"
enforcer, Melissa Click, an associate professor of communications,
drew nationwide condemnation when she took it upon herself to have
the journalist ejected. "Who wants to help me get this reporter out of
here?" she asked the crowd. "I need some muscle over here." Video of
her attempted intimidation went viral and Click was dismissed from
her job (only to resurface at Gonzaga University a year later). If you're
wondering whether Click was humbled, wonder no more. She, too, was
apparently a victim. "This is all about racial politics," she told the
Chronicle of Higher Education in April 2016. "I'm a white lady. I'm an

easy target." Besides, she added, "there was no reason to think I was doing something that wasn't sanctioned by the university." She had a point there.

The demonstrations snowballed. Soon, the African-American members of the football team joined the ongoing protests. The rest of the team followed suit, threatening the school's football program, a major revenue stream. When the national political press turned its eyes to the chaos and controversy at Mizzou, Wolfe's position became untenable. Fewer than eight weeks after the initial charge of racism on campus was made, he resigned. The school's chancellor followed him into exile soon thereafter. Governor Jay Nixon called the resignations a necessary step toward "healing and reconciliation."[18]

But there was no healing and no reconciliation. This episode only demonstrated the extent to which even an unproved charge of racial resentment—not discrimination with accompanying material losses, but verbal abuse—conferred real power upon claimants. At Mizzou, this charge mobilized an army, ended careers, ruined lives, paralyzed a state university system, and dominated national headlines for weeks.

By the summer of 2017, the wages of chaos and appeasement at the University of Missouri had come due. Freshman enrollment at the flagship Columbia campus was down 35 percent, and its 2017 freshman class was the smallest this century. A university that was growing steadily before the protests, Mizzou had begun to contract. "Now, with budget cuts due to lost tuition and a decline in state funding, the university is temporarily closing seven dormitories and cutting more than 400 positions, including those of some non-tenured faculty members, through layoffs and by leaving open jobs unfilled," the *New York Times* reported.[19]

The University of Missouri is just one example of an institution that was faced with a claim to victimization and, in the interests of social justice, dispensed with an investigation and simply awarded the petitioner undue authority and legitimacy. This sad tale has been repeated across the country for decades. When America's responsible institutional stakeholders cave in to a mob, they sow the seeds of more mobs. The currency associated with establishing a legitimate claim to victimization, particularly victimization that is the result of bigotry and discrimination, is self-evident. Just look to the wave of hate-crime hoaxes.

The Epidemic that Wasn't

In the spring of 2013, Oberlin College was paralyzed with terror. The college, one of the most reliably liberal institutions in the nation with a famously progressive professoriate, was suddenly plagued by racist vandalism. Vile anti-black, anti-Semitic, anti-Chinese, and homophobic graffiti was everywhere. In an abundance of caution, the school publicized this graffiti, replete with "trigger warnings," to raise public awareness and mobilize a response.

"A sizable cohort of 460 students, faculty, staff and community members marched on Wednesday in solidarity," the *Oberlin Review* reported. The protests were covered on cable news and in major newspapers like the *New York Times*. Some had already denounced the famously liberal school for fostering the conditions in which this kind of naked bigotry might thrive just beneath the surface. "It's not just about these big events," said one student. "No one wants to address the micro-aggressions that happen every day."

Less than one month after the graffiti began appearing around campus, Oberlin authorities fired off an emergency email. "A person wearing a hood and robe resembling a KKK outfit" had been spotted on campus near the school's Afrikan Heritage House. In response to this threat, the school immediately canceled all classes and non-essential activities. Only after panic swept the school and students were cheated out of the classes they paid for did the sprawling plot begin to unravel.[20]

"Officers checked the area and were unable to locate anybody," the police reported. "College security later saw a student wrapped in a blanket"—an "innocent mistake." The rest of it wasn't so innocent at all. Police later identified two students responsible for the graffiti. The motives of one of them were particularly transparent. On his social media accounts, he described himself as an organizer for Barack Obama's 2012 reelection campaign and a member of a group dedicated to the eradication of "structural racism." Perhaps worst of all, as Legal Insurrection's William Jacobson confirmed, "School officials and local police knew the identity of the culprits, who were responsible for most if not all of such incidents on campus, yet remained silent as the campus reacted as if the incidents were real."[21]

A year before the siege of Oberlin, a twenty-one-year-old junior at the University of Wisconsin, Parkside, was the focus of national attention when she discovered a "hit list" with her name on it, along with the names of a dozen other African-American students. The incident sparked outrage and fear on campus, resulting in a college-wide awareness campaign and a series of student body meetings to address public concern and flush out racist sentiment on campus. It was all a lie. Police confronted the hoaxer, who confessed that she had made the list after another attempted hoax—involving nooses made from rubber bands— failed to elicit a properly panicked response. Bad spelling proved to be her downfall. According to the sheriff, she had misspelled every name on the list but her own.[22]

Even as Alexandra Pennell was addressing an anti-hate rally at Central Connecticut State University organized in her honor with the school's cooperation, police were eyeing her with suspicion. "All I have to say is that I'm not going to be run out of my home, and I will not be intimidated by hate," she declared to hundreds of supporters.[23] Pennell claimed to be the target of harassment, routinely discovering notes attacking her for being a lesbian. The university took the allegations seriously and involved the police, who installed a recording device in her dorm room to identify the culprit. When that device was mysteriously disabled twice, police set up another recorder without Pennell's knowledge. That camera discovered that the source of these harassing letters was Pennell herself. Eventually confessing her fraud, the nineteen-year-old was expelled from her program and criminally charged.[24]

In mid-2013, Vassar College changed the name of its Campus Life Response Team to the Bias Incident Response Team, since the most urgent matters related to student life on campus had become episodes of racial intolerance. Over three months, there had been a number of incidents of vandalism targeting transgender and African-American students. In December of that year, that reign of terror was ended. Vassar's dean of college life revealed in a campus email that they had caught the culprits. Unmentioned in that email, however, was that one of the guilty parties was the school's vice president of student life; black and transgender herself, and a member of the vaunted Bias Incident Response Team. Nearly a week later, the school's vice president admitted that the students behind these episodes of alleged racial intolerance also "falsely reported these as anonymous messages."[25]

On April 29, 2017, a racist, threatening, and anonymous note was found on the windshield of a black student's car at Minnesota's St. Olaf College, touching off a firestorm. Classes were canceled. Marches were organized. Demonstrations rocked the school for days, the target of the threat "tearfully relaying the discovery of the note and how unsafe it made her feel on campus."[26] Neither administrators nor law enforcement could thoroughly investigate the note because its recipient had, in a dramatic display of defiance, burnt it. By now, you know the drill. According to St. Olaf's president, the hoaxer's noble intention was "to draw attention to concerns about the campus climate."

These are just a few examples of a proliferating plague of hoaxes. Racism has not been expunged from our country, but something has gone very wrong when so many are pretending to be the victims of trauma. Surely some of these student hoaxers simply enjoyed the attention their fabricated persecution afforded them, but others probably thought their actions were justified because they publicized a real threat that affects tens of thousands of people.

If bigotry and discrimination are to be banished from polite society, these hoaxers reasoned, then society is obliged to adopt a zero-tolerance policy. So what if a few episodes of prejudice have to be fabricated as long as it generates attention for a very real problem? This is Plato's "noble lie" turned on its head. The Platonic ideal is the untruth proffered in service to continued social cohesion and harmony. These are lies dedicated to shattering civic comity, all in the name of educating the supposedly unenlightened.

Trumping the Truth

The self-serving racial hoax is not exclusive to college campuses. Donald Trump's unexpected rise prompted a period of particular energy among those who fancy themselves so attuned to the ubiquitous scourge of racism that they have to make it up.

Amid a spasm of white racial anxiety in 2015 and 2016 coinciding with Trump's rising political prospects, it was understandable if some thought the bad old days were back. That was surely the assumption shared by hundreds of protesters who turned out in 2016 to demonstrate against a grotesque incident of racism at the University of Albany in New York. It was alleged that three black female students had been attacked by a group of white men on a bus. They were battered, bombarded with racial slurs, and degraded as the other passengers and driver looked on silently.

"There's no excuse for racism and violence on a college campus," Hillary Clinton wrote in solidarity with the mass of protesters who were enraged by the incident. But the evidence that began to trickle in did not support the allegations. Passengers did not corroborate their story, nor did the bus's surveillance footage. In fact, authorities later alleged, these three women weren't victims but aggressors.

The conveyance's security camera showed that these three women had attacked a nineteen-year-old white woman on the bus. "It was a turnabout tailor-made to delight conservative media outlets and to ignite social-media recriminations," read the *New York Times* account.[27] The *Times* had put its finger on the real offense committed by these women. Their alleged assault was bad enough, but providing fodder for conservative arguments that racist violence is not, in fact, endemic? That is truly unforgivable.

A University of Michigan student became a symbol of the plight of American Muslim women who wear the hijab when she alleged that a Trump-supporting man approached her and threatened to set her on fire. The charge turned out to be false, and she faced felony charges of lying to investigators, but she wasn't the last of her kind. Weeks later, a Muslim woman riding the New York City subway home from Baruch College, where she was a student, alleged that three drunken men screaming "Donald Trump" assaulted her, tearing her hijab from her head. "Shortly after, dozens of New Yorkers turned up at Grand Central Terminal in midtown Manhattan in solidarity with her, carrying signs that read 'Fight hate' and '#NotInOurCity,'" the *Washington Post* reported. It was another a lie, and this alleged victim was charged with filing a false police report and obstructing government administration.[28]

"Vote Trump" was found spray-painted on the burnt-out husk of a historic black church in Mississippi a week before the 2016 elections, leading authorities to suspect that a horrific feature of the resistance to civil rights legislation in the 1960s had made a comeback. Journalists began hounding the state GOP to comment on this vandalism done in their name. "This is a tense time in American politics," wrote *The Atlantic*'s Emma Green.[29] "The burning of Hopewell M.B. Church is a sign of how bad things have gotten, and what may be still to come." Indeed, it was, but not in the way that Green anticipated. Less than two months later, a forty-five-year-old parishioner was charged with arson in the first degree. "There may have been some efforts to make it appear politically motivated," said the state's insurance commissioner and fire marshal.[30]

A week after the 2016 vote, another church was vandalized, allegedly by pro-Trump racists. "Fag church," "Heil Trump," and swastikas were found spray-painted on the exterior walls of a house of worship in Indiana. "It's no secret that the atmosphere of hatred has kind of permeated the nation right now," said the church's pastor. In the end, the only suspect arrested for the crime was the church's organist, a self-identified gay man who eventually confessed. Investigators said the suspect hoped to "mobilize a movement after being disappointed in and fearful of the outcome of the national election."[31]

For about a week in late 2017, Lieutenant General Jay Silveria became a national celebrity when he ordered his U.S. Air Force Academy students to take out their phones and film him delivering an emotional call to arms on the matter of race. "If you can't treat someone with dignity and respect, get out," he declared.[32] The speech was prompted by the revelation that five African-American cadets at the academy's preparatory school in Colorado Springs awoke one morning to find racial slurs on the message boards affixed to their dorm room doors. Six weeks later, the investigation concluded that one of the cadets targeted was, in fact, responsible for all of them. The cadet confessed, and the matter was concluded, but the sparse coverage generated by the resolution of this episode paled in comparison to the abundance of headlines advertising the discovery of a racism problem at the U.S. Air Force Academy.[33]

Trump's election also seemed to be the trigger for a wave of bomb threats targeting Jewish Community Centers (JCCs) across the United States and Canada. More than a hundred threats were called in between December 2016 and February 2017, terrifying North American Jews. Because there was an anti-Semitic movement that appeared dedicated to the president—a cohort whose fealty Trump had only recently disavowed—political observers held Trump responsible for the threats.

That chorus of opprobrium intensified when the Democratic attorney general of Pennsylvania, Josh Shapiro, alleged that Trump had said of the threats, "The reverse may be true." "I don't know what the president meant by that statement," Shapiro said, but many interpreted it to mean that Trump thought the threats were coming from within the Jewish community. "False flags," the *Washington Post* declared.[34] "Trump echoes David Duke," Think Progress insisted.[35] "We're astonished," remarked the Anti-Defamation League's Jonathan Greenblatt.[36] The bomb threats were a hoax, of course, most of them the work of a mentally-disturbed teenager with dual U.S.-Israeli citizenship and criminal connections.[37]

Authorities attributed another twelve threats against JCCs around the country to thirty-one-year-old Juan Thompson, an already disgraced former journalist for the left-wing online publication The Intercept. The false threats were part of a plot by Thompson to cast himself as the victim of a setup. He was even bold enough to lament the increase in threats to community centers on Twitter. "You know who's at a JCC? Kids," he wrote. "KIDS." Much of his time was spent in online forums ranting against racism and capitalism. Thompson resented the "white media" and insisted that "white people have no shame." "With threats [and] hate crimes on the rise," he wrote, "we shouldn't have to tell [President Trump] to do his part."[38]

There is a simple explanation for this epidemic of hoaxes: victimhood bestows credentials. If you reward certain behavior, you'll get more of it.

Part of what makes this outbreak of false victimization so egregious is that it taints legitimate allegations of bigotry and discrimination. I've recounted only a few of the documented hate-crime hoaxes. They happen so frequently that you'd expect establishment journalists to exercise some restraint when publicizing allegations of overt bigotry, but they never do. The rewards for confirming social justice activists' preconceptions about the ubiquity and intractability of American prejudice far outweigh the cost of being wrong.

Justice Inverted

It is the nature of social justice to expand the meaning of injustice beyond what can be addressed in a courtroom. Indeed, in the eyes of its advocates, that is the whole point; "justice" as traditionally defined is too narrow. And when the definition of justice becomes so expansive that the judicial system cannot provide it, the judicial system becomes the enemy.

Tragically, racial injustice has been abetted, in some cases, by American courts. This has convinced some activists that extrajudicial restorative mechanisms akin to those practiced in post-conflict societies—from the community-level Gacaca courts of Rwanda to South Africa's national Truth and Reconciliation Commission—are necessary in the West. Those are extreme examples, but some social justice advocates truly believe that the American justice system is incapable of addressing some injustices that are so culturally ingrained they are not even recognized as such. Among them is the left's new idée fixe: "rape culture."

For a particular type of social justice devotee, blind justice is not just. Blindness fails to address grievances that span the generations, overlapping networks of oppression, institutional biases, and the intangible privileges enjoyed by the majority. When it comes to sexual violence like rape—distinct from sexual abuse or harassment—activists have endorsed an accuser's "right to be believed" as a means of beating back these insidious prejudices. An effort to tip the scales in the direction of the oppressed has, however, produced some new and inconvenient victims.

In 2011, the Department of Education's Office for Civil Rights distributed to some seven thousand universities a set of guidelines and recommendations for handling campus sexual assault complaints. This document, known as the "Dear Colleague" letter, "reinterpreted Title IX [of the Education Amendments of 1972] as giving the federal government authority to dictate the specific procedures that colleges must use to adjudicate student-on-student sexual assault allegations."[39] The letter was released amid increasing worries that sexual assault on campus had become an unseen epidemic. It was believed not only that the undeniable stigma of being a rape victim was discouraging reports of violence, but also that sexual violence had been too narrowly defined.[40]

David Lisak, a psychologist at the University of Massachusetts at Boston, conducted a study of 1,882 college men in Boston and reported his results in 2002. Of the men interviewed, 120—6.4 percent—admitted to committing rape or attempted rape, often by taking advantage of an intoxicated partner. Seventy-six of them confessed to numerous violations. Lisak concluded that serial rapists commit the majority of criminal assaults, calculating that repeat violators average 5.8 rapes apiece. A follow-up study published in 2011 confirmed these findings and issued a set of recommendations for handling repeat offenders.[41]

Lisak's study has been sharply criticized, and it is clearly an incomplete portrait of the phenomenon of sexual assault. College-educated females are statistically less likely to be subjected to sexual violence than women without a degree.

A study of the Department of Justice's National Crime Victimization Survey data from 1995 to 2013 has found that rates of sexual assault among women aged eighteen to twenty-four are higher for non-students than for students. In rural areas, the rate of assault on non-matriculated women was almost twice that of students.[42] What's more, women without a college degree or a high school diploma are at far greater risk, as are women who report lower household incomes.[43] This is perhaps an intuitive statistic that is the result of a variety of complex social phenomena, none of which lends itself to a narrative as simple as the privileged fraternity brother taking advantage of his inebriated date.

For activists, the absence of evidence is evidence. Rates of sexual abuse on campus *must* be higher than in the general population. Those missing assaults are probably unreported. And so academics, college faculty, and policymakers convince themselves that there is a rape epidemic on American campuses.

In 2014, the journalist Emily Yoffe set out to chronicle for the online publication Slate the extent to which these and other foundational studies resulted in the misuse of Title IX, the federal law designed to protect against discriminatory practices in the education system. Her exhaustive study identified the myriad ways in which this law and the Obama administration's guidelines had been misused to deprive students—most of them men—of their constitutional rights.[44]

The "Dear Colleague" letter, she showed, compelled schools to act as tribunals in which the rights of the accused are often overlooked. The accuser, for instance, has access to an appeals process, ensuring that the accused faces multiple prosecutions for the same alleged offense. The rules also lower the standard of proof for conviction from "beyond a reasonable doubt"—the standard that applies in the criminal justice system—to the much looser "preponderance of the evidence."

Under the "Dear Colleague" regime, students are often deprived of their Fifth and Sixth Amendment rights in these campus Star Chambers. For the accused, access to independent counsel, witnesses, or evidence is limited or entirely prohibited. Activists who favor easy convictions object to moving the adjudication of violent crimes like campus rape into a courtroom precisely because of the protections afforded the accused there. Testifying in public and being confronted by the accused is too traumatic, they say, for victims of sexual violence, and the evidentiary standards for conviction are too high. This conception of justice is downright dystopian.

In the name of helping the victims of sexual assault come out of the shadows, new victims were produced in mass quantities. *Reason* magazine's Robby Soave has chronicled case after case in which both accuser and accused were deprived of the protections afforded to all parties in a court of law: [45]

- At Stony Brook University, a woman who alleged sexual assault was denied counsel and had to act as her own attorney.
- An alleged rapist at George Mason University whom the school found responsible for assault appealed his tribunal conviction in court and won because his constitutional rights had been violated.
- Despite evidence in the form of timestamped text messages demonstrating a woman at Amherst College admitted to taking advantage of an intoxicated man, the school still found the man guilty of assault and expelled him.

- On several occasions, women have been informed by authorities that they were raped, regardless of their repeated denials. If they insist too loudly to the contrary, they are accused of evincing stereotyped "battered woman syndrome."

- Two athletes at the University of Southern California in a monogamous relationship were seen by a neighbor playfully roughhousing. The neighbor reported an assault to the campus authorities, and despite the couple's assertions to the contrary, the man was expelled, barred from campus, and denied access to his girlfriend, against her will.

- At the University of Texas at Arlington, a gay male student was supposedly told to "consider killing yourself" by a straight classmate. That allegation was not supported by any evidence and may have been an attempt at revenge for the straight student's rejection of the gay student's advances. The gay student filed a complaint under Title IX. Found responsible for sexual harassment, the straight student believed his "conviction" would keep him out of graduate school and committed suicide.

"The higher education insurance group United Educators did a study of the 262 insurance claims it paid to students between 2006 and 2010 because of campus sexual assault, at a cost to the group of $36 million," Emily Yoffe reported in 2014. "The vast majority of the payouts, 72 percent, went to the accused—young men who protested their treatment by universities." The number was undoubtedly higher by 2017, when a Republican presidential administration finally devoted itself to addressing these injustices.

Title IX hasn't just been abused. In some cases, it has been weaponized. Perhaps the most famous example is that of Northwestern University's Professor Laura Kipnis—a self-described feminist and liberal—who challenged her students to think critically about the new guidelines for combating sexual assault on campus.

"[T]he climate of sanctimony about student vulnerability has grown too thick to penetrate; no one dares question it lest you're labeled antifeminist," Kipnis wrote in 2015 for the *Chronicle of Higher Education*. "Or worse, a sex criminal." She immediately found herself the target of a Title IX complaint. The students who marched against Kipnis denounced her "toxic ideas," and formally alleged that she created a hostile environment by proffering challenging ideas.[46]

Kipnis was not intimidated by her accusers. She went public, wrote extensively about her experience, and publicized her ordeal for a universe of readers that had never lent any credence to conservative criticisms of Title IX. "I was deluged with desperate emails from professors and students around the country with stories about *their* Title IX tribunals," Kipnis recalls. "I soon learned that rampant accusation is the new norm on American campuses; the place is a secret cornucopia of accusation, especially when it comes to sex. Including merely speaking about sex."[47]

One of the priorities of the new Trump administration was to contain the injustices spawned by the Obama administration's "Dear Colleague" letter. "One rape is one too many, one assault is one too many, one aggressive act of harassment is one too many," declared Secretary of Education Betsy DeVos in September 2017. "One person denied due process is one too many." That seemingly unobjectionable assertion whipped the social justice left into a frenzy.

"This administration's lack of compassion for the survivors of sexual assault is shameful," declared Jess O'Connell, the Democratic National Committee CEO. She was far blunter on Twitter, where she accused DeVos of being a traitor to her sex: "Banner day when Republicans can find women to do their dirty work against other women. Another day, another attack on civil rights."

Her fellow social justice advocates were no more measured. "Survivors of sexual assault deserve to be believed and supported, not brushed off and blamed," said Planned Parenthood's president, Cecile Richards. Amy Siskind, the president and co-founder of the liberal advocacy group The New Agenda, displayed her mastery of Orwellian doubletalk when she called DeVos's review of Title IX "the next stop on our path to authoritarianism." When confronted by *National Review*'s David French about her antipathy to blind justice and due process, Siskind replied, charmingly, "Oh STFU with your hackneyed due process talking point and do some f—ing research on the issue!" She saved her most incisive riposte for later, puncturing her critics' arguments with the observation that they were "all white men."[48]

Why all the scene-chewing theatrics from the left? Because when the facts aren't with you, the only recourse is to pound the table. These injustices are a feature of the system they built, and the abuses they abet have produced an army of sympathetic victims. More grotesquely, they have made unsympathetic figures of the real victims of sexual abuse and harassment, who now have to shout above the clamor of the falsely accused. The real victims of sexual assault are forced to appeal to a corrupt system for justice. The verdicts reached in their cases—just or unjust—will forever be tainted by their association with unethical institutions.

In these cases, the social justice left demands that the justice system determine not who has been genuinely wronged and who is spinning a capricious or even malicious tale for personal gain, but which identity group deserves a boot in the face. This is discrimination by any definition. Its advocates call it positive discrimination—the supposedly noble kind—but it is still a prejudgment based on accidents of birth.

Of course, racism, sexism, and other vile forms of prejudice in America are not hoaxes. Historically, incidents in which perpetrators with the right identity (male, white, and heterosexual) were protected from the consequences of their actions both by private and governmental institutions were not uncommon. That is a great injustice. But many of the left's attempts to rectify these injustices have been an immoral disgrace. They have only made true justice and equality harder to achieve.

The Dark Enlightenment

Liberals are not the only Americans who are seduced by social justice fanaticism. Donald Trump's insurgent presidential campaign revealed that victimization has bipartisan appeal. By presenting himself as a defender of the status quo ante—being unspecific enough to allow his listeners to imagine their own preferred "ante"—Trump tapped into a brand of identity politics that resonates with a considerable subset of the Republican electorate.

By neglecting to denounce prominent racists like David Duke and the Klan during the primaries, Donald Trump emboldened them. In the process, racially anxious factions on the right were encouraged to poke their heads out from the shadows. Their sudden courage revealed a curious fact: the ideology animating aggressive white racists is not all that distinct from what motivates racial hoaxers—the desire to be a victim.

The so-called alt-right's world is a labyrinth of persecution. Foreign labor steals their jobs, global free trade renders their work obsolete, a permissive immigration system dilutes their gene pool, police and government bureaucrats conspire to rob them of their due. White supremacists and the social justice left use different vocabulary but speak the same language.

Central to Trump's initial appeal as a candidate was his hawkish approach to both legal and illegal immigration. He promised the construction of an unbroken barrier across a vast expanse of rugged terrain and the deportation of more than eleven million illegal immigrants—many of whom have been in the country for decades— over an extremely short period. Even the boldest immigration skeptics doubted the seriousness of these schemes, but that is what made them attractive to Trump's earliest committed supporters. The very audacity and impracticability of his proposals communicated to them that Trump understood the righteousness of their anger and the urgency of their circumstances. It didn't matter if Trump's ideas were unfeasible or even incoherent; someone was finally mirroring their anxiety.

Republicans attracted to Trump's audacity forgot the admonitions of Dwight Eisenhower and Ronald Reagan, who routinely dismissed appeals to solidarity based solely on ethnicity, religion, or sex as dangerous anti-republicanism. But Trump's movement was not an entirely conservative movement. In fact, it was plainly hostile not only to the GOP but also to the limited-government philosophy that had animated the party for so many years.[49]

The social justice left seems incapable of seeing prejudice in itself, but it is hyper-aware of racial anxiety in others. Occasionally, the temptation to abandon nuance and complexity and to build a theory of everything around that anxiety is too great to resist. Many of Trump's opponents convinced themselves that the movement he commanded was animated by racism alone. Perhaps some of the angst into which Trump tapped was rooted in racial paranoia, but it is the height of arrogance to assert that ignoble sentiments animate the average Trump voter. A substantial number of Trump's core supporters live in what the left would freely describe as "marginalized communities" if they were inhabited by people of color.

Writing in *Commentary* magazine in early 2017, the demographer Nicholas Eberstadt observed that a substantial but overlooked segment of Americans saw their health, income, and prospects for social mobility begin to decline around the turn of the twenty-first century. "Work rates have fallen off a cliff since the year 2000 and are at their lowest levels in decades," he wrote. Even today, the country has not fully recovered from the "lost decade" ushered in after the financial collapse of 2008. These doldrums seem to be disproportionately pushing men in their prime earning years out of the workforce.[50]

As financial prospects for Americans in predominantly white middle America deteriorated, so too did their physical condition. In 2000, for the first time since World War II, life expectancy among middle-aged, non-Hispanic whites began to decline. This deterioration was exacerbated by a rise in "deaths of despair"—fatalities attributed to suicide, liver cirrhosis, and drug overdose. Citing a study conducted by Alan Krueger, the former chairman of President Obama's council of economic advisors, Eberstadt observed that roughly seven million men today are taking daily pain medication. "In our mind's eye we can now picture many millions of un-working men in the prime of life, out of work and not looking for jobs, sitting in front of screens—stoned," he concluded.

This epidemic went largely unnoticed until Donald Trump won the White House. To many of those affected, the reason elites on the coasts were ignoring their plight was painfully obvious: mostly white and male, the suffering had the wrong identity. That self-pity is as crippling as the narcotics-induced haze into which many of the afflicted escape.

This embittering dysfunction and hopelessness are fertile ground for the narrative of victimization. Donald Trump reaped the benefits. He did not inculcate a persecution complex in his most alienated supporters; he merely exploited it. Long before Trump's presidential candidacy, beyond the realm of respectable sociopolitical analysts and sober academics, the right's dispossessed developed a set of racial and cultural anxieties that evolved into an organizing principle. And they called it the "Dark Enlightenment."

That's exactly what it sounds like: an antagonistic reaction to egalitarian philosophers like John Locke, Francis Bacon, and Montesquieu. These thinkers set the foundation for the modern democratic republic as we know it, and they had a profound influence on America's founding generation. This period was, the Dark Enlightenment's philosophers contend, an aberration in human political evolution.

Few journalists have shed more light on the luminaries of the "neo-reactionary" movement than Rosie Gray. Richard Spencer, the founder of the white supremacist National Policy Institute, is perhaps the most conspicuous character in the cast Gray has highlighted over the years. Spencer is, however, the white nationalist equivalent of Abbie Hoffman—more an agitator and organizer than a thought-leader. The Dark Enlightenment's Paulo Freires are still in the shadows.

"The movement is undergirded by some of the ideas espoused by Dark Enlightenment or neo-reactionary thinkers like the English philosopher Nick Land and the American computer programmer Curtis Yarvin (aka 'Mencius Moldbug')," Gray writes. These figures and their disciples reject democracy, pluralism, and a colorblind society, but they are not the gap-toothed hill folk that liberals think of when they imagine white nationalists. This new generation lives well-heeled, refined lifestyles in upwardly mobile occupations, and they write verbose tomes promoting their views using language that mimics academic rigor.[51]

So-called "neo-reactionary" thought has attracted some prominent fellow travelers over the years. It has intrigued figures ranging from former Business Insider CTO Pax Dixon to PayPal founder and libertarian activist Peter Thiel. Uniting this movement's disparate elements is an antipathy for democratic systems. "I no longer believe that freedom and democracy are compatible," Thiel wrote in 2009.[52]

Neo-reactionaries have varying ideas about what should replace the classically liberal state as we know it. "Demotist systems, that is, systems ruled by the 'People,' such as Democracy and Communism, are predictably less financially stable than aristocratic systems," writes self-described neo-reactionary Michael Anissimov. "Each dollar goes further towards improving standard of living for the average person in an aristocratic system than in a Democratic one."[53]

For his part, Yarvin seems to endorse a kind of mercantile despotism in which the state is subsumed into a vast corporate enterprise with a shareholder aristocracy and a legal dictator resembling the chairman of the board. In an earlier essay, Yarvin confessed to having given up on democracy, a form of social organization he equates now with "war, tyranny, destruction, and poverty." Yarvin exercises some influence. In 2017, *Politico* magazine reported that he was in close contact with Steve Bannon, Trump's onetime campaign chairman and chief strategist in the White House.[54] For neo-reactionary thinkers like Yarvin, the ills of multiculturalism cannot be separated from the shortcomings of the democratic republican system itself. In a 2008 essay provocatively titled "What's so bad about the Nazis?" he condemns the Holocaust but questions the moral authority of the allies.

In a sprawling, unwieldy manifesto outlining his authoritarian and racist alternative to classical liberalism, Nick Land provokes for provocation's sake. "A distinctive silence accompanies the broken, half-expression of a mute tide of racial separatism, driven by civilizationally disabling terrors and animosities, whose depths, and structures of reciprocity, remain unavowable," reads a tortured sentence typical of Land's ponderous style.[55]

It is obviously not Land's insight that makes him so dangerous but his ability to impersonate the overburdened prose of the humanities professorate. His readers don't need to know what is being said, which is often nothing. They can derive assurance merely from the highfalutin tone packaging what is essentially a crude case for authoritarianism, oppression, and racial segregation.

Land frequently congratulates himself for saying what others will not, particularly about race. He insists "barbarity" is an accepted feature of the Western world where law does not apply. This condition is native to "inner cities" but not exclusive to them. "Quite clearly, these are places where civilization has fundamentally collapsed," he wrote, "and a society that includes them has to some substantial extent *failed*" (Land's italics).[56]

Fatalism, victimization, identity-obsession—these are all the characteristics we associate with the typical social justice advocate on the left. Following Trump's ascension to political prominence and eventually power, a brand of identity politics that appeals to white Americans rapidly developed traits that have distinguished history's most effective tyrannies. Perhaps by observing these characteristics on the right, the Identitarian left might also begin to see them in themselves.

The Tie That Binds

It is a sad fact that whole classes of people have been deprived of the chance to exercise free will. It must be said again that discrimination, racism, and bigotry are real and detestable. But victimhood also conveys authority. More troubling, those who fancy themselves champions of the allegedly victimized classes have developed an unhealthy antipathy toward institutions that mete out objective, blind justice. This is nothing short of an attack on the foundational principles of classical liberalism.

For those who believe that they have been shut out of life's great game—whether on the right or the left—two courses are available. The first is resignation, depression, and crippling cynicism. The second is to lash out. The most militant social justice advocates believe that, for the most part, the nation's political and cultural elites do not share their dire view of modern life, and they resent that. They convince themselves that only a strong hand can restore what has been stolen from them. Bitterness, resentment, and a sense of betrayal make a potent cocktail.

From some remove, the pursuit of Identitarian social justice looks a lot like tyranny. But that's the final phase of a long process. After the radicalization of the vanguard, the next stage of any successful revolution is terror.

CHAPTER 7

Violent Delights

What happens to a people when it becomes convinced that its public and private institutions serve only to keep it in chains? What happens when it becomes insular, narrow-minded, and petty? When good news is rejected because it undermines its woeful narrative, when it prefers societal alienation to integration, when provocateurs profit from ignorance and disillusionment? How does it all end?

Too often, the answer is in bloodshed.

Regression

"Not all value opinions are the result of social conditioning. For if they were, then there could be no non-conformity to society based on moral values," the philosopher Peter Kreeft declares in his famous attack on moral relativism. "There could only be rebellions of force, rather than principle."[1] But to the most fanatical social justice activists, conditioning is inescapable and transcendent moral values are chimerical. The present is all that matters, and the present is rather terrible. Their worldview favors raw power over moral authority for advancing the interests of any individual or group. And if those interests are advanced by fomenting violence, a growing number seem prepared to answer, "So be it."

"So strong is this propensity of mankind to fall into mutual animosities," James Madison wrote in Federalist Paper No. 10, "that where no substantial occasion presents itself, the most frivolous and fanciful distinctions have been sufficient to kindle their unfriendly passions and excite their most violent conflicts." The Founders knew us better than we know ourselves. As partisan affiliation suffices for or enhances personal identity, political disagreements become personal disagreements. The more trivial our differences, the more those who benefit from conflict must exaggerate them.[2]

Both ends of the political spectrum are guilty of embracing elements who make a virtue of moral relativism. These elements convince themselves that their adversaries are aggressors with no remorse or compunction. To observe civility and decorum in the face of their opponents' attacks is tantamount to unilateral surrender. They whip themselves and their supporters into a frenzy. They inflate virtually every cultural clash or policy disagreement into a battle for primacy or even survival. They cheapen the concept of self-defense by treating the most modest offense as a grave injury that demands retribution.

These movements, with their unrealistic view of what circumspect constitutional governance is capable of achieving, make demands of government that can never be met. The rise of social justice and grievance politics has therefore been accompanied by bitterness and increasing resentment toward government and the governing class. And when these movements perceive the political process as having failed them and their cause, they become convinced that it is only logical to take matters into their own hands.

With rare exceptions, America's political culture has not been marked by organized violence. While violent conflict has not been entirely unknown, it has been dormant in our public for more than a generation. Regrettably, that may be changing.

In *Pedagogy of the Oppressed*, Paulo Freire insists that students should be encouraged to see themselves as victims of systemic oppression, but he also advises educators to teach them to see violence as a legitimate remedy for their plights. "He defends violence and terror by redefining them," Bruce Bawer observes. "[F]or the oppressed to resist [oppression] actively, in however bloody a manner, does not constitute violence or terror," Bawer writes, "for '[v]iolence is initiated by those who oppress' and '[i]t is not the helpless...who initiate terror' but their oppressors." In other words, any action in service to class war, even violent action, is justified.[3]

As we'll see, this self-serving rationalization for potentially murderous violence outside the context of self-defense has taken root in the imaginations of many otherwise rational people. Identitarian movements erode the ethical and social safeguards against violence while erecting elaborate moral justifications for physical attacks on their perceived enemies. This is how organized political violence begins, as it has begun again in America.

The Fanatical Left

The type of violence we have seen from Identitarian factions on both the right and the left in the second decade of the twenty-first century presages a grim future. In many ways, this ugly moment in American political history began at an inconspicuous corporate park in Lower Manhattan.

Zuccotti Park was, in many ways, an apt site for the birth of the Occupy Wall Street movement. Two and a half centuries before it was damaged in the 9/11 attacks, rebuilt by a corporate consortium, and renamed for Mayor Abe Beame's city planning commission chairman, the site had been home to a coffee house.

Though the English have acquired a reputation as tea-drinkers, the British Empire had a far more robust coffee culture in the seventeenth and eighteenth centuries. Coffee houses were ubiquitous in Great Britain, and the coffee was the least interesting thing about them. They were places where British subjects discussed current events, debated political philosophy, read their newspapers, and conducted commerce. The same was true in America, where, in the autumn of 1773, the Sons of Liberty held one of their first demonstrations against the Tea Act outside this Lower Manhattan coffee house.[4]

In 2011, the expression of financial anxiety that would become known as the Occupy movement made its appearance on this spot. In the wake of the Republican Party's resurgence in the third year of a sluggish economic recovery and the abrupt end of the legislative period of Barack Obama's presidency, here was a band of progressives demanding more. That demand won the hearts of many liberal champions, and they lent their support to this rabble despite their illegal occupation of private property. It was a grave misjudgment.

"I support the message to the establishment," Democratic Minority Leader Nancy Pelosi told reporters when asked about the nascent Occupy movement. "God bless them for their spontaneity," she later added. "It's young, it's spontaneous, and it's focused. And it's going to be effective."[5] Even President Obama, abandoning prudence, embraced this group despite its criminal inclinations. "The protesters are giving voice to a more broad-based frustration about how our financial system works," he said.[6] On another occasion he compared them to Martin Luther King Jr. because both "rightly challenge the excesses of Wall Street." Like the protesters, King had been "vilified by many, denounced as a rabble-rouser and an agitator, a communist, and a radical."[7]

The irresponsibility of these assertions should have been obvious by the time a genuine civil rights leader, Congressman John Lewis, attempted to address an Occupy encampment in Atlanta. After making him sit through a bizarre confab about the relevancy of his African-American heritage and a cascade of self-referential speechifying, the occupiers voted not to let Lewis speak. The civil rights icon was forced to shuffle sheepishly back to Washington, having never addressed the movement he sought to co-opt.[8]

While Occupy was a leftist movement dedicated to a social democratic economic agenda, it was also a social justice movement. Soon, activist "facilitators" of Occupy's various jaw sessions began to introduce the concept of the "progressive stack" into the mix. As one Occupier in Virginia explained it, "if you have your name on the list and you come from a traditionally marginalized background—race, gender, ethnicity, anything that is traditionally marginalized—you get bumped up the list." Further, "white men, white women, people who've been privileged," are obliged to "step back."[9]

By Occupy's fourth week in Zuccotti Park, it had given birth to chapters in urban centers all over the Western world. That was when the violence started.

News of the squalid, lawless conditions in these encampments began to filter out, prompting officials to wonder if they had a public health crisis on their hands. In places like Rome, "Occupiers" exploded from their bivouacs to make war on the symbols of capitalism all around them. They smashed windows, destroyed ATMs, attacked television crews, and set vehicles on fire. In New York City, seven hundred protesters were arrested amid an attempt to shut down half the town by seizing the Brooklyn Bridge. These warning signs did not dissuade high-profile Democratic lawmakers from making common cause with a movement they wanted to believe could form the nucleus of a liberal Tea Party.[10]

Then things really spiraled out of control.

Supplies dwindled as the weather grew colder, and conditions in the camps became desperate. Occupy violence soon developed into something more organized and widespread. Tales of chronic drug use and overdoses, muggings and theft, assaults and protected spaces in which women were spared the threat of sexual violence began to escape the camps. In Washington, D.C., a mob overpowered security guards and invaded the National Air and Space Museum.[11] A riot erupted in Denver when police attempted to break up the encampment there.[12] Emboldened by the endorsement of labor unions, including the Service Employees International Union, AFL-CIO, Teamsters, and United Auto Workers, three thousand Occupiers in Oakland, California, stormed and captured an abandoned port facility. Their intention wasn't to hold the ground but to destroy it. They broke windows, set vacant buildings on fire, and engaged in running street battles with police.[13]

As bad as the Occupy demonstrations became, they could have been much worse. In Ohio, five members of the local Occupy branch were arrested and charged with plotting to affix eight packages of what they thought were plastic explosives to the support structures of a local bridge. This failed attack was supposed to be part of a campaign of terrorism aimed at what they dubbed symbols of "corporate America."[14]

Rationalizing Violence

The left, in particular, has grown comfortable drawing moral equivalencies between disagreeable speech and physical violence. When speech becomes indistinguishable from violence, a violent response to speech is justified—even morally necessary.

"When someone calls a black person the 'n' word out of hatred, he or she is not expressing a new idea or outlining a valuable thought," read a 2012 editorial in the *Harvard Crimson*. "They are committing an act of violence." When the feminist lecturer Christina Hoff

Sommers was marched off campus in the spring of 2015, the student editors at the *Oberlin Review* penned a self-soothing "love letter to ourselves." It was a fatuous mound of false equivalencies justifying the censorship of inconvenient statistical analysis that called into question the scope of the supposed epidemic of sexual violence on campus—or as the students called it, "rape denialism."[15] In 2017, editors at Wellesley College's student newspaper offered an ominous endorsement of "appropriate measures" against speakers who bucked the leftist consensus. They weren't being coy: "[I]f people are given the resources to learn and either continue to speak hate speech or refuse to adapt their beliefs, then hostility may be warranted."[16]

These sentiments are, apparently, broadly shared. A survey conducted in 2015 by the Higher Education Research Institute at the University of California at Los Angeles found that almost 71 percent of that year's freshman class believed that colleges should "prohibit racist/sexist speech." Another 43 percent of incoming freshmen agreed that colleges should "have the right to ban extreme speakers" from campus. These censorious ideas trickled down from their mentors. In 2010–11, the institute's survey of faculty found that 70 percent of female university staff and nearly half their male counterparts believed that colleges should "prohibit" speech determined to be racist or sexist.

A poll conducted in 2017 by John Villasenor of UCLA and the Brookings Institution confirmed that students were prepared to take action to enforce their contemptuous dogma. That poll, funded by the Charles Koch Foundation, revealed that a plurality (44 percent) of students do not believe that the First Amendment protects "hate speech." A majority of respondents said it was acceptable to shout down "a very controversial speaker" who is "known for making offensive and hurtful statements." Most disturbingly, nearly one-fifth of college students polled said it was acceptable to engage in violence to silence a challenging speaker.[17]

This violent creed has begun to yield violent actions. When the right-leaning provocateur Milo Yiannopoulos was scheduled to appear at Cal Berkeley, the students set their campus ablaze.[18] Professors at Middlebury College were physically assaulted and even injured by the dozens of students who violently protested the appearance of the political scientist Charles Murray.[19] The inauguration of Donald Trump to the presidency was met with violent demonstrations across the country from college-age protesters who assaulted police, set vehicles on fire, and destroyed property.[20]

The tens of thousands who participated in the Women's March against Trump in January 2017 were criticized by some on the left, like the *New Republic*'s Jess Zimmerman, for not being violent enough. She attributed the lack of brutality not just to the pacific nature of the march's participants but also to their predominately white skin color. "If the police stay their hand with you, white women, it is not a compliment," she wrote. "It's condescension."[21]

By legitimizing violence committed in defense of their shared values, these students and agitators were only mimicking their elders. When Islamist terrorists murdered the editorial staff of the satirical French magazine *Charlie Hebdo* in 2015, for example, a variety of prominent members of the liberal intelligentsia insisted the dead had it coming.

"*Charlie Hebdo* has a long record of mocking, baiting and needling French Muslims," read a loaded sentence by Tony Barber in the *Financial Times*. This massacre is "what happens when you get a culture that, rather than asking to what end we defend free speech, valorizes free speech for its own sake and thus perversely values speech more the more pointlessly offensive it is," The Daily Beast's Arthur Chu insisted. Even Secretary of State John Kerry contended that these murderers had "a rationale that you could attach yourself to somehow and say, 'Okay, they're really angry because of this and that.'"

Just four months after the *Charlie Hebdo* slaughter, the conservative activist Pamela Geller staged a well-publicized "cartoon drawing contest" in a Dallas suburb to demonstrate solidarity with the cartoonists at the Danish magazine *Jyllands-Posten*, which had been targeted with violence following a contest in which readers submitted satirical drawings of the prophet Mohammed. It worked. Two Islamist gunmen attacked Geller's event and were summarily killed by security.

For conducting a successful experiment to demonstrate the barbaric illiberalism of her antagonists, Geller was pilloried. The *Washington Post* insinuated that she should apologize. MSNBC host Chris Matthews castigated her for "taunting," "daring," and "provoking" her would-be murderers. CNN's Erin Burnett accused her of enjoying "being a target of these attacks," and the *New York Daily News* columnist Linda Stasi wrote that Geller "will get her wish: More dead Americans at the hands of radical Muslims."[22]

These are the logical foundations that lead otherwise decent and rational people to excuse murderous violence. This abhorrent phenomenon is not limited to the political left.

In August 2017, Donald Trump's national security advisor, H. R. McMaster, ousted a conspiracy theorist from the president's National Security Council. Rich Higgins was let go, however, only after he penned an addlebrained memorandum, to which the president himself was privy, that was so untethered as to be downright unnerving.

Headlined "POTUS & Political Warfare," the memo is one long hysterical delusion. Higgins warns that the president may be forced out of office not because of his own incompetence but by the efficacy of "memes" spread anonymously on social media. He warns of "cultural Marxist drivers" who have seized the commanding heights of culture. He engages the contemptibly familiar straw man of "International Banking," which supposedly benefits from immigrant labor and

America's "debtor status"—thinly-veiled anti-Semitism that gives away the game.

"Atomization of society must also occur at the individual level; with attacks directed against all levels of group and personal identity," the memo continues. "Hence the sexism, racism, and xenophobia memes. ... [T]his is a form of population control by certain business cartels in league with cultural Marxists/corporatists/Islamists who will leverage Islamic terrorism threats to justify the creation of a police state."[23]

That this kind of neurosis was able to find its way to the president's desk is, to put it mildly, disconcerting. Equating the president's domestic political opposition with a "Maoist insurgency" is a caricature that any sense of republican civic decency would prohibit. The memo reduces Trump's opponents to a one-dimensional, monomaniacal horde of People's Liberation Army soldiers pouring over the hilltops to overwhelm the valiant, outmanned defenders in the White House. It was a radical effort to dehumanize, and dehumanization of a set of targets is a historically effective tool for fomenting political violence.

Through a quirk of American political history, this kind of thinking, common on fringe white supremacist blogs, came to be legitimized by the American president and the head of the Republican Party.

America's Weimar Moment

In March 2016, as the political temperature rose to a boiling point, a Trump supporter at one of the candidate's rallies in North Carolina sucker-punched an African-American protester in the back of the head. Following his arrest, the attacker was utterly unapologetic, promising that the next time he had the opportunity to come to blows with an anti-Trump demonstrator, his intent would be murder.[24]

The attack followed weeks of incitement by Trump himself. The future president reveled in the notion that his supporters were so passionate about his candidacy that they might harm his detractors. He talked openly about meting out violence himself—"I'd like to punch him in the face"—and complained, "We're not allowed to push back anymore." "In the old days," Trump told a crowd, protesters "would be carried out on a stretcher."[25] He promised to pay the legal bills of those who were arrested for committing violence in his name, and not just on the stump but on *Meet the Press*.[26]

In the weeks that followed, attendees at Trump rallies were comfortable enough in the company of like minds that they were filmed giving Nazi salutes and yelling at onlookers to "go to f—ing Auschwitz" or "go back to Africa," depending on the look of their targets.[27] The attack on a black protester by a white Trump supporter had the feel of an opening salvo in a war. And, in a way, it was.

One day, when Trump traveled to downtown Chicago for another scheduled rally, his opponents were ready for him. At the nearby University of Illinois at Chicago campus, a mob of students, many of them self-described supporters of Senator Bernie Sanders, showed up with a simple mission: "Shut shit down." Demonstrators flooded the streets outside the Trump rally and infiltrated the arena. Fist fights broke out and demonstrators clashed with police. By the end of the night, two police officers were injured—one was hit in the head with a bottle—and two demonstrators were arrested. This was a harbinger of unrest to come.[28]

The following month, twenty protesters were arrested in Costa Mesa, California, attempting to shut down another Trump event. The month after that, Trump rally-goers were attacked in San Jose by demonstrators waving Mexico's flag while burning America's. Some peaceful rally-goers were pelted with eggs. Others had their clothes torn off. One pro-Trump rally-goer was photographed bleeding profusely from the head and face following an encounter with attackers. "Violence against supporters of any candidate has no place in this election," wrote Hillary Clinton's campaign chairman, John Podesta. If it were not for the unambiguous hostility of the anti-Trump demonstrators, Podesta would not have felt compelled to take ownership of these protesters, albeit only to disown them.[29]

In June 2016, a collection of self-described "white nationalists" descended on Sacramento, California. Emboldened by the ascendance of Donald Trump and his apparent tolerance for their repugnant racism, they sought and secured a license from the city to promote their views. Their widely-publicized rally did not go unnoticed by their foes, some of them self-styled "anti-fascists." They, too, gathered in the city's center, intending to force the white supremacists to disperse.

"White supremacists should not be entitled to 'free speech' to preach their hateful messages and incite beatings and murders," declared the socialist magazine *Liberation*. "They were met with a huge crowd that was there, committed and determined, very courageous, to take action, shut them down, and stop them from organizing for genocide and for lynch mobs," asserted the counter-protest's organizer, the diminutive middle-school teacher Yvette Felarca. A peaceful demonstration was not in the cards.

Armed with knives, clubs, broken bottles, and rocks, both groups were ready for a melee, and they soon got one—captured on video from multiple angles. Ten people were injured, two critically. "The Nazis did not recruit anyone new today, and our side did," Felarca proclaimed triumphantly.

For whatever reason, Americans didn't talk much about this episode. Perhaps its villains were not clear-cut enough. There is no moral ambiguity about opposing white supremacists, but some observers seemed conflicted over whether to condemn "anti-fascists," even if they inaugurate violence. "If I had to say who started it and who didn't, I'd say the permitted group didn't start it," said George Granada, a California highway patrolman and head of the department's protective services division. A year later, Felarca's arrest on charges of inciting a riot confirmed that Granada's suspicions were shared by California's department of justice.[30]

Maybe the inability to honestly blame this attack entirely on racist Trump supporters discouraged a media complex invested in his loss from delving too deeply into the story. Perhaps the thought of unapologetic fascists and communists coming to blows in the American streets was too terrifyingly evocative of the Weimar Republic's final days to elicit much public discussion. Maybe we just didn't want to see what was happening to us.

The scene was repeated in February 2017 when a group of so-called "alt-right" agitators targeted a lawful socialist demonstration. "Heil Trump," they shouted in an effort to drown out the socialists, who barked, in Spanish, "One class, one struggle—against borders!" The clash of words soon escalated into a violent confrontation.

Hundreds were involved in a similar episode of politically-inspired mob violence the following April in Berkeley, California, where a large gathering of pro-Trump demonstrators was met by counter-protesters—a tense situation that prompted many businesses, fearing imminent violence, to close preemptively. They were right.

"Both groups threw rocks and sticks at each other and used a large trash bin as a battering ram as the crowd moved around the perimeter of the park," the *Los Angeles Times* reported. Twenty-one people were arrested. Eleven were injured and six, including a stabbing victim, were taken to the hospital.[31]

In retrospect, these events deserved more attention than they received. They were a prelude to atrocities yet to come.

Racial Terror in the Age of Trump

On the night of Thursday, July 7, 2016, twenty-five-year-old Micah Johnson resolved to get his revenge. An African-American veteran of the war in Afghanistan, Johnson was steeped in racial resentment. He had no formal ties to any political organization, but he was a supporter of the Black Lives Matter movement. His Facebook page revealed his support for the New Black Panther Party, which, according to the *New York Times*, "has advocated violence against whites, and Jews in particular."[32]

His home was full of weapons—ballistic vests, bomb-making equipment and fuses, ammunition, a journal of combat tactics, and, of course, guns. But it was a sniper rifle that Johnson would use to mete out vengeance that night. Ascending to the top of a parking garage in downtown Dallas, Johnson set up his position, took aim at any policemen he could find, and opened fire. By the end of the night, five Dallas officers were dead. "The suspect said he was upset at white people," said Dallas Police Chief David Brown. "The suspect stated he wanted to kill white people, especially white officers."

In February 2017, Adam Purinton walked into a bar in Olathe, Kansas, and quickly became agitated by the presence of two Indian men. He demanded to know their immigration status and, unsatisfied with their response, insisted that they "get out of my country." Purinton was escorted out of the bar, but he returned thirty minutes later with a handgun and opened fire. "There is a kind of hysteria spreading," a relative of one of the victims observed.[33]

Twenty-eight-year-old James Jackson was a U.S. Army veteran and a fan of the alt-right and Richard Spencer. He watched alt-right YouTube videos and cut his blond hair in a severe style that deliberately mimicked the haircuts of young men in Hitler's Germany. In March 2017, Jackson traveled from Baltimore to New York City, where he encountered Timothy Caughman, a sixty-six-year-old African-American he had not previously met. Without warning or provocation, Jackson plunged a twenty-six-inch sword into Caughman's chest, killing him. Prosecutors alleged that the murder was a trial run for a racist killing spree Jackson had planned to execute in Times Square.[34]

"Allahu Akbar!" shouted Kori Ali Muhammad in the act of murdering three white people in downtown Fresno, California, in April 2017. But despite his name and battle cry, Muhammad was no devout Muslim, and this was not a typical act of lone-wolf Islamist terrorism. A few days earlier, Muhammad had killed a security guard at a local Motel 6, a man police believe was targeted because he was white. Muhammad expressed hatred for white people on social media and in interviews with police and had an affinity for violent black liberationist rhetoric.[35]

The following month, twenty-three-year-old Richard Collins III, a newly commissioned lieutenant in the United States Army, was three days from graduating from college when he was stabbed to death by a random attacker. Collins was black and his murderer, Sean Urbanski, was a member of a racist Facebook group called the Alt-Reich Nation. That same day, Mississippi state representative Karl Oliver said that those seeking to remove Confederate monuments "should be lynched."[36]

"I stabbed the two motherf—ers in the neck and I'm happy now," yelled Jeremy Joseph Christian of Portland, Oregon. His unhinged rant was delivered into courtroom microphones as he was being arraigned for killing two men who came to the defense of Muslim girls whom Christian was harassing. "Death to the enemies of America!" he raved. "You call it terrorism. I call it patriotism."[37]

The slaying of two good Samaritans provoked a national outpouring of grief and solidarity. A week later, organizers of a previously scheduled "free speech" pro-Trump rally (which Portland's mayor sought unsuccessfully to have canceled) were swamped by a semi-spontaneous gathering of demonstrators rallying "against hate." A clash ensued. "Protesters threw bricks, mortars, and balloons filled with 'unknown, foul-smelling liquid,'" *USA Today* reported. Police used chemical munitions and impact weapons to subdue the crowds. Fourteen people were arrested.[38]

These violent assailants were no doubt mentally disturbed, as are almost all people who engage in murderous violence against strangers. But the vile sentiments that inspired them are promoted by people who know exactly what they are doing. In Portland, this kind of racist violence showed that it had the capacity to incite a mob. The worst was yet to come.

Charlottesville

The white supremacist march on the campus of the University of Virginia in Charlottesville was already an un-American abomination well before the violence broke out.

On the night of August 12, 2017, approximately one hundred alt-right demonstrators gathered in Emancipation Park for the first of a set of weekend events dubbed "Unite the Right." Bearing torches, chanting Nazi slogans, throwing Hitler salutes, and vowing that "Jews will not replace us," these demonstrators made their intentions clear. They wore khaki pants and white golf shirts. Their faces were uncovered. They wanted to be identified, and they were looking for a fight. They soon found one.

"Stay in formation!" one rally organizer shouted to his compatriots, according to the *Washington Post* reporter Joe Heim. The mob of white nationalists swarmed a gathering of about thirty student counter-demonstrators. A scuffle ensued. "Shoves. Punches. Both groups sprayed chemical irritants," Heim reports. Law enforcement was slow to intervene in what was eventually dubbed an "unlawful assembly," allowing plenty of time for the nation to drink in the images of violent neo-Nazis swarming a college campus in the heart of the so-called New South. It was a sickening display that presaged a catastrophe.[39]

The following morning, the "Unite the Right" white nationalist demonstrators took to the streets for a sanctioned demonstration. They were met with a phalanx of peaceful counter-demonstrators: clergy and local political figures united in their opposition to white nationalism.

"[T]hen brawls broke out," Hawes Spencer reported in the *New York Times*, describing a scene in which protesters sprayed one another with mace and beat one other with clubs, flagpoles, and "makeshift weapons." White supremacists clad in black wearing mock militia garb and bearing white riot shields marked uniformly with a black "X" plunged into a gang of counter-demonstrators identified only by their black and red banners.[40]

Soon, the ranks of the white nationalists were augmented by uniformed and hooded Klan members, but the white supremacist presence was outnumbered by approximately one thousand counter-demonstrators. "A few minutes before 11 a.m.," Heim recalled, "a swelling group of white nationalists carrying large shields and long wooden clubs approached the park on Market Street. About two dozen counter-protesters formed a line across the street, blocking their path. With a roar, the marchers charged through the line, swinging sticks, punching and spraying chemicals."

As the clashes escalated, police tried to clear out the demonstrations, deploying tear gas and pepper spray. Twenty-three people were arrested, but only three were taken to the hospital—two for exposure to heat and one for over-imbibing. Elsewhere, a gang of white supremacists were photographed kicking and beating a black man in a parking garage—images reminiscent of a terrible era in American race relations. The images went viral and resulted in the arrest of two of the young men two weeks later.

So far the unrest, though regrettable, had not been as bad as it might have been, and by early afternoon, it seemed like disaster had been averted. It had not.

Several blocks from the park in which torch-bearing white suprem-acists had rallied the day before, anti-racist protesters ambled peace-fully down a local thoroughfare. Without warning, a Dodge Challenger with tinted windows and no plates sped through the narrow streets of Charlottesville and collided with the back of a sedan. That sedan and the minivan in front of it lurched into the crowd of protesters, injuring nineteen persons, some quite badly. Thirty-two-year-old Heather Heyer died of her wounds. Her murderer, James Alex Fields, was cap-tured on camera just hours earlier marching with members of the organization Vanguard America—a white nationalist group that advo-cates "a government based in the natural law," which "must not cater to the false notion of equality."[41]

Fuel to the Fire

Nearly a month after the attack, the independent journalistic collective ProPublica published the results of an investigation into the behavior of the online communities that organized the "Unite the Right" rally. What they found was disgusting, although not surprising.

ProPublica reported that white supremacist groups spent months tracking the efforts of their adversaries to counter-organize ahead of Charlottesville. Racist online communities like the Daily Stormer prepared to present evidence of violent agitation by the left. They advised participants against bringing cell phones that might compro-mise their "affinity group," a term they had borrowed from liberal social justice activists to describe a network of unaffiliated organizations working together on a common cause.

They prepared for violence and joked ominously about committing it—jokes that notably featured acts of vehicular violence. One user of a white supremacist message board posted an image of vehicles plowing through a crowd in response to a discussion about car insurance and logistics. "Another user replied, claiming that in North Carolina 'driving over protesters blocking roadways isn't an offense,'" ProPublica reported. "The user then posted a meme showing a combine harvester that could be a 'digestor' for multiple lanes of protesters, saying, 'Sure would be nice.'"[42]

Typical of his compulsion to excuse the inexcusable and validate the self-pity that animates white supremacists, President Donald Trump spent the next week wrestling with himself over just how forcefully to condemn those who participated in this incident. The traumatic terroristic event could not be divorced entirely from the abhorrent white supremacism that had been on display for the better part of twenty-four hours. In its wake, the president appeared on camera and delivered a prepared statement denouncing the violence. But in a deviation from the script, Trump took the opportunity to suggest a moral equivalence and pointedly condemned "both sides."

In fact, there *was* violence on both sides, but there was time enough for equivalencies after the blood had been washed off Charlottesville streets. In fact, the time for equivalencies was a year earlier, when revanchist fascists and proto-Bolsheviks were knifing each other on the streets of Sacramento. But that was a missed opportunity.

A firestorm erupted over Trump's comments. Republican lawmakers, one after the other, criticized the president, and an exodus of business and labor leaders from Trump's advisory councils eventually led to their dissolution.

Under pressure, Trump delivered another set of prepared remarks unequivocally condemning the white supremacists and the terrorism to which they were a party. But the president resents being controlled and, the following day, he contradicted himself in a free-flowing exchange with reporters at a press conference.

"What about the alt-left that came charging at the, as you say, alt-right?" a visibly agitated Trump barked at reporters. "Do they have any semblance of guilt?" The president added that he believed "not all of those people" who attended the white nationalist demonstrations "the night before" were racists. "Not all of those people were neo-Nazis, believe me," Trump contended. "Not all of those people were white supremacists by any stretch."[43]

These remarks undid any good the president had done by sticking to the script the day earlier. Not only had he validated the cause to which white supremacists were rallying—as members of the alt-right were quick to point out—but he compelled his liberal opponents to valorize the abhorrent political violence being meted out by the costumed sociopaths calling themselves "Antifa."

Antifa

Following the clashes at Charlottesville, members of the liberal intelligentsia declared any and all opposition to fascist white nationalists a noble enterprise—even if that resistance was violent.

Prominent liberal commentators disseminated simplistic memes comparing masked vandals to the American soldiers who landed on Omaha Beach,[44] and there were glowing profiles in mainstream media outlets. "They relish in punching Nazis. They protest in all black. And they've vowed to physically confront racists and extremists across the country," an NBC News report read,[45] while Mark Bray of Dartmouth College praised "their willingness to physically defend themselves and others from white supremacist violence and preemptively shut down fascist organizing efforts before they turn deadly."[46]

This impulse was the culmination of a campaign on the left to glorify violence committed in the name of "anti-fascism." In January 2017, the *Nation*'s Natasha Lennard heaped praise upon the organization for being willing to "fight fascism in the streets." She mocked liberals who "cling to institutions" and approvingly observed how this loose amalgam of leftist thugs had adopted twentieth-century tactics "rooted in militant left-wing and anarchist politics."[47]

This admiration for authoritarian violence only became more overt after Charlottesville. "We're not asking for Nazi speech rights to be curtailed," Lennard wrote. "Antifa is not about asking."[48] The left-wing magazine *Mother Jones* joined the lionization of Antifa with a less-than-condemnatory profile of the "new wave of left-wing militants" who "pledged to resist right-wing extremists by any means necessary."[49]

This wave of militancy has an unmistakably Identitarian flavor. Years before Charlottesville, the Antifa organizing website ItsGoingDown.org, which in late 2017 boasted a following of more than twenty-five thousand on Facebook and another thirty-five thousand on Twitter, prescribed violence against white nationalists within the framework of identity politics. One pseudonymous manifesto posted on the site calls for "the queerest insurrection":

> A fag is bashed because his gender presentation is far too femme. A poor transman can't afford his life-saving hormones. A sex worker is murdered by their client. A gender-queer persyn is raped because ze just needed to be "f—ed straight." Four black lesbians are sent to prison for daring to defend themselves against a straight-male attacker. Cops beat us on the streets and our bodies are being destroyed by pharmaceutical companies because we can't give them a

dime...Queers experience, directly with our bodies, the violence and domination of this world.[50]

This rhetoric is restrained compared with some of the other documents on this pro-Antifa website. Another essay, titled "Dangerous Spaces: Violent Resistance, Self-Defense, & Insurrectional Struggle against Gender," is as despicable a revolutionary screed as you're ever likely to read.

A compendium of radical tracts published by Untorelli Press begins by defining rape, vivisection, "gay bashing," the conduct of commerce, full-time occupations, monthly rent bills, and a variety of medical ailments as "violence that dominates." Except for rape and, bizarrely, involuntary surgery, these things are not violence. Confusing the tedium and trials of everyday life with acts of grotesque oppression is, as we will see, a common trait among members of Antifa.

The author of this unsigned document seems, though, to know what constitutes real violence. That kind of carnage is the violence he likes: "the violence that liberates."

> It is the murdered homophobe. It is the knee-capped rapist. It is the arson and the mink liberation. It is the smashed window and the expropriated food. It is the cop on fire and the riot behind bars. It is work avoidance, squatting, criminal friendship, and the total refusal of compromise. It is the chaos that can never be stopped.[51]

"I am never peaceful," the introduction concludes. "The world does violence to me, and I desire nothing but violence toward the world. Anyone who attempts to keep me from my lust for blood and fire will burn with the world they cling so desperately to." Sincerely and "until the last rapist is hung with the guts of the last frat boy," yours truly, Untorelli Press.

These savage indulgences are prefaced with a "trigger warning" for the faint of heart.

These provocative assertions—the overwrought prose typical of pitiful, angsty, sexually repressed youth—should not be given undue significance. Replace the objects of their hatred (homophobes, frat boys, bank tellers, etc.) with the objects of white nationalist hatred (miscegenation, minorities, "social justice warriors," etc.), and these ugly sentiments are almost ideologically interchangeable. But while it would be an error to suggest that manifestos like this are highly regarded on the social justice left, it would also be a mistake to dismiss their potential to incite.

Trump's remarks might have led white nationalist sympathizers to get off the sidelines and into their misguided fight. The left's esteem for violent "anti-fascists" might have had the same effect.

News from the Front

Berkeley, California, had been the scene of several brutal clashes. The riotous street battle in April 2017 was preceded by one in February, when the Berkeley College Republicans invited Milo Yiannopoulos to address the campus. Then, a mix of students and what the university called "150 masked agitators" took their anger out on their surroundings.

That reptilian tide broke windows, set fires, and torched a generator-powered spotlight before police used chemical irritants to disperse the crowd. Before the mob had scattered, they left behind one hundred thousand dollars in damages and several bloodied persons whom the mob had fingered as Yiannopoulos supporters. Though the images of the walking wounded quickly populated social media and were prominently featured in journalistic accounts of the violence on campus, Sergeant Sabrina Reich of the UCPD revealed that "no one has come forward and made a police report regarding being assaulted or injured."[52]

The violence of February and April was merely a prelude to the events in Berkeley in August.

"We have neither the legal right [n]or [the] desire to interfere with or cancel their invitations based on the perspectives and beliefs of the speakers," declared UC Berkeley spokesman Dan Mogulof about the mob's demand that Yiannopoulos be permanently barred from campus. The local college Republicans tried again to get the provocative performance artist to address their campus as part of "Berkeley Free Speech Week," and the university was keen to stand aside. But the city's mayor, Jesse Arreguin, protested. To treat "free speech week" as an opportunity to exercise the right to free speech, he said, had the potential "to create mayhem."[53] He knew his town well.

Antifa brigades clad in improvised armor with bandanas covering their faces arrived in the thousands at Berkeley's Martin Luther King Jr. Civic Center Park, ready to meet their adversaries. Arranging themselves in a Greek phalanx, linking together homemade riot shields on which the words "No Hate" were stenciled, Antifa formed the vanguard of the legion assembled to "Rally Against Hate."

Their outnumbered adversaries were not, in this case, white supremacists, but average Trump supporters and anti-communists. They gathered in smaller numbers because the event they wanted to attend, the "Freedom Rally" at Crissy Field Beach, had been canceled by its organizers. Joey Gibson, a peaceful pro-Trump activist, told reporters with the *Los Angeles Times* that he feared "extreme or racist figures might try to co-opt his event." Moreover, the agitated counter-demonstrators could not be trusted to observe any decencies. "It doesn't seem safe," Gibson said. "A lot of people's lives are going to be in danger tomorrow."[54] He was right.

Roving gangs of Antifa beat whoever looked to them like a Trump sympathizer. They set upon a handful of activists, including Gibson and his friends, who were clad in patriotic regalia (including one with an American flag do-rag) and had raised their hands in a sign of submission. The mob swung at them, hit them with bear repellent, and threw bottles in their direction. "Pete catches a shot right on his stars 'n' stripes dome from a two-by-four and goes down," reported the *Weekly Standard*'s Matt Labash, who was on the scene. "Someone crashes a flagpole smack on Joey's head."[55]

In retreat, Gibson walked backward into a line of police. They took him into custody, presumably because police were so vastly outmanned by the park's menacing, so-called anti-fascist demonstrators. Six people were injured in the melee. Two were hospitalized. At least one police officer was injured while making one of the day's thirteen arrests, but those were only the most egregious violators. "Berkeley Police Chief Andrew Greenwood said officers were told not to actively confront the anarchists," the Associated Press reported.[56]

Bloodlust of the Bored

Those who engaged in violence in 2016 and 2017 were born in the most fortunate period in the safest and most stable country mankind has ever known. They were born into stability and relative prosperity, regardless of their personal circumstances. Unless they have migrated from elsewhere, most have never known organized, state-supported political terror. But they have nevertheless romanticized political violence and, to some extent, welcomed it.

"There is going to be some kind of change, and even if it's like a Nazi-type change, people are so drama-filled," predicted Victor

Vizcarra, a forty-eight-year-old Trump-curious Bernie Sanders supporter who spoke with the *New York Times* in early 2016. It was not
uncommon to hear that kind of nihilism expressed freely in 2016.[57]

We are too far gone, this worldview holds, too tainted by elitist
condescension, too decadent to survive in our present state. Those were
the assumptions behind Michael Anton's widely read pro-Trump essay,
"The Flight 93 Election," published by the Claremont Institute two
months before the election of 2016. If the plane is going down no matter what, it is incumbent on its passengers to rage against their fate.
Facing certain death, the hijacked are obliged to perform one last
desperate act of defiance, even if it's suicidal. For Anton, that meant
supporting Trump not because of what he stood for but because of the
hypocrites and moralizers who stood against him.

This anxiety and despair is not the kind of sentiment you'd expect
to hear from a successful and connected financier residing comfortably
in Manhattan. That's the problem—our stereotypes do not match reality. A potentially violent movement becomes a kinetically violent
movement when its unreasonable expectations are not met, not as a
result of perceived deprivation.

Studies have demonstrated that poverty is not a predictive factor
when examining the causes of extremism and terror. In fact, in 2010,
the sociologist Diego Gambetta and the political scientist Steffen
Hertog noticed a trend among the perpetrators of Islamist terrorism—an engineering degree. A reasonably advanced education is a
unifying feature of many violent groups: from Irish Republican
rebels, to pre-independence Israeli radicals, to the Weather Under-
ground in the United States. "[T]o a large extent, those historically
attracted to terrorism have, in fact, tended to be reasonably well, if
not, highly educated; financially comfortable and, in some cases,
quite well off; and, often gainfully employed," writes the *National
Interest*'s Bruce Hoffman.[58]

This should be intuitive, but it is not. The liberal myth holds that privation and dispossession will drive people to acts of political violence, because the liberal myth is a reductionist philosophy that boils down every sociopolitical development to privation and dispossession. When all you have is a hammer, everything looks like an opportunity to redistribute incomes. It does not require uncommon insight to conclude that those who steep themselves in violent revolutionary fantasies and class envy are at least familiar with similar movements throughout history. Whether the effect is intended or not, those who bend over backward to justify the violent injustices that characterize the social justice movement have helped to catalyze them.

Our Challenge

It must be said that it is more depraved for an individual to conduct a terroristic attack like the one that occurred in the streets of Charlottesville than for a mob to act like a mob.

History is, in many ways, the study of mobs, and they all have a similar nature. The mob that murdered African-American children in the streets of New York City in 1863 is the same mob that was moved to violence by the sight of Caesar's bloody tunic. The coldblooded desire to surrender individuality and flow with the human tide seems instinctual. It takes only collective passion to transform a thoughtful person into a cog in a machine capable of astonishing brutishness.

"The crowd is the same everywhere, in all periods and cultures," Elias Canetti wrote in his seminal work, *Crowds and Power*. "Once in being, it spreads with the utmost violence." Canetti observed that the crowd that becomes a mob is a fickle instrument for those seeking power. The kind of crowd capable of mob violence must continually expand, and once it ceases to expand, it dissipates quickly. It may have to be baited into existence, but it can quickly resolve to perform acts of collective vengeance almost spontaneously, especially in stratified societies in which oppressed classes seeks to engineer a "reversal" of the power dynamic that benefits their oppressors.[59]

Premeditated acts of gross criminality by an individual amount to terrorism, but a healthy society can endure terrorism. Violent, politically programmatic mobs are more threatening to society's foundations. The mob is a greater threat to societies that are already riddled with contradictions and stricken by self-doubt. Those sickly societies are apt to crumble under even weak pressure. Contrary to the braying of professional pessimists, the United States is not such a fragile society. Not yet, anyway.

The violence America witnessed in Sacramento and Charlottesville is likely to be repeated. It is the fruit of a potent anti-egalitarian trend, a trend that America desperately needs to confront.

For whatever reason, Americans barely noticed these incidents of violence when they began. In the days that followed the attack in Charlottesville, conservatives and Trump supporters (two groups that often overlap but are nevertheless distinct) observed that the rising tide of Identitarian violence did not materialize overnight. It is a wave that was building even before Sacramento. This observation prompted emotional outbursts from those who are fond of identity politics. They insisted that it was "whataboutism" or "moral equivalency" to invoke violence committed by leftists condemning white racist terrorism. But the time for burying our heads in the sand is over. The crisis is upon us.

No amount of opprobrium heaped upon white supremacists will ever be too much. But the initial reluctance of elite opinion-makers to condemn Antifa with equal fervor suggests that in their eyes some violent mobs are more abhorrent than others. That is corruption; it is the rot that eats away at the foundations of a healthy society. And one day, when the rot has been ignored for so long that no one believes it can be expunged, another mob will come along. And that time, the republic's weakened edifice may not withstand the pressure.

The fate of a gathering of peaceful Trump-supporting Republicans in Minnesota in May 2017 illustrates the threat posed by the rise of the radical fringe. Trump fans, with a permit, assembled to celebrate the president's first hundred days in office, but their rally was quickly hijacked by what the Minneapolis *Star-Tribune* described as a "small group" of white supremacist fanatics. "They show up everywhere," an exasperated pro-Trump organizer told the reporters. "Please go away," another attendee told the hijackers. "We have nothing to do with you guys." To these displays of typical Midwestern courtesy, the demonstrators responded by chanting, "We are the future!"

The white supremacists had advertised their intention to hijack the event on social media, and their Antifa opponents were ready for them. Bearing their signature black and red banners, the anti-fascist counter-protesters became aggressive with the alt-right usurpers. Profanity and insults were exchanged between the two groups, who were kept apart by police. "Go home, fascists!" one group screamed. "No Nazis on our streets!" The other barked back, "Law and order!"[60]

By the end of the afternoon, the peaceful pro-Trump rally inside Minnesota's capitol building had been forgotten. The action outside made all the headlines. It was all anyone would remember about the day, and it is a symbol of the challenge before conventional liberals and conservatives as their fringes secure more power and attention.

From the nation's highest elected and appointed officials to its most obscure activists and students, a culture that confuses speech and violence has taken hold of the social justice left. The Identitarian right, too, has begun rendering its political opponents as one-dimensional stick figures against whom it can, and indeed must, lash out. Together, these groups presage a new age of political violence in America.

But the United States is a remarkable place, with an unrivaled capacity for reinvention and renewal. These are not the first poisonous ideas to root themselves in American minds. How can the rational people that make up the majority of American voters reassert their authority? Can they rescue the country from the charismatic fanatics in their midst?

If history is a guide, violent and prejudicial ideas can be expelled from the public square. It has been done before, and both the right and the left have models in their respective histories to which they might turn for guidance.

CHAPTER 8

"Throw It the Hell Out"

T he humble republican civic ethic that guided the political development of the United States for generations seems to have fallen out of favor among our opinion-makers. The mechanisms the Founders put in place as a bulwark against tyranny are increasingly derided by the West's most fortunate children as impediments to achieving their preferred ends and, in their minds, a just society. But the changes they seek are radical, whether they know it or not. If they are not careful, they may get what they're asking for.

Maybe these quasi-revolutionaries think they are the leading edge of some new paradigm for American political life, but they are only the latest in a series of fanatics who have tried to take a sledgehammer to the republic's legal and intellectual foundations. The danger this wave of authoritarianism poses is exceptional not because its champions are uniquely skilled or their philosophy especially appealing. They are dangerous because the forces that could once be counted on to oppose their paranoid, reactionary politics seem to have lost the will to resist.

A catastrophe may be approaching, but it is not inevitable. The appeal of radical identity politics is limited by its practical shortcomings. Retributive social justice is incompatible with the egal-itarianism that is at the foundation of America's understanding of itself, so advocates for tiered justice and functional caste systems are forever asking Americans to abandon their most cherished conceptions of themselves. The threat of identity politics and retributive justice is contained for now within small groups of activists who attract far more attention than their influence warrants, fostering a perception that these groups are larger than they actually are. But perception has a habit of becoming reality.

Politics is a game of addition, and any successful political coalition will be tempted to ignore its ugliest components if they help win elec-tions. Neither traditional conservatives nor their progressive counter-parts should be allowed to take refuge in the meager numbers of the authoritarians in their midst. These elements must be called out, shamed, and relegated to the fringes of American life in as public a manner as possible. Their rejection and the defeat of their ideas cannot be ambiguous.

Classical liberals in both parties who want to purge their move-ments of Identitarianism may have no idea how to go about it, and those who try may be tempted to use a meat cleaver when what's called for is a scalpel. The political philosophies associated with hardline social justice militancy deserve to be isolated and margin-alized, but the otherwise reasonable and judicious people who might find those ideas attractive should not be so rashly ejected from their political homes. No rational political movement with a sense of self-preservation would engage in a purge of its own mem-bers anyway.

So how do you exile a bankrupt idea while keeping most of those who find it alluring inside the tent? Both the progressive left and the conservative right know how to do this. They've done it before.

Buckley and the Birchers

Robert Henry Winborne Welch Jr. was confectioner before he was a conspiracy theorist. An unremarkable anti-Communist with strong anti–New Deal views and a lot of money, he mounted an unsuccessful campaign for lieutenant governor of Massachusetts in 1950. Senator Robert Taft's loss of the GOP presidential nomination to Dwight Eisenhower in 1952 and the Republican Party's failure to unite behind Senator Joseph McCarthy's paranoid campaign to root out Soviet sympathizers in American society left Welch embittered. He felt that these men and their righteous causes had been "betrayed" by "the Republican political establishment"[1]—a complaint that has a familiar ring.

In the transcript of an obscure congressional hearing, Welch read about a man named John Birch, an American missionary to China killed by Communist soldiers in 1945. In 1953, he wrote a brief book about Birch, whom he considered America's first casualty in the Cold War, convinced that this crime had been covered up by Communist agents inside the United States.

Birch's mother had hoped her son would be remembered as a Christian martyr, but by consenting to Welch's request to name his new political society after him, she ensured that the name John Birch would forever be associated with right-wing fanaticism instead.

The notion that the American government had conspired to keep the name John Birch from the lips of average Americans while also clumsily forgetting to destroy the congressional transcript to which Welch was privy wasn't the Birchers' only daft theory. The candy mogul became convinced that Boris Pasternak's *Doctor Zhivago* was a piece of Soviet propaganda smuggled into the West to undermine capitalism. In fact, the precise oppposite was the case. Boris Pasternak's novel was initially distributed inside the Soviet Union with the help of the CIA to destabilize the regime in Moscow.

Welch thought the Communist advances around the world, such as their victories in China and Cuba, were possible only with the covert aid of American policymakers secretly loyal to the Communist cause. And he saw Communists everywhere.[2]

According to Welch, Henry Kissinger was a Communist. President Eisenhower engaged in "conscious treason" and was a "dedicated, conscious agent of the Communist conspiracy." Secretary of State John Foster Dulles and his brother, Allen, the director of the Central Intelligence Agency, were both fellow travelers. Even former Secretary of State George Marshall, architect of the Marshall Plan, which had kept much of Western Europe from falling to Communist insurgencies after World War II, was counted among the left-wing conspirators. In 1961, Welch estimated that Communist agents had infiltrated between 50 and 70 percent of the American government.

William F. Buckley Jr. did not seem to dislike Robert Welch Jr. personally. Not at first, anyway. In their initial correspondence, Buckley always emphasized that they agreed on more than they disagreed on. They shared similar pedigrees and political predispositions. Both men edited political journals (Buckley founded *National Review*; Welch, *American Opinion*). Both were deeply suspicious of John Kennedy, who had taken to speaking out about "extremism" on the right and who used Welch's paranoid accusations as fodder to discredit both the John Birch Society and American conservatism more broadly. Buckley feared Welch's fringe positions would help Kennedy achieve that objective, but Welch—ever the conspiratorial thinker—insisted that his unfavorable coverage in the press was "communist-inspired."[3]

Kennedy's effort to couple conservatism and Bircherism might have driven even sober-minded conservatives into the arms of their paranoid brethren out of tribal solidarity. But, as Buckley later reflected, Welch's reckless charges "placed a great weight on the back of responsible conservatives."

The final straw for Buckley and his acolytes was the attention that the John Birch Society's campaign to impeach Chief Justice Earl Warren attracted. The famously liberal jurist had presided over a string of decisions the Birchers detested: declaring loyalty oaths and school prayer unconstitutional, extending First Amendment protections to overt Communists, and overturning the "separate but equal" doctrine that permitted racial segregation. Welch and the addlebrained theories he promoted became a fixation of the press and political elites. Richard Nixon denounced him in writing. He was spoken of with contempt on the Senate floor. Legislators in Washington were talking about holding hearings. Something had to be done.

"Once they began to appear regularly in the mainstream media, Buckley and others found it difficult to draw distinctions in the public mind between the JBS founder and his organization," writes the historian Alvin Felzenberg. That distinction had to be made. But how? The society had an estimated one hundred thousand members, a number of whom were wealthy and influential. "Every other person in Phoenix is a member of the John Birch Society," Senator Barry Goldwater famously quipped. "I'm not talking about commie-haunted apple pickers or cactus drunks; I'm talking about the highest cast of men of affairs."[4]

Though he privately agreed that Welch's paranoia was an albatross around conservative necks, Goldwater publicly praised the society's members as the "type of people we need in politics." After all, it was true. Even some on the *National Review* masthead were society members. If conservatism was to be saved from guilt by association with the John Birch Society, someone was going to have to make a swift and forceful move.

Plan of Attack

In 1962, Goldwater convened a summit that included Buckley as well as Russell Kirk, the political philosopher and author of *The Conservative Mind*. The most important item on the agenda was not the 1964 presidential campaign but what was to be done about Welch. Resolved that the John Birch Society had to be dealt with, the meeting's participants assigned responsibilities. "Goldwater would seek out an opportunity to dissociate himself from the 'findings' of the Society's leader, without, however, casting any aspersions on the Society itself," Buckley wrote. "I, in *National Review* and in my other writing, would continue to expose Welch and his thinking to scorn and derision."

Buckley recognized that the John Birch Society was organized around a fallacy that is common to just about every paranoid crank—"the assumption that you can infer subjective intention from objective consequence." Hanlon's Razor posits that it is a fallacy to presume malice when incompetence suffices for a comprehensive explanation of events. Neither Welch nor the John Birch Society had any use for Hanlon's Razor.

Opposing this organization was not easy. It was rigidly structured, and its members were disciplined. They mounted withering pressure campaigns against any institution they believed had been too friendly to leftist thought, and they organized successful boycotts of stores that stocked goods made in a Communist country. To isolate the movement but not its members, Buckley's arguments had to be carefully calibrated.

Buckley's first shot across Welch's bow, titled "The Uproar," opened with an attack on the unscrupulous left and the press, which were "opportuning on the mistaken conclusions of Robert Welch to anathematize the entire American right wing." It was an appeal to unity across the conservative spectrum, since all conservatives could be counted on to despise the mainstream press. "In professing themselves to be scandalized at the false imputation of pro-communism to a few people, the critics do not hesitate to impute pro-fascism to a lot of people," Buckley continued. Only after the beaches had been softened did Buckley turn his attention toward Welch. The piece proceeded to savage the founder of the John Birch Society for his unhealthy habit of eschewing a simple explanation for events in favor of absurdly complex and nefarious rationalizations.[5]

Buckley later confessed that he wished there had been a way to attack the society and its founder "without pleasing the people I cannot stand to please." The piece received much praise from outside conservative circles, but the reaction inside the conservative tent was far more fractious. Even today, the desire among activists to avoid receiving compromising praise from their political adversaries keeps well-meaning dissenters from speaking out against their supposed "allies." But Buckley felt a duty to posterity, and there was no going back. The door having been cracked, he moved to thrust it open.

In the following issue of *National Review*, Buckley adopted a less ideological line of attack on Welch, suggesting that the conspiracy theorist and his society had reached the point of diminishing returns for conservatives. The society's unfavorable press outweighed the benefits of its organizational competence. Buckley also lined up conservative leaders to echo his attack on Welch, including Goldwater and Ronald Reagan. "Mr. Welch is only one man, and I do not believe his views, far removed from reality and common sense as they are, represent the feelings of most members of the John Birch Society," Goldwater wrote. Praising the organization but attacking its leadership, he called on Welch to resign from the society he had founded. "We cannot allow the emblem of irresponsibility to attach to the conservative banner," Goldwater concluded.

Russell Kirk had hoped that the Birchers and Welch would be excommunicated from the conservative movement. That had not happened, though their positions had been weakened. During Buckley's bid for the mayoralty of New York City in 1965, the Birchers made themselves an issue once again, and the editor of *National Review* dubbed the Republican candidate for mayor, John V. Lindsay, a "pro-Communist." Buckley now abandoned caution. No longer would he make utilitarian arguments or draw subtle distinctions between the society and its misguided leadership.

In three columns published in August of that year, Buckley attacked the poisonous delusions in which the John Birch Society, members and leadership alike, seemed to wallow—including the notion that the majority of Supreme Court justices were the agents of a "foreign dictatorship." "One continues to wonder how it is that the membership of the John Birch Society tolerates such paranoid and unpatriotic drivel," he wrote.

In response, Buckley received no shortage of hate mail. Near the end of his life, he often reflected on this period, and he appeared to see identity politics as central to the Bircher ethos, though he didn't put it in those terms. Among the achievements of which he was proudest, he recalled, was "the absolute exclusion of anything anti-Semitic or kooky from the conservative movement."[6]

Nothing Lasts Forever

Buckley had succeeded. Welch was isolated and discredited, the society he founded synonymous with addled, conspiratorial thinking. Even today, "Bircher" remains a synonym for a paranoiac. But nothing lasts forever. The conservative movement has again found itself attracted to conspiratorial thinking. Again it is beset by agitators who insist that the "Republican political establishment" has sold the movement out and that its so-called conservative leaders are secretly in league with equivocators, saboteurs, and crypto-liberals. As conspiracies have begun to make a comeback, so, too, have the conspiracy theorists.

Writing for The Daily Caller in 2010, the future Breitbart editor Matt Boyle observed that with the rise of the Tea Party movement, "the John Birch Society is making a comeback." The society's president at the time, John McManus, told Boyle that his organization was utterly unrepentant and that it maintained the same beliefs that it had at its founding in 1958.[7]

That's largely true. A casual review of the group's website today includes eye-openers about a government conspiracy to "curtail your freedom of travel" and the revelation that the Islamist terrorist group ISIS "is a charade to help build a New World Order." But McManus was wrong on at least one count. In a section on the alleged "myths" about the society that persist, the group disavows the idea that "JBS considers public water fluoridation part of a Communist mind-control plot." There, at least, the organization has matured considerably.

McManus defended Welch's claim that Eisenhower was a Communist and implied that the threat of Communism had merely evolved into the threat posed by a global world order. "In 1990, President George H. W. Bush stated over and over again his intentions to create the New World Order," he told Boyle. "We had people calling us up saying, 'looks like you guys were right all along.'"[8]

In 2009, the first year of Barack Obama's presidency, the John Birch Society appeared at the annual Conservative Political Action Conference for the first time in decades. "To the extent that the JBS is an advocate for our core ideals, they're a welcome element of the tea party," said Tea Party Express spokesman Levi Russell. As in Goldwater's day, these conservatives wear the epithet "extremist" as a badge of honor. Perhaps they see the John Birch Society as provocative; a group that has all the right enemies. Then, as now, the conservative movement's reasonable center has undesirable elements descending upon it from the fringes.

Conservatives know that if they criticize their more extreme brethren on the right, they may be praised by center-left political and media elites. But that praise, they fear, reflects a desire to see the conservative movement mortally wounded, not a stronger, more compelling conservative presence in American public life. So those on the right have tended to express criticism of their compatriots only among themselves.

But there is no honor in stifling necessary rebukes merely because unloading the burden of a troubled conscience means, as Buckley put it, "pleasing the people [we] cannot stand to please." It is incumbent on Republicans to follow the examples of Kirk, Goldwater, and Buckley to expel white racism and paranoia from their ranks. Conspiratorial thinking and prejudice are not justified simply because they irritate Democrats. Responsible Republicans are obliged to stigmatize their own Identitarian social justice advocates until they are again consigned to the shadows. Anyone who believes that conservative values and policies are the best hope for this country will gladly join a fight to prevent their being hijacked by charlatans, no matter how much that internecine conflict might please the left.[9]

Buckley's experience with the Birchers demonstrates how this stigmatization can be achieved without sacrificing political influence or alienating irreplaceable elements of the conservative coalition.

Surrounded by Reds

In a way, the John Birch Society came along too late. They were preoccupied with the notion that much of American society had been penetrated by Communists aligned with the Soviet Union, when that charge had become baseless. A decade before Welch founded the society, though, the claim had some merit. Much of the organized labor movement in the United States was once shot through with Communists and Soviet sympathizers. In their equally important effort to rid themselves of authoritarian social justice militants, the progressive left might look at how the labor movement in the United States rid itself of the Communists.

The academic consensus is that the Red Scare of the 1920s and renewed anti-Communist fears in the late 1940s and early 1950s were simply bouts of national hysteria. Some historians maintain that there was, in fact, never any significant Communist infiltration of American institutions. That's patently false. Maurice Halperin, the chief of the Latin American division of the Office of Strategic Services, was an agent working for the NKVD (the predecessor of the KGB). So, too, was Lieutenant Colonel Duncan Lee, a confidential assistant to the head of the OSS, Major General William "Wild Bill" Donovan. Alger Hiss helped organize the Yalta conference and was involved with the establishment of the United Nations. From the public sector to the journalistic establishment, Soviet agents had thoroughly sunk their hooks into American institutions. But nowhere was Soviet influence more pervasive than within organized labor.[10]

The global labor movement was an explicit target of Marxist indoctrination. Solomon Abramovich Lozovsky's 1922 book *Marx and the Trade Unions* called labor organizations "schools of socialism" in which workers received "elementary class training." In the brief period in which the young Soviet Union advocated global socialist revolution, Vladimir Lenin insisted that Communists around the world were obliged to "get into the trade unions, to remain in them, and to carry on communist work within them at all costs." He wrote in detail about the necessity of infiltrating unions, winning the confidence of their members, and removing "reactionary" labor leaders from their posts.

The "Profintern," established by the Kremlin in 1921, was designed to coordinate the actions of Soviet sympathizers inside trade unions around the world.[11]

By the 1880s, radical socialists in the United States were already effective and well-organized. One of the founders of the American Federation of Labor, Samuel Gompers, was initially a committed socialist.[12] Eugene V. Debs, the perennial presidential candidate of the Socialist Party, founded the American Railway Union. In the early twentieth century, the labor movement in the United States was engaged in a passionate, occasionally violent, intramural debate over whether to pursue its objectives through political avenues or strikes and insurrectionary tactics. The radical Industrial Workers of the World, which advocated the abolition of individual unions and the formation of an amalgamated coalition of laborers, explicitly advocated the "abolition of the wage system."[13]

The Trade Union Educational League (TUEL), founded in 1922 by the Native American Communist activist William Foster, was even friendlier toward Bolshevism, debunking the idea of "harmonizing the interests of capital and labor" as "demoralizing nonsense" and insisting that the labor movement's objective should be "the abolition of capitalism and the establishment of a workers' republic." Foster's organization successfully infiltrated independent unions of machinists, painters, textile manufacturers, carpenters, railroad workers, and various other tradespeople.

Some of this work was done at Moscow's behest. According to the account of the former Communist Benjamin Gitlow, Foster revealed his plan in 1922 at a convention of American Communists in Michigan "called by Moscow." The TUEL leader revealed that "the Communists were to build up their own organization within the trade union structure [and] hide their identity and establish secret trade union cells in the unions in which the Communists got a foot-hold." The Kremlin lavishly financed this activity. "When the Communists attempted to take over the United Mine Workers of America, Moscow made an initial contribution of $100,000," Gitlow wrote, adding another $150,000 later.[14]

In a report he prepared for Congress in 1949, William H. Chartener—who would later serve as an assistant secretary of commerce—revealed the extent to which the "communists still take pride in their part in establishing" the Congress of Industrial Organizations (CIO). During World War II, however, the Soviet Union and the American labor movement had something of a falling out. John L. Lewis, the former president of the CIO, continued to toe Moscow's noninterventionist line even after the Nazis tore up the Molotov-Ribbentrop Pact and invaded the Soviet Union. This display of principle angered the Kremlin and resulted in pointed attacks on Lewis in the left-wing press.

"In the years of the United War Effort, the communists were among the foremost supporters of labor-management cooperation and the no-strike policy," Chartener wrote, noting that the Roosevelt administration and military brass enjoyed good working relations with admitted Communists in organized labor during the war. Chartener emphasized that union members who declined to support the few labor-backed strikes that did occur during the war were condemned as "Stalinist-minded." Both labor and Lewis lost much of their clout in a widely condemned miner's strike that crippled national production in 1943 and led to FDR's temporarily seizing the coal mining industry.[15]

Communist infiltration of American labor organizations was no figment of Joe McCarthy's imagination. And yet, as the Iron Curtain descended across Europe and the fear of Soviet penetration of American institutions reasserted itself, efforts to undermine the power of socialists in the labor movement verged on excess, though attempts to deport Communist labor organizers or hold them in contempt of

Congress occasionally ran afoul of the courts. Eventually, the anti-Communist fervor that led to the expulsion of Soviet-sympathizers from the labor movement affected innocent persons and institutions, ruining some lives.

Many still regard the fervid anti-Communism of the McCarthy era as a bout of collective madness. Nevertheless, the anti-Communism of that period forced organized labor to choose between continued sympathy to Communism and ridding its ranks of Soviet apologists. Since association with Communists would spell the end of their power, it was no choice at all.

"The Chopping Block"

Antipathy toward the Communist sympathizers in labor's ranks had been building since the surrender of Nazi Germany, and many unions moved preemptively to isolate and oust them.

In 1946, the CIO passed a resolution attacking the Communists in its midst: "We resent and reject efforts of the Communist Party or other political parties and their adherents to interfere in the affairs of the CIO." "If communism is an issue in any of your unions," its new president, Philip Murray, said, "throw it the hell out, and throw out its advocates along with it." Local CIO affiliates responded with their own resolutions barring "Fascists, Klansmen, and Communists" from union posts.[16]

These efforts were vehemently resisted by pro-Communist organizations, which maintained a broad constituency among the rank and file. "A leader who denies class division must, sooner or later, deny the necessity of struggle by labor and must come to the conclusion, as Murray does, that the interests of a union can best be served through a policy of servility to employers or, as some choose to call it, 'labor-management cooperation,'" read an attack on Murray's leadership of the CIO in the Communist-affiliated *Daily Worker.*[17]

The confrontation with Communism came to a head after a series of crippling strikes in 1946 contributed to a Republican takeover of both houses of Congress. The following year, Congress passed the Labor Management Relations Act, better known as "Taft-Hartley," over President Harry Truman's veto.

The act prohibited a variety of previously protected labor activities, including jurisdictional strikes. It outlawed mandatory union membership, certain political activities, and union donations to political campaigns. Most importantly, the law compelled the National Labor Relations Board to forego the provision of aid and support to any union that had not submitted signed affidavits from its leaders attesting that they were not members of the Communist Party and did not support Communist activities in America.

Some, including both Lewis and Murray, refused to sign affidavits despite their general hostility toward the Communist cause. The majority of union leaders, though, quietly complied with this new demand, and anti-Communist elements took the opportunity to force socialists in the labor movement out into the open.

The anti-Communist Walter Reuther, narrowly elected president of the CIO's United Automobile Workers (UAW) in 1946, won a resounding reelection victory in 1947 and removed left-wing elements from the union's executive committee in the process. Upon securing his role as leader of the UAW, he pledged to dismiss all Communist officers in his union. Through clever legislative maneuvers in the summer of 1947, Joseph Curran shattered Communist influence over the National Maritime Union. And in August of that year, Murray ousted the overtly Communist editor of the CIO's newsletter. "Before the CIO convention in November 1948," Chartener recalled, "the executive council revoked the charter of the New York City CIO council for 'slavish adherence' to the communist line."[18]

The end of the influence of Soviet sympathizers over organized labor was in sight by 1948, when FDR's sometime vice president and the former editor of the *New Republic* Henry Wallace challenged Truman for the presidency from the left. Particularly critical of Truman's staunchly anti-Communist foreign policy, Wallace was plagued by the accusation that he harbored Soviet sympathies and that his Progressive Party was a Communist-controlled apparatus. Were it not for Wallace's campaign, labor's break with Communism might not have been as total as it was.

The president's advisors knew he needed the help of organized labor to win reelection and reverse Republican gains in Congress. In 1940 and 1944, Communists had helped FDR win reelection, knocking on doors and rallying to the president and the Democrats. But labor needed Truman, too. The CIO's Murray, like a host of other labor leaders, was no fan of FDR's successor, but he reasoned that Wallace's candidacy threatened to split the Democratic vote. If Truman lost, Taft-Hartley would never be repealed.[19]

Murray publicly backed Truman's anti-Soviet foreign policy, compelling those who agreed with Wallace's attacks to reveal themselves. "In August, the CIO formally endorsed Truman for reelection," writes the historian Gary Donaldson. "The purged communists in organized labor were forced into the waiting arms of Henry Wallace, where they all went down to defeat together."[20]

Communism's excommunication from the organized labor movement in America provoked a grudge that socialists continued to nurse even a half-century later. "Rather than conducting a principled defense of their right to be part of the labor movement," read an editorial in a 1990 issue of *Socialist Worker*, "CP leaders acquiesced to the attacks, hoping to curry favor. In reality, they merely offered themselves up to the chopping block."[21]

Today's Democrats are increasingly dependent upon the energy and enthusiasm that Identitarian social justice advocates provide for their candidates and causes. They are the party's activist base, and Democrats cannot afford to lose them. Skillful political navigators on the left have been attempting to decouple identity politics from Democratic politics, but the effort will not succeed until Democratic lawmakers of stature join the fight. This crusade cannot be the province of academics and essay writers alone. Liberals in good standing must communicate in clear terms why the social justice left's brand of politics is not only a dead-end but also a threat to the egalitarian system they profess to love.

Bringing Civics Back

F. A. Hayek said that the prefix "social" destroys the meaning of every word to which it is attached. Perhaps he overstated his case, as "social studies" used to refer to the exploration of political history, geography, and rudimentary civics. But today social studies is being redefined and deprioritized. The country is suffering as a result.

In 1993–94, students in grade school spent approximately 9.5 percent of the school week in social studies classes. By 2003–04, that figure had declined to 7.6 percent. In 2007–08, it was down to 7.1 percent. Those are the most recent numbers available from the Department of Education, but they are unlikely to have improved in the past decade.[22]

Following the implementation of the No Child Left Behind education reform law in 2007, the Center for Education Policy found that 36 percent of the departments it surveyed were cutting back on social studies education. With budgetary constraints came hard decisions. Social studies was once regarded as a core subject along with arithmetic, language arts, and the sciences. However, when education became a matter of triage due to test-driven pressures, social studies was deemed a low priority.[23]

Studies have shown that students who receive a modest civic education are more likely to vote, to dedicate their time to their communities and charities, to engage with their local, state, and federal elected representatives, and to understand and appreciate the American system of government. A lack of civic education leaves students confused about their government and susceptible to cynical and propagandist revisionism.

Americans are losing touch with the country's core values. Thirty-seven percent of Americans polled in 2017 could not name a single right enshrined in the First Amendment. One-third of those polled were unable to name one of the three branches of the federal government.[24] A Cato Institute poll of 2,300 people that same year found that a majority of respondents believe "it would be hard to ban hate speech because people can't agree what speech is hateful," not because a ban would be antithetical to the First Amendment. Nevertheless, 46 percent of respondents expressed support for a law that would make it illegal to say negative things about African-Americans; 41 percent said the same about Jews, 40 percent about immigrants, and 39 percent about Hispanics.[25]

The American republic cannot survive if its citizens do not know what they must preserve or why it's worth the effort. American schools must restore civic education to its proper place.

This is not a partisan issue. "Today more than ever, the social studies are not a luxury, but a necessity," Barack Obama's education secretary, Arne Duncan, wrote in 2011.[26] But the discipline of social studies has been subsumed under the broader rubric of diversity studies and multiculturalism. Whatever their value, such studies cannot replace civics and political history. Social studies have become an exploration of demography, identity, the problem of stereotyping, and the virtues of pluralism. There are no more absolutes; no more narrow-minded value judgments. Perhaps children should explore those ideas, but they do not suffice for a civic education.

Duncan's successor, Betsy DeVos, has a more hands-off philosophy when it comes to government, but she too has expressed support for civic education. The Department of Education has enormous influence on schools' priorities. The study of American history and government should be chief among those priorities.

Conservatives are correct to be mindful of the unintended consequences of excessive legislation, but it would also be prudent for legislators to study the prospect of tying federal funding of public education to the completion of a certain number of hours per week dedicated to civic education. It was not that long ago that an average of between 2.7 and 3 hours per week was standard, and that's not much to ask. Math, science, and other core courses are critical, but the nation cannot afford to make the study of the legacy bequeathed to us by the Founders an ancillary exercise.

Lessons Learned

Civic education has the potential to impart not just an understanding of the unique American system of government but also respect for what it took to build it. But civic education is not a panacea. All the patriotic civics instruction that American schoolchildren received in the first half of the twentieth century did not prevent fringe elements from achieving an unhealthy level of influence in both political parties.

The successful effort to expel those elements from mainstream American politics targeted not persons but ideas—ideas that clever leaders convinced their movements were obstacles to their common objectives. Those who went on the offense against the Communists in labor and the Birchers in the GOP weren't hostile and condescending as much as sympathetic. Whether these problematic ideas are sound is surely debatable, they conceded; you have every right to believe them, but they are making the work of our movement more difficult.

The point of these efforts wasn't to divide their respective coalitions into small cliques defined by ideological conformity. Quite the opposite. The goal was to secure power. In the near-term, the goal of this stigmatization was, in part, to make conservatism or organized labor more attractive to moderate, non-ideological voters. Ultimately, though, the point was to render these movements an indispensable part of any winning political coalition. And it worked.

Radicalism occasionally tempts the politically engaged, but it is not an irresistible force of history. In the United States, the radicals are almost always a vocal minority. Identitarianism and vindictive social justice are radical philosophies, antithetical to the American idea. But rank-and-file social justice advocates must be handled with sympathy and care. They are not anti-American insurgents; they are our neighbors with valid concerns about the future of the country. They have been led astray.

These productive and engaged Americans must be convinced that the ideology they find so attractive is a blind alley. It's possible. It has been done before. And it's a pressing project that must begin today, before it is too late.

CONCLUSION

For years, I kept a framed poster on my wall. It was bequeathed to me by my parents, and I loved it because it provided me with a link to their pasts and to what I thought might be my future.

That poster announced a forthcoming general student strike across the country in response to the revelation that Richard Nixon had ordered the bombing of Cambodia. That call to action, typical of the Vietnam War era, advocated the student-led occupation of various facilities on campuses across the country. Using vaguely revolutionary language and closing with the image of a clenched fist, this beacon was suggestive of any number of so-called people's liberation movements.

It's no accident that youthful political engagement tends to take this form. Absolutism, moral righteousness, and a willingness to offend the sensibilities of a staid class of elders is a feature of young political movements throughout history. I was young myself once, but that poster appeals less to my idealism than to my desire to see myself as a participant in the making of history, as I'm sure it did to the students who mobilized behind it a half-century ago.

It is surely no coincidence that the identity-fueled social justice movements examined in this book are populated predominantly by young idealists. Such movements are vaguely authoritarian, entirely uncompromising, and exceedingly self-referential. They have little regard for the generations that came before them. Their "Year Zero" mentality excuses them from studying the past and learning from the mistakes made by wiser men and women.

It is not uncommon to hear young social justice advocates accept as fact the idea that American political history—history in general, really—is just the story of identity politics. The most fanatical among them would add, however, that the idea of America is entirely dishonest. Stop me if you've heard this before: Americans pretend to reject identity politics in favor of false notions of egalitarianism and equal rights, but the United States never truly aspired to these ideals. This is cynicism masquerading as enlightened and dispassionate analysis, and it does the country a disservice. The United States, like every other human endeavor, is flawed, but its imperfections are outshone by the beauty of its promise, its manifest historical successes, and the people and minds it has liberated.

On a cosmetic level, social justice is a noble pursuit—one perfectly in keeping with the American political tradition. In practice, though, it has been corrupted, perhaps beyond the point of redemption.

Social justice is no longer the pursuit of pure equality but of retribution, often for intangible, ill-defined, and occasionally even conjectural offenses committed by generations long departed. It is an ideology that cannot be distinguished from the identity-based grievance politics that animate its proponents. It compels its adherents to fixate on trivialities and to elevate perceived slights to the level of grave personal injuries. It steals from its enthusiasts a sense of charity, forces them to compete for victim status, and in the end to wallow in self-pity.

Social justice turns its devotees into imperious hall monitors. It demands that they judge others not on their individual merit but on their group identity. And it insists that its champions abandon the traditions of Anglo-American common law and the foundational principles of Western jurisprudence—the bedrocks of civilization—in service to arbitrary, capricious, and ultimately unsatisfying vengeance.

To justify their predilections, social justice activists have deluded themselves into believing that the United States—the most selfless, prosperous, freedom-loving society the world has ever known—is a myth. They seem to want to believe America is a generally exploitative society struggling with institutional prejudices and internal conflicts that render it unable to deliver impartial justice. Of course, the kind of pure justice that social justice advocates insist upon is a moving target. They do not reckon with their definition problem because to nail down social justice is to expose it for what it is: the antithesis of fairness and impartiality. It is arbitrary, impulsive, and often spiteful. And when their impossible standards are not met, when social justice advocates are thoroughly marinated in radicalism and filled with revolutionary zeal, the violence begins. Right or left, the vicious Identitarian factions clashing on American streets are two sides of the same coin.

This book offers some suggestions as to how sober-minded members of both Republican and Democratic political establishments can identify, isolate, and expel violence and prejudice from their ranks. Those suggestions admittedly fall short of a surefire solution to this problem. In many ways, the rise of Identitarianism represents a crisis of confidence in the legitimacy of the United States itself.

This crisis has been many years in the making, and it will not be reversed overnight. Most certainly, though, the first step toward untangling this mess is to embrace a paradigmatic shift. The successful civil rights movements of the mid-twentieth century were effective not because they were bitter and vengeful and violent, but because they held tight to the Founders' ideals. Indeed, these movements seemed to exemplify those ideals far more fully than their opponents did. The moral authority of the pacifist, colorblind resistance movements of the last century was undeniable.

Among a particular set of activists, the tenets of non-violence and colorblindness are the subject of scorn and ridicule. Colorblindness is dismissed as an illusion that only those with white skin can afford to entertain. Gender neutrality is rejected as a form of paternalism. Non-discrimination is, in fact, discriminatory. Violence is simply a means to an end. And if the end doesn't justify the means, then what does? This is a bankrupt worldview.

The United States is an exceptional nation in many ways, and not all of those ways are worthy of celebration. And yet those who bank on the fundamental goodness of the United States and the virtue of its people rarely regret that decision. Those who are optimistic about America's future and the blind justice it has championed and struggled to achieve throughout its history have the easier case to make. The burden of proof is on those who fancy themselves justice's redistributionists. Our system, a product of countless generations who spilled their blood and that of tyrants to preserve the freedoms we take for granted today, speaks for itself. It is not perfect, but it gets more right than wrong.

The smoldering self-confidence present in the majority of patriotic Americans, who want nothing to do with extremism and violence, is often lost in the glare of political fireworks. Identitarian social justice advocates are loud and passionate. They are prepared to fight for their beliefs, and that is their greatest advantage. Their numbers appear inflated by the disproportionate influence they wield and the fact that they encounter so little resistance from the center. That has to end.

Nations exist only as long as their citizens are committed to their preservation. Systems implode when those who believe in their purpose and rectitude are outnumbered by the cynical, disengaged, and exhausted. That tipping point is nowhere near, but it may be coming.

That's especially true if America's responsible and historically literate citizens—both Republican and Democratic—do nothing to protest injustice committed in the name of tackling injustice.

This burning imperative cannot wait for a savior to emerge. The cavalry is not coming. No messiah will save us from ourselves. This urgent responsibility and the hard work ahead fall on all of us. And it must begin today.

ACKNOWLEDGMENTS

Having spent most of my professional writing career as a blogger, I presumed that writing a book couldn't be that hard. I could churn out a thousand words per day and have a fully conceptualized manuscript in my editor's hands in about ten weeks. That is not, I was to learn, how books are written. Writing this book was a challenge, but it was also one of the greatest privileges of my life. It a great honor to be able to think and write about matters of great importance, and I am indebted to you for devoting your time to reading this book.

I owe quite a bit to a number of people who made this work possible. I would like to acknowledge them in no particular order, but with one exception: my wife, Jaryn Rothman. Her saintly patience as I retreated on weekends and after working hours to our home office for months on end was, I'm sure, a hardship. That's especially true considering I abandoned her to raise our boys, Jace Arnold and Elias Murphy, then one and three years old. I owe her some much-deserved kid sitting and a day at the spa.

This book would have remained an unpublishable rant without the input and editorial guidance of my mentors and role models, John and

Patricia Rothman. My parents helped me to reconsider my opinions, forced me to murder overwritten sentences with which I'd imprudently fallen in love, and challenged conceptions that I had adopted without critically analyzing them. Their charitable efforts on my behalf extend well beyond reading and reviewing rough drafts of my work, but a full accounting of those efforts would require another book.

I am especially indebted to my agent, Andrew Stuart, who transformed the stale and duplicative pitch for this book into a salable commercial product. The idea for *Unjust* is as much Andrew's as anyone's, and it was his guidance that resulted in a book that is viable in a marketplace I did not understand. He helped to conceptualize this book and then found a publisher willing to take a risk on a first-time author. I'm grateful to be able to call him a colleague and a friend.

Everyone at Regnery Publishing deserves a lot of credit for this book. I am particularly grateful to Marjory Ross and my editor, Tom Spence, for turning this book into a polished product worthy of your time.

Unjust would never have been written without the careful mentoring and guidance of my boss, *Commentary* editor John Podhoretz. He has had a profound effect on my thinking and has sharpened my writing immeasurably. I am also thankful to my colleague, editor, and podcast partner, Abe Greenwald. The entire team at *Commentary* is like a second family. I am uniquely privileged and grateful to be able to work in such a stimulating environment.

I would also like to extend my thanks to the people who helped me to navigate the publishing world and who helped me polish and expand on the themes in this book. That list includes, but is not limited to, Dana Perino, Neal Freeman, Jay Nordlinger, Eddie Glaude Jr., Kat Rosenfield, Jane Coaston, and Charles C. W. Cooke. I would also like to extend my thanks to some who helped me along the way and to whom I owe my career: John Batchelor, Jonathan Garthwaite, Michael

J. Hennessy, Dan Abrams, Jon Nicosia, Ed Morrissey, Allahpundit, Mary Katharine Ham, and Guy Benson.

Finally, and though it is admittedly a little bit maudlin, I owe a debt of gratitude to this country, in which I was fortunate enough to be born. The United States of America is an ongoing experiment to determine whether a people whose rights are derived from God are sovereign. It is a study to see whether all the peoples of the world can live harmoniously on top of one another. Like all experiments, it has had successes and disappointments. But the United States remains the indispensable nation. I am indebted to those who serve this country both in and out of uniform.

Chapter 1: Identitarianism

1. K-Sue Park, "The A.C.L.U. Needs to Rethink Free Speech," *New York Times*, August 17, 2017.

2. Laura Weinrib, "The ACLU's free speech stance should be about social justice, not 'timeless' principles," *Los Angeles Times*, August 30, 2017.

3. Joseph Goldstein, "After Charlottesville, A.C.L.U. Braces for the Next Alt-Right Case," *New York Times*, October 4, 2017.

4. "White, Right, and Pretentious: How 'Identitarian' Politics is Changing Europe," *Economist*, March 28, 2018.

5. Eugene Volokh, "You can be fined for not calling people 'ze' or 'hir,' if that's the pronoun they demand that you use," *Washington Post*, May 17, 2016.

6. Emily Rella, "Citigroup just changed the game with this unbelievable work perk for millennials," AOL, March 16, 2016, https://www.aol.com/article/2016/03/16/citigroup-inc-just-changed-the-game-with-this-unbelievable-work/21328736/.

7. Susan Johnston Taylor, "Could 'Social Justice Benefits' Be the Newest Employment Trend?" *Fast Company*, April 20, 2017.

8. UCLA Diversity & Faculty Development, "Diversity in the Classroom," 2014, adapted from Derald Wing Sue, *Microaggressions in Everyday Life: Race,*

Gender and Sexual Orientation (Hoboken, New Jersey: John Wiley & Sons, 2010), https://academicaffairs.ucsc.edu/events/documents/Microaggressions_Examples_Arial_2014_11_12.pdf.

9. Jonathan Foreman, "The Timothy Hunt Witch Hunt," *Commentary*, September 1, 2015.

10. Lisa Respers France, "Philae researcher criticized for shirt covered in scantily clad women," CNN, November 14, 2014.

11. Matthew Reade, "Students Demand Administrators 'Take Action' Against Conservative Journalists," *Claremont Independent*, April 17, 2017.

12. Morton Schapiro,"I'm Northwestern's president. Here's why safe spaces for students are important," *Washington Post*, January 15, 2016.

13. Bre Payton, "University Of Michigan Protesters Demand a Separate But Equal Safe Space For Black Students," The Federalist, November 16, 2016.

14. Frank Furedi, "Campuses are breaking apart into 'safe spaces,'" *Los Angeles Times*, January 5, 2017.

15. Kimberlé Crenshaw, "Mapping the Margins: Intersectionality, Identity Politics, and Violence against Women of Color," *Stanford Law Review* 43, No. 6. (July 1991), 1241–99.

16. Noah Rothman, "The 'Intersectionality' Trap," *Commentary*, July 18, 2017.

17. Christina Cauterucci, "Embracing Farrakhan Betrays the Most Essential Principles of the Women's March," Slate, March 8, 2018, https://slate.com/news-and-politics/2018/03/the-womens-marchs-embrace-of-louis-farrakhan-betrays-its-most-essential-principles.html.

18. Noah Rothman, "Otto Warmbier, Moral Perversion, and the Social Justice Left," *Commentary*, June 19, 2017.

19. Eileen Reynolds, "What if Donald Trump and Hillary Clinton Had Swapped Genders?" *New York University News*, February 28, 2017.

20. Rebecca Savransky, "Text 'you have right to be believed' edited out of Clinton website," *The Hill*, August 15, 2016.

21. Steve Gorman, "Rolling Stone to pay Virginia fraternity $1.65 million in defamation suit," Reuters, June 13, 2017, https://www.reuters.com/article/us-virginia-rollingstone-idUSKBN1942ZN.

22. William Blackstone, *Commentaries on the Laws of England*, Book 4, Chapter 27 (1769).

23. Alex Griswold, "Dem Rep. on Campus Rape: Better to Expel More Students, Even if 80% Are Innocent," Mediaite, September 10, 2015.

24. William Voegeli, "Liberals, Shipwrecked: Democrat Mark Lilla seeks an alternative to identity politics, but it's a lonely quest," *City Journal*, August 24, 2017.

25. Edmund Kozak, "Alt-Right vs. Conservative Inc.," LifeZette, August 21, 2016, https://www.lifezette.com/2016/08/alt-right-vs-conservative-inc/.

26. Ramesh Ponnuru, "The Great Immigration Non-Debate," Bloomberg, February 20, 2015.

27. Ben Domenech, "Are Republicans for Freedom or White Identity Politics?" The Federalist, August 21, 2015.

Chapter 2: A Nation or a People?

1. Thomas Patrick Burke, "The Origins of Social Justice: Taparelli d'Azeglio," *Modern Age*, Vol. 52, No. 2 (Spring 2010), 99.

2. Gene Van Son, "Catholic Social Justice Is Not What the SJWs Are Pitching," *Catholic Stand*, June 20, 2016.

3. Thomas Behr, "Luigi Taparelli and a Catholic Economics," *Journal of Markets & Morality*, Vol. 14, No. 2 (Fall 2011), 610, quoted in Van Son, *supra*.

4. Caitlin Fitz, *Our Sister Republics: The United States in the Age of American Revolutions* (New York: Norton, 2016), 32–33.

5. Ibid., 60.

6. Walter F. Willcox, ed., *International Migrations, Volume II: Interpretations* (Cambridge, Mass.: National Bureau of Economic Research, 1931), 86–93.

7. Lorraine Boissoneault, "How the 19th-Century Know Nothing Party Reshaped American Politics," *Smithsonian*, January 26, 2017.

8. Douglas R. Egerton, *Year of Meteors: Stephen Douglas, Abraham Lincoln, and the Election that Brought on the Civil War* (New York: Bloomsbury Press, 2013), 134–35.

9. *Evening Post*, New York, April 25, 1817.

10. Terry Golway, *Machine Made: Tammany Hall and the Creation of Modern American Politics* (New York: Norton, 2014), 4.

11. Padraig McAuliffe, *Transitional Justice and Rule of Law Reconstruction: A Contentious Relationship* (New York: Routledge, 2013), 244.

12. Michael Perman, *Reunion Without Compromise: The South and Reconstruction: 1865-1868* (Cambridge: Cambridge University Press, 1973), 4–5.

13. Charles Sumner, "Clemency and Common Sense: A Curiosity of Literature; with a Moral, *Atlantic Monthly* 16, no. 98 (December 1865), 759.

14. Edwin Percy Whipple, "Reconstruction and Negro Suffrage, *Atlantic Monthly* 16, no. 94 (August 1865), 238.

15. Ibid., 241–42, 244.

16. C. C. Pearson, "The Readjuster Movement in Virginia," *American Historical Review* 21, no. 4 (July 1916), 734–49.

17. Terry Martin, *The Affirmative Action Empire: Nations and Nationalism in the Soviet Union*, 1923–1939 (Ithaca, N.Y.: Cornell University Press, 2001), 17.

18. Ibid.

19. Ibid., 334.

20. Hubert Poetschke, *Memoirs from the Turbulent Years and Beyond: Analysis and Consequences of the World War II* (Xlibris, 2008), 293–94.

21. Emily Badger, "How Redlining's Racist Effects Lasted for Decades," *New York Times*, August 24, 2017.

22. Ibid.

23. *New York: A Documentary Film*, Episode 6: "A City of Tomorrow," directed by Ric Burns, Public Broadcasting Service, 1999.

24. Jeremy Bauer-Wolf, "ACLU Speaker Shouted Down at William & Mary," Inside Higher Ed, October 5, 2017.

25. Bruce Bawer, *The Victims' Revolution: The Rise of Identity Studies and the Closing of the Liberal Mind* (New York: HarperCollins, 2012), 251.

26. Aimee Picchi, "Nobel winner Stiglitz: 'American Dream is a myth,'" CBS News, April 23, 2015.

27. Carlos Lozada, "A Berkeley sociologist made some tea party friends—and wrote a condescending book about them," *Washington Post*, September 1, 2016.

28. Jason D. Hill, "An Open Letter to Ta-Nehisi Coates," *Commentary*, September, 2017.

29. Peter Edelman, "Poverty in America: Why Can't We End It?" *New York Times*, July 28, 2012.

30. Aparna Mathur, "Families are the real issue for opportunity, not inequality," Brookings Institution, May 26, 2015.

31. William J. Clinton, Remarks on the National Homeownership Strategy, June 5, 1995. Online by Gerhard Peters and John T. Woolley, The American Presidency Project. http://www.presidency.ucsb.edu/ws/?pid=51448.

Chapter 3: Truths and Transgressions

1. *In re Tam*, 808 F.3d 1321 (D.C. Cir. 2015); Associated Press, "The Slants, Washington Football Team Battle Government in Trademark Fight," September 21, 2016.

2. *Matal v. Tam*. 582 U.S. _____ (2017).

3. Ann Marimow and Ian Shapira, "Washington Redskins win trademark fight over the team's name," *Washington Post*, June 29, 2017.

4. Kate Conger, "Exclusive: Here's The Full 10-Page Anti-Diversity Screed Circulating Internally at Google," Gizmodo, August 5, 2017.

5. Nash Jenkins, "The Mark Zuckerberg vs. Ted Cruz Showdown Was the Most Explosive Part of Today's Facebook Testimony," *Time*, April 10, 2018.

6. U.S. Department of Education, National Center for Education Statistics, Integrated Postsecondary Education Data System (IPEDS), October, 2016, https://nces.ed.gov/programs/digest/d16/tables/dt16_318.45.asp?current=yes.

7. Deborah Bach, "Why do some STEM fields have fewer women than others? UW study may have the answer," *University of Washington News*, October 12, 2016.

8. Melanie Ehrenkranz, "Google Reportedly Fires Author of Anti-Diversity Screed," Gizmodo, August 7, 2017.

9. Jackie Wattles, "Storm at Google over engineer's anti-diversity manifesto," CNN, August 7, 2017.

10. Bill Chappell and Laura Sydell, "Google Reportedly Fires Employee Who Slammed Diversity Efforts," August 7, 2017.

11. Mahita Gajanan, "Read Google CEO Sundar Pichai's Letter About the Controversial Anti-Diversity Memo," *Fortune*, August 7, 2017.

12. Scott Thurm, "The Guy Who Wrote the 'Google Memo' Might Just Sue," *Wired*, August 8, 2017.

13. Ulrich Baer, "What 'Snowflakes' Get Right about Free Speech, *New York Times*, April 24, 2017.

14. Noah Rothman, "The Courage to Confront Campus Radicalism," *Commentary*, February 14, 2018.

15. Daniel Cox, Betsy Cooper, Rachel Lienesch, and Robert P. Jones; "Majority of Americans Oppose Transgender Bathroom Restrictions," PRRI, 2017, http://www.prri.org/research/lgbt-transgender-bathroom-discrimination-religious-liberty/.

16. Noah Rothman, "Charleston and Our Tragic Impotence," *Commentary*, June 22, 2015.

17. Katie Reilly, "Here Are All the Times Donald Trump Insulted Mexico," *Time*, August 31, 2016.

18. Jenna Johnson, "Trump calls for 'total and complete shutdown of Muslims entering the United States,'" *Washington Post*, December 7, 2015.

19. Eric Bradner, "Donald Trump stumbles on David Duke, KKK," CNN, February 29, 2016.

20. Alex Altman, "How Donald Trump Is Bringing the Alt-Right to the White House," *Time*, November 14, 2016.

21. Jacob Levy, "The Defense of Liberty Can't Do Without Identity Politics," Niskanen Center, December 13, 2016.

22. Roland G. Fryer, "An Empirical Analysis of Racial Differences in Police Use of Force," National Bureau of Economic Research, Working Paper No. 22399, July 2016, revised January 2018.

23. Tami Luhby, "Worsening wealth inequality by race," CNN Money, June 21, 2012.

24. Noah Rothman, "Capitalism: Bad Again After All These Years," *Commentary*, May 17, 2018.

25. Kurt Bauman and Camille L. Ryan, "Educational Attainment in the United States: 2015," U.S. Census Bureau, March 2016.

26. Lisa Selin Davis, "My Daughter Is Not Transgender. She's a Tomboy," *New York Times*, April 18, 2017.

27. Debra Soh, "No, the Google manifesto isn't sexist or anti-diversity. It's science," *Globe and Mail*, August 8, 2017.

28. Karalee Katsambanis, "At four years old, identifying a child as transgender is too early," *Sydney Morning Herald*, September 6, 2016.

29. Daniel Trotta, "U.S. parents accept children's transgender identity by age three," Reuters, December 22, 2016.

30. Editor, "The Controversial Research on 'Desistance' in Transgender Youth," KHSU, May 23, 2018.

31. BBC News Magazine, "The extraordinary case of the Guevedoces," September 20, 2015.

32. Michelle Goldberg, "What Is a Woman? The Dispute Between Radical Feminism and Transgenderism," *New Yorker*, August 4, 2014.

33. Anne Barnhill and Jessica Martucci, "Unintended Consequences of Invoking the 'Natural' in Breastfeeding Promotion," American Academy of Pediatrics, March 4, 2016.

34. Rachael Pells, "Oxford University Student Union denies telling students to use gender neutral pronoun 'ze,'" *Independent*, December 13, 2016.

35. Scott Jaschik, "Fear of New Pronouns," Inside Higher Ed, September 8, 2015.

36.   Sohrab Ahmari, "The Associated Press and the Pronoun Wars," *Commentary*, October 11, 2017.

37.   Jason Phipps and Ian Sample, "Science Weekly Extra: Simon Baron-Cohen on empathy and evil," *Guardian*, May 5, 2011.

38.   UNESCO, "The Race Question," July 18, 1950.

39.   Robert Wald Sussman, "There Is No Such Thing as Race," *Newsweek*, November 8, 2014.

40.   Guilaine Kinouani, "Why black women feel so betrayed by Rachel Dolezal," *Telegraph*, June 26, 2015.

41.   Denene Millner, "Why Rachel Dolezal Can Never Be Black," NPR, March 3, 2017.

42.   Jesse Singal, "This Is What a Modern-Day Witch Hunt Looks Like," *New York Magazine*, May 2, 2017.

43.   Pew Research Center, "First- and Second-Generation Share of the Population to Reach Record High in 2065," September 23, 2015, http://www.pewhispanic. org/2015/09/28/modern-immigration-wave-brings-59-million-to-u-s-driving-population-growth-and-change-through-2065/ph_2015-09-28_immigration-through-2065-11/.

44.   Pew Research Center, "Second-Generation Americans: A portrait of the Adult Children of Immigrants," February 7, 2013.

45.   Amy Wax and Larry Alexander, "Paying the price for breakdown of the country's bourgeois culture," *Philadelphia Inquirer*, August 9, 2017.

46.   Jack Citrin et al., "Testing Huntington: Is Hispanic Immigration a Threat to American Identity?" *Perspectives on Politics* 5, no. 1 (2007), 31–48.

47.   Stephen Dinan, "Mexican, Central American immigrants lag behind at assimilating into U.S. culture," *Washington Times*, September 21, 2015.

48.   Nate Cohn, "More Hispanics Declaring Themselves White" *New York Times*, May 21, 2014.

49.   Pew Research Center, "Muslim Americans: Middle Class and Mostly Mainstream," May 22, 2007.

50. Pew Research Center, "Muslim Americans: No Signs of Growth in Alienation or Support for Extremism," August 30, 2011.

51. Noah Rothman, "Are American Muslims Assimilating?" *Commentary*, June 16, 2016.

52. Pew Research Center. "Demographic portrait of Muslim Americans," July 26, 2017.

Chapter 4: Lifting the Veil

1. Stephanie Saul, "Arizona Republicans Inject Schools of Conservative Thought into State Universities," *New York Times*, February 26, 2018.

2. Lucy Pasha-Robinson, "SOAS students call for 'white philosophers to be dropped from curriculum,'" *Independent*, January 8, 2017.

3. Minna Salami, "Philosophy has to be about more than white men," *Guardian*, March 23, 2015.

4. Pbier, "Courageous Students Demand Ban of White Philosophers Such as Plato, Socrates and Kant," *Accredited Times*, January 9, 2017, https://www.accredited-times.com/2017/01/09/courageous-students-demand-ban-on-white-philosophers-like-plato-socrates-and-kant/.

5. Aristotle, *The Politics*, Benjamin Lowett, trans. (Oxford: Clarendon Press, 1885), Vol. 1, Book 3.

6. Leo XIII, *Rerum novarum* (On the Condition of Workers), 15 May 1891, in *Acta Sanctae Sedis* No. 23.

7. David Harvey, *Social Justice and the City* (Athens: University of Georgia Press, 1973), 109.

8. Carl L. Bankston, "Social Justice: Cultural Origins of a Perspective and a Theory," *Independent Review* 15, no. 2 (Fall 2010), 174.

9. Ibid., 173.

10. Andrew Lister, "The 'Mirage' of Social Justice: Hayek Against (and for) Rawls," Centre for the Study of Social Justice, Working Paper SJ017, June 2011, 2–4.

11. "Firing Line with William F. Buckley Jr.," Public Broadcasting Service, Episode S0300, November 7, 1977.

12. F. A. Hayek, *Law, Legislation, and Liberty, Volume 2: The Mirage of Social Justice* (Chicago: University of Chicago Press, 2012), 74.

13. Hayek quoted by Lister, 27.

14. Lister, 18.

15. Lister, 24.

16. Richard Arneson, "Luck Egalitarianism and Prioritarianism," *Ethics* 110, no. 2 (January 2000), 339.

17. Anca Gheaus, "Hikers in Flip-Flops: Luck Egalitarianism, Democratic Equality and the Distribuenda of Justice," *Journal of Applied Philosophy* 35, no. 1 (February 2016), 66.

18. Jane Jacobs, *The Death and Life of Great American Cities* (New York: Vintage, 1961), 4.

19. Karl Detzer, "Our Great Big Highway Bungle," *Reader's Digest*, July 1960, 46.

20. Arthur Brooks, "The Social Justice Fight," *USA Today*, March 5, 2014.

21. *Fisher v. University of Texas*, 579 U.S. ___ (2016).

22. Ariane de Vogue, "Supreme Court releases audio of Justice Antonin Scalia saying maybe black students don't belong at elite universities," CNN, December 11, 2015.

Chapter 5: Entry-Level Politics

1. Jason Rhode, "The Girl On Wall Street: Why a Statue is Not Enough," *Paste*, March 8, 2017.

2. Colin Kruger, "Stereotypes aplenty as global wealth group State Street Global Advisors hunts alpha female investors," *Sydney Morning Herald*, March 13, 2017.

3. Matt Stevens, "Firm Behind 'Fearless Girl' Statue Underpaid Women, U.S. Says," *New York Times*, October 6, 2017.

4. Kieran Shiach, "Is Marvel's fascist Captain America losing command of his fans?" *Guardian*, May 19, 2017.

5. Abraham Riesman, "First Captain America Became Evil, Then the Comics World Erupted," *Vulture*, June 27, 2017.

6. Michael Rothman, "Marvel on Captain America's turn to Hydra: 'We hear your concerns,'" ABC News, May 2, 2017.

7. Alex Abad-Santos, "The outrage over Marvel's alleged diversity blaming, explained," Vox, April 8, 2017, https://www.vox.com/culture/2017/4/4/15169572/marvel-diversity-outrage-gabriel.

8. Ashley Rodriguez, "Too much diversity? Marvel says some comic-book readers are pushing back against its relaunched titles," *Quartz*, April 4, 2017.

9. Brad Slager, "Yes, Marvel Comics, Going Full Identity Politics Is Hurting Your Sales," The Federalist, April 25, 2017.

10. Wesley Morris, "The Year We Obsessed Over Identity," *New York Times*, October 6, 2015.

11. M. Choueiti, K. Pieper, and S.L. Smith; "Inequality in 700 popular films: Examining portrayals of gender, race, & LGBT status from 2007 to 2014," (Los Angeles, CA: USC Annenberg, 2015).

12. Reece Ristau, "Study: Film Still Mostly White, Straight and Male," *Variety*, August 5, 2015.

13. Stephen Miller, "If the Oscars Are So Liberal, Why Are the #OscarsSoWhite?" *National Review*, January 27, 2016.

14. Noah Rothman, "How to Manipulate a Democrat," *Commentary*, October 6, 2017.

15. Kat Rosenfield, "The Toxic Drama on YA Twitter," Vulture, August 7, 2017, http://www.vulture.com/2017/08/the-toxic-drama-of-ya-twitter.html.

16. Ruth Graham, "YA Novel About 'Mob Mentalities' Punished After Online Backlash" Slate, October 16, 2017.

17. "A Note from the Editor in Chief," Kirkus, https://www.kirkusreviews.com/statement/laura-moriarty/american-heart/.

18. Noah Rothman, "To Get History Right, Democrats Would Erase It," *Commentary*, July 24, 2015.

19. Thomas Jefferson, "Sixth Annual Message," December 2, 1806. Online by Gerhard Peters and John T. Woolley, The American Presidency Project, http://www.presidency.ucsb.edu/ws/?pid=29448.

20. Noah Rothman, "Whitewashing the $20 Controversy," *Commentary*, September 12, 2017.

21. Jackie Calmes, "Success of 'Hamilton' May Have Saved Hamilton on the $10 Bill," *New York Times*, April 15, 2016.

22. Emily Shire, "The Dumbest College Renaming Debate Yet," The Daily Beast, December 10, 2015, https://www.thedailybeast.com/the-dumbest-college-renaming-debate-yet.

23. Susan Scafidi, *Who Owns Culture? Appropriation and Authenticity in American Law* (New Brunswick, N.J.: Rutgers University Press, 2005), 9, quoting Bruce Ziff and Pratima V. Rao, "Introduction to Cultural Appropriation: A Framework for Analysis," in *Borrowed Power: Essays on Cultural Appropriation*, ed. Bruce Ziff and Pratima V. Rao (New Brunswick, N.J.: Rutgers University Press, 1998), 100.

24. Katie J. M. Baker, "A Much-Needed Primer on Cultural Appropriation," Jezebel, November 13, 2012, https://jezebel.com/a-much-needed-primer-on-cultural-appropriation-30768539.

25. Marcus Gilmer, "Yale students rally against racism in campus 'March of Resilience,'" Mashable, November 9, 2015, https://mashable.com/2015/11/09/racism-yale-rally/#VS2vPEWt3iqy.

26. Isaac Stanley-Becker, "A confrontation over race at Yale: Hundreds of students demand answers from the school's first black dean," *Washington Post*, November 5, 2012.

27. Karin Agness Lips, "Yale vs. Princeton: The Battle For Free Speech On Campus," *Forbes*, November 12, 2015.

28. Redbook Editor, "Maybe Don't Dress Your Kid Up As Moana This Halloween?" *Cosmopolitan*, October 23, 2017.

29. Mary Wakefield, "The mad, bad crusade against 'cultural appropriation,'" *Spectator*, April 1, 2017.

30. Michael Harriot, "This White Woman's Painting of Emmett Till Belongs Under the Definition of White-Peopleing, Not on a Museum Wall," The Root,

March 21, 2017, https://www.theroot.com/this-white-womans-painting-of-emmett-till-belongs-under-1793483717.

31. Roberta Smith, "Should Art That Infuriates Be Removed?" *New York Times*, March 27, 2017.

32. Jamilah King, "These White Cooks Bragged About Stealing Tortilla Recipes from Mexico to Start a Business," May 19, 2017, https://mic.com/articles/177642/these-white-cooks-bragged-about-stealing-tortilla-recipes-from-mexico-to-start-a-portland#.PeNe8vqaA.

33. Tim Carman, "Should white chefs sell burritos? A Portland food cart's revealing controversy," *Washington Post*, May 26, 2017.

34. Steven Humphrey, "Regarding This Week in Appropriation: Kooks Burritos and Willamette Week," *Portland Mercury*, May 21, 2017.

35. Sam Meier, "You Could Be the Writer PolicyMic's New Vertical Is Looking For," October 8, 2013, https://mic.com/articles/66885/you-could-be-the-writer-policymic-s-new-vertical-is-looking-for#.2wn9RfFnS.

36. Adrianne Jeffries, "Mic's Drop," The Outline. August 22, 2017, https://theoutline.com/post/2156/mic-com-and-the-cynicism-of-modern-media?zd=1&zi=tcfurqpo.

37. Manil Suri, "Why Is Science So Straight?" *New York Times*, September 4, 2015.

38. Glenn Nelson, "Why Are Our Parks So White?" *New York Times*, July 10, 2015.

39. Maura Judkis, "Discomfort food: Using dinners to talk about race, violence and America," *Washington Post*, August 23, 3016.

40. Jesse Byrnes, "Trump on transgender bathroom debate: 'Leave it the way it is,'" *The Hill*, April 21, 2016.

41. Corinne Jurney, "North Carolina's Bathroom Bill Flushes Away $630 Million In Lost Business," *Forbes*, November 23, 2016.

42. Erik Eckholm, "Pfizer Blocks the Use of Its Drugs in Executions," *New York Times*, May 13, 2016.

43. Jeff Swiatek, "Salesforce packed a punch in galvanizing RFRA opposition," IndyStar, April 2, 2015, https://www.indystar.com/story/money/2015/04/02/salesforce-packed-punch-galvanizing-rfra-opposition/70842680/.

44. Tony Romm, "Apple, Amazon and Google spent record sums to lobby Trump earlier this summer," Recode, July 21, 2017, https://www.recode.net/2017/7/21/16008504/apple-amazon-google-record-lobby-trump-immigration-science-privacy.

45. Joanna Piacenza, "Consumers Want Brands to Get Political, but Companies Need to Tread Carefully," Morning Consult, February 6, 2018, https://morningconsult.com/2018/02/06/consumers-want-brands-to-get-political-but-companies-need-to-tread-carefully/.

46. Daniel Gross, "Corporations are suddenly jumping into political fights. Here's why," *Los Angeles Times*, May 27, 2016.

47. Stephen J. Dubner, prod. Greg Rosalsky, "The True Story of the Gender Pay Gap." Freakonomics, January 7, 2016, http://freakonomics.com/podcast/the-true-story-of-the-gender-pay-gap-a-new-freakonomics-radio-podcast/.

48. White House website archives, "Did You Know That Women Are Still Paid Less Than Men?" https://obamawhitehouse.archives.gov/equal-pay/myth.

49. Lawrence H. Leith, "Why do women still earn less than men?" Bureau of Labor Statistics, June, 2014.

50. Andrew Biggs and Mark Perry, "The '77 Cents on the Dollar' Myth About Women's Pay," *Wall Street Journal*, April 7, 2014.

51. Shira Tarlo, "What Is Equal Pay Day? Here's Everything You Need to Know," NBC News, April 4, 2017.

52. Jessica Guynn, "Sheryl Sandberg's new mission on Equal Pay Day: #20PercentCounts," *USA Today*, April 3, 2017.

53. ThinkProgress, "The Republican Brain: The Science of Why They Don't Believe in Science (or Many Other Inconvenient Truths)," November 8, 2011, https://thinkprogress.org/the-republican-brain-the-science-of-why-they-dont-believe-in-science-or-many-other-inconvenient-5e079356463/.

54. Katie Palmer, "Cool Catchphrase, Hillary, But Science Isn't About Belief," *Wired*, July 29, 2016.

55. Emily Atkin, "Is the March for Science Bad for Scientists?" *New Republic*, March 1, 2017.

56. Benedict Carey, "For sex researcher, a never-ending backlash," *New York Times*, August 21, 2017.

57. Alice Dreger, *Galileo's Middle Finger: Heretics, Activists, and One Scholar's Search for Justice*, (New York: Penguin Books, 2016), 10–11.

58. Indrek Wichman, "Engineering Education: Social Engineering Rather than Actual Engineering," The James G. Martin Center for Academic Renewal, August 2, 2017.

59. Kyle Smith, "Bill Nye, the Scientism Guy," *National Review*, April 27, 2017.

60. Christine Roussell, "Bill Nye The Eugenics Guy: Maybe We Should Penalize People With 'Extra Kids,'" TownHall, April 26, 2017, https://townhall.com/tipsheet/christinerousselle/2017/04/26/bill-nye-the-eugenics-guy-maybe-we-should-penalize-people-with-extra-kids-n2318527.

Chapter 6: Victimocracy

1. Paulo Freire, *Pedagogy of the Oppressed* (New York: Continuum, 1970), 66.

2. Sol Stern, "Pedagogy of the Oppressor," *City Journal*, Spring 2009.

3. Freire, 46.

4. Noah Rothman, "Blameless," *Commentary*, May 26, 2017.

5. Issie Lapowsky, "Author of Trump's Favorite Voter Fraud Study Says Everyone's Wrong," *Wired*, January 25, 2017.

6. Ilya Somin, "Political ignorance, partisan bias, and belief in conspiracy theories," *Washington Post*, December 30, 2016.

7. Rush Transcript, "Hillary Clinton Speaks at Women for Women International," CNN, May 2, 2017, http://transcripts.cnn.com/TRANSCRIPTS/1705/02/wolf.02.html.

8. Callum Borchers, "Hillary Clinton's revisionist history of debating Donald Trump," *Washington Post*, May 2, 2017.

9. CBS/AP, "Center Of Debate: An 'SNL' Skit," CBS News, February 28, 2008.

10. Abe Greenwald, "Because It's 2015," *Commentary*, November 5, 2015.

11. Rush Transcript, "Transcript of the Democratic Presidential Debate in Milwaukee," Federal News Service, *New York Times*, February 11, 2016.

12.   Amanda Jackson, "Hillary Clinton to hold election night party under real glass ceiling," CNN, October 26, 2016

13.   Edwin Rios, "How Campus Racism Just Became the Biggest Story in America," *Mother Jones*, November 9, 2015.

14.   Elahe Izadi, "The incidents that led to the University of Missouri president's resignation," *Washington Post*, November 9, 2015.

15.   Kendall Foley, "How MU has come face-to-face with racism on campus," *Columbia Missourian*, October 21, 2015.

16.   Kasia Kovacs, "Protesters say talks with President Wolfe did not achieve resolution," *Columbia Missourian*, October 27, 2015.

17.   Rush Transcript, "Univ. of Missouri President Resigns; Giant Hole Swallows Cars," CNN, November 9, 2015.

18.   John Elignon, Richard Perez-Pena, "University of Missouri Protests Spur a Day of Change," *New York Times*, November 9, 2015.

19.   Anemona Hartocollis, "Long After Protests, Students Shun the University of Missouri," *New York Times*, July 9, 2017.

20.   Noah Rothman, "A Plague of Racial Hoaxes on Campus," *Commentary*, November 12, 2015.

21.   William Jacobson, "Psychoanalyzing The Great Oberlin College Racism Hoax of 2013," Legal Insurrection, July 24, 2015, https://legalinsurrection.com/2015/07/psychoanalyzing-the-oberlin-college-2013-racism-hoax/.

22.   Sharita Erves, Henry Rosoff, "21-year-old UW-Parkside junior created hit list," February 6, 2012, https://fox6now.com/2012/02/06/student-on-uw-parkside-hit-list-admits-to-hoax/.

23.   William Wier, "After Threats To Gay Students, CCSU Holds Rally Against Hate Crimes," *Hartford Courant*, March 13, 2012.

24.   Hilda Munoz, David Owens, "CCSU Police Say Student Faked Anti-Gay Notes," *Hartford Courant*, July 2, 2012.

25.   Robby Soave, "Exclusive: Shocking Discovery in Hoax Bias Incident at Vassar College," The Daily Caller, November 27, 2013, https://dailycaller.

com/2013/11/27/exclusive-shocking-discovery-in-hoax-bias-incident-at-vassar-college/.

26. Jennifer Brooks, Paul Walsh, "St. Olaf: Report of racist note on black student's windshield was 'fabricated,'" *Star Tribune*, May 11, 2017.

27. Vivian Yee, "Racism Charges in Bus Incident, and Their Unraveling, Upset University at Albany," *New York Times*, March 1, 2016.

28. Kristine Phillips, "A Muslim student in Michigan claimed a man threatened to set her on fire. Police say it's a hoax," *Washington Post*, December 21, 2016.

29. Emma Green, "A Black Church Burned in the Name of Trump," *The Atlantic*, November 2, 2016.

30. Camila Domonoske, "'Parishioner Arrested For November Arson Of Black Church In Mississippi," NPR, December 22, 2016.

31. Sarah Larimer, "This Indiana church was defaced with 'HEIL TRUMP' graffiti — and is keeping it," *Washington Post*, November 15, 2016.

32. Max Greenwood, "Air Force general: 'If you can't treat someone with dignity and respect get out' of Academy," *The Hill*, September 29, 2017.

33. Joshua Rhett Miller, "Black cadet admits to writing racial slurs outside Air Force Academy dorm room," *New York Post*, November 8, 2017.

34. Aaron Blake, "Trump is flirting with the idea that anti-Semitic incidents are false flags again," *Washington Post,* February 28 2017.

35. Aaron Rupar, "Trump echoes David Duke, reportedly suggests Jews are behind threats to Jewish schools," ThinkProgress, February 28, 2017, https://thinkprogress.org/trump-anti-semitism-false-flag-david-duke-ee29668fa101/.

36. Mark Berman, "Trump questions who is really behind anti-Semitic threats and vandalism," *Washington Post*, March 1, 2017.

37. Reuters, "Israeli-U.S. teen indicted for bomb threats, hate crimes: U.S. Justice Department," February 28, 2017, https://www.reuters.com/article/us-usa-security-jewish/israeli-u-s-teen-indicted-for-bomb-threats-hate-crimes-u-s-justice-department-idUSKCN1GD3MN.

38. Jamiles Lartey, "Jewish community center threats: man arrested in alleged cyberstalking plot," *Guardian*, March 3, 2017.

39. K. C. Johnson, Stuart Taylor, "The path to Obama's 'Dear Colleague' letter," "The Volokh Conspiracy," *Washington Post*, January 31, 2017, https://www. washingtonpost.com/news/volokh-conspiracy/wp/2017/01/31/the-path-to-obamas-dear-colleague-letter/?utm_term=.84c17f48130d.

40. U.S. Department of Education, "Dear Colleague Letter," Office of the Assistant Secretary, April 4, 2011, https://www2.ed.gov/about/offices/list/ocr/letters/ colleague-201104.html?exp=1.

41. David Lisak, "Understanding the Predatory Nature of Sexual Violence," *Sexual Assault Report* 14, no. 4 (March/April 2011), 56–57.

42. Lynn Langton, Sofi Sinozich, "Rape And Sexual Assault Among College-Age Females, 1995-2013," Bureau of Justice Statistics, December 11, 2014, http:// www.bjs.gov/index.cfm?ty=pbdetail&iid=5176.

43. Beatrice Dupuy, "Women who didn't go to college are twice as likely to be sexually assaulted than those with a degree," *Newsweek*, November 23, 2017.

44. Emily Yoffe, "The College Rape Overcorrection," Slate, December 7, 2014, http://www.slate.com/articles/double_x/doublex/2014/12/college_rape_ campus_sexual_assault_is_a_serious_problem_but_the_efforts.html.

45. Robby Soave, "Here Is Every Crazy Title IX Rape Case Betsy DeVos Referenced, Plus a Bunch More," *Reason*, September 7, 2017.

46. Laura Kipnis,"Sexual Paranoia Strikes Academe," *Chronicle of Higher Education*, February 27, 2015.

47. Laura Kipnis, "Eyewitness to a Title IX Witch Trial," *Chronicle of Higher Education*, April 2, 2017.

48. Noah Rothman, "This Is Not Justice," *Commentary*, September 8, 2017.

49. Noah Rothman, "What Has Conservatism Conserved," *Commentary*, October 18, 2016.

50. Nicholas Eberstadt, "Our Miserable 21st Century," February 15, 2017.

51. Rosie Gray, "Behind the Internet's Anti-Democracy Movement," *The Atlantic*, February 10, 2017.

52. Peter Thiel, "The Education of a Libertarian," Cato Unbound, April 13, 2009, https://www.cato-unbound.org/2009/04/13/peter-thiel/education-libertarian.

53. Klint Finley, "Geeks for Monarchy: The Rise of the Neoreactionaries," Tech Crunch, November 23, 2013, https://techcrunch.com/2013/11/22/geeks-for-monarchy/.

54. Eliana Johnson, Eli Stokols, "What Steve Bannon Wants You to Read," *Politico Magazine*, February 7, 2017.

55. Nick Land, "The Dark Enlightenment: Part 4: Re-running the race to ruin," 2008, http://www.thedarkenlightenment.com/the-dark-enlightenment-by-nick-land/.

56. Nick Land, "The Dark Enlightenment: Part 4a: A multi-part sub-digression into racial terror," 2008, http://www.thedarkenlightenment.com/the-dark-enlightenment-by-nick-land/.

Chapter 7: Violent Delights

1. Peter Kreeft, "A Refutation of Moral Relativism," transcription, Integritas Institute, February 24, 2003, http://www.peterkreeft.com/audio/05_relativism/relativism_transcription.htm.

2. James Madison, "The Same Subject Continued The Union as a Safeguard Against Domestic Faction and Insurrection," The Federalist Papers No. 10, November 23, 1787.

3. Bruce Bawer, *The Victims' Revolution: The Rise of Identity Studies and the Closing of the Liberal Mind* (New York: HarperCollins, 2012), 18.

4. Eden Gordon, "The Top 10 Secrets of NYC's Zuccotti Park," Untapped Cities, June 12, 2017, https://untappedcities.com/2017/06/12/the-top-10-secrets-of-nycs-zuccotti-park/.

5. Ian Schwartz, "Pelosi On Occupy Wall Street Activists: 'God Bless Them,'" RealClearPolitics, October 6, 2011.

6. Ian Schwartz, "Obama: Wall St. Protesters Giving 'Voice' To Frustration," RealClearPolitics, October 6, 2011.

7. Transcript, "Full text: President Obama's speech at MLK Memorial," *Washington Post*, October 16, 2011.

8.   conservARTive, "Occupy Atlanta Silences Civil Rights Hero John Lewis!"
      October 8, 2011, https://www.youtube.com/watch?v=3QZlp3eGMNI&feature=
      youtu.be.

9.   OccupyRichmond2011, "Occupy Richmond 10/6/11 Intro to 'Progressive
      Stack,'" October 8, 2011, https://www.youtube.com/watch?v=SCwhlZtHhWs.

10.   Kenneth Rapoza, "Global 'Occupy' Protests Lead To Violence In Rome, Arrests
      In Chicago," *Forbes*, October 16, 2011.

11.   Emma Brown, Wilber Del Quentin, "Air and Space Museum closes after
      guards clash with protesters," *Washington Post*, October 8, 2011.

12.   CNN Wire Staff, "DA: 3 Occupy Denver activists charged with felonies," CNN,
      November 18, 2011.

13.   Matt Flegenheimer, Sarah Maslin Nir, "Hundreds Held in Oakland Occupy
      Protest," *New York Times*, January 29, 2012.

14.   Michael Scott, "FBI arrests 5 accused of plotting to blow up Ohio 82 bridge in
      Cuyahoga valley," *Plain Dealer*, May 1, 2012.

15.   Noah Rothman, "When Will Colleges Fight Back Against Their Coddled
      Student Bodies?" April 24, 2015, https://hotair.com/archives/2015/04/24/when-
      will-colleges-fight-back-against-their-coddled-student-bodies/.

16.   Alice Lloyd, "Wellesley's Student Paper Mounts a Barely Literate Defense of
      Censorship, " *Weekly Standard*, April 14, 2017.

17.   Noah Rothman, "Conservatives are increasingly hostile to higher ed. Who can
      blame them?" *USA Today*, July 20, 2017.

18.   Kyung Lah, Madison Park, "Berkeley protests of Yiannopoulos caused
      $100,000 in damage," CNN, February 2, 2017.

19.   Stephanie Saul, "Dozens of Middlebury Students Are Disciplined for Charles
      Murray Protest," *New York Times*, May 24, 2017.

20.   Sean Rossman, "U.S. drops charges against 129 inauguration day protesters,"
      USA Today, January 18, 2018.

21.   Jess Zimmerman, "The Myth of the Well-Behaved Women's March," *New
      Republic*, January 24, 2017.

22.   Noah Rothman, "Whose Violence Is It?" *Commentary*, August, 2016.

23. Elias Groll, Jana Winter, "Here's the Memo that Blew Up the NSC," *Foreign Policy*, August 10, 2017.

24. Sarah Larimer, Justin Moyer, Jenny Starrs, "Trump supporter charged after sucker-punching protester at North Carolina rally," *Washington Post*, March 11, 2016.

25. Jeremy Diamond, "Donald Trump on protester: 'I'd like to punch him in the face,'" CNN, February 23, 2016.

26. *Meet the Press with Chuck Todd*, "Will Donald Trump Pay Supporter's Legal Fees?" NBC News, March 13, 2016.

27. Jim Geraghty, "No, Let's Not Burn the System Down," *National Review*, March 14, 2016.

28. Charles Bramesco, "Protesters Shut Down Trump Rally, Clash with Supporters in Chicago," *Vanity Fair*, March 12, 2016.

29. Noah Rothman, "Whose Violence Is It?" *Commentary*, August, 2016.

30. Joseph Serna, "Neo-Nazis didn't start the violence at state Capitol, police say." *Los Angeles Times*, June 27, 2016.

31. Paige St. John, "Hundreds of Trump supporters and counter-protesters clash at Berkeley rally," *Los Angeles Times*, April 15, 2017.

32. Alan Blinder, Richard Fausset, Manny Fernandez, "Micah Johnson, Gunman in Dallas, Honed Military Skills to a Deadly Conclusion," *New York Times*, July 9, 2016.

33. Ishaan Tharoor, "An act of American terror in Trump's heartland," *Washington Post*, February 27, 2017.

34. Mark Berman, "Fatal stabbing in New York was 'practice' for more attacks on black men, police say," *Washington Post*, March 23, 2017.

35. CBS/AP, "Fresno shooting spree suspect charged with 3 counts of first-degree murder," CBS News, April 26, 2017.

36. David Love, "Lynching re-emerges in new rhetoric of hate," CNN, May 23, 2017.

37. Lydia O'Connor, "Portland Murder Suspect Calls Stabbings 'Patriotism' In First Court Appearance," *Huffington Post*, May 30, 2017.

38. KGW-TV, "14 arrested during competing protests in Portland in wake of train stabbing," USA Today, June 5, 2017.

39. Joe Heim, "Recounting a day of rage, hate, violence and death," *Washington Post*, August 14, 2017.

40. Hawes Spencer, "A Far-Right Gathering Bursts Into Brawls," *New York Times*, August 13, 2017.

41. Alan Blinder, Jonah Engel Bromwich, "What We Know About James Alex Fields, Driver Charged in Charlottesville Killing," *New York Times*, August 13, 2017.

42. George Joseph, "White Supremacists Joked About Using Cars to Run Over Opponents Before Charlottesville," August 28, 2017, https://www.propublica.org/article/white-supremacists-joked-about-using-cars-to-run-over-opponents-before-charlottesville.

43. Noah Rothman, "What Trump Voters Heard," *Commentary*, August 16, 2017.

44. Alex Pfeiffer, "Major Figures Work to Mainstream Violent Antifa Protesters," The Daily Caller, August 16, 2017.

45. Chelsea Bailey, "What Is 'Antifa'? Meet the Fascist-Fighting Coalition Dubbed the 'Alt-Left' by President," NBC News, August 16, 2017.

46. Mark Bray, "Who Are the Antifa?" *Washington Post*, August 16, 2017.

47. Natasha Lennard, "Anti-Fascists Will Fight Trump's Fascism in the Streets," *Nation*, January 19, 2017.

48. Natasha Lennard, "Not Rights but Justice: It's Time to Make Nazis Afraid Again," *Nation*, August 16, 2017.

49. Madison Pauly, "A New Wave of Left-Wing Militants Is Ready to Rumble in Portland—and Beyond," *Mother Jones*, (May/June, 2017).

50. Mary Nardini Gang, "Toward the queerest insurrection," The Anarchist Library, 2014, https://theanarchistlibrary.org/library/mary-nardini-gang-toward-the-queerest-insurrection.

51. Anonymous, "Dangerous Spaces: Violent Resistance, Self-Defense, and Insurrectional Struggle Against Gender," (Untorelli Press, 2012), https://untorellipress.noblogs.org/files/2011/12/dangerous.pdf.

52. Gretchen Kell, "Campus investigates, assesses damage from Feb. 1 violence," Berkeley News, February 2, 2017, http://news.berkeley.edu/2017/02/02/campus-investigates-assesses-damage-from-feb-1-violence/.

53. Phillip Matier, Andrew Ross, "After melees, Berkeley mayor asks Cal to cancel right-wing Free Speech Week," *San Francisco Chronicle*, August 28, 2017.

54. Daniel Uria, "California rally accused of attracting white supremacists is canceled," August 26, 2017, https://www.upi.com/California-rally-accused-of-attracting-white-supremacists-is-canceled/7781503754400/.

55. Matt Labash, "A Beating in Berkeley" *Weekly Standard*, September 1, 2017.

56. Paul Elias, Jocelyn Gecker, "Black-clad anarchists swarm anti-hate rally in California," AP, August 28, 2017.

57. Noah Rothman, "A Revolt of the Comfy and Bored," *Commentary*, June 9, 2016.

58. Bruce Hoffman, "Today's Highly Educated Terrorists," *National Interest*, September 15, 2010.

59. Elias Canetti, "Crowds and Power," (New York: Farrar, Straus and Giroux, 1960), 58–59, 77–78.

60. Liz Sawyer, "Alt-right nationalists, protesters clash at Minnesota State Capitol," *Star Tribune*, May 6, 2017.

Chapter 8: "Throw It the Hell Out"

1. Thomas Mallon, "A View from the Fringe," *New Yorker*, January 11, 2016.

2. Alvin Felzenberg, "How William F. Buckley Became the Gatekeeper of the Conservative Movement," *National Review*, June 19, 2017.

3. Alvin Felzenberg, "The Inside Story of William F. Buckley Jr.'s Crusade Against the John Birch Society," *National Review*, June 20, 2017.

4. William F. Buckley, "Goldwater, the John Birch Society, and Me," *Commentary*, March, 2008.

5. Alvin Felzenberg, "A Man and His Presidents: The Political Odyssey of William F. Buckley Jr.," (New Haven: Yale University Press, 2017), 142.

6.   Alvin Felzenberg, "A Man and His Presidents: The Political Odyssey of William F. Buckley Jr.," (New Haven: Yale University Press, 2017), 136.

7.   Matthew Boyle, "Conservatives Question Whether John Birch Society Should Be Accepted as Part of the Tea Party Movement," The Daily Caller, December 3, 2010.

8.   James Kirchick, "The Ron Paul Institute: Be Afraid, Very Afraid," The Daily Beast, April 25, 2013.

9.   Alvin Felzenberg, "The Inside Story of William F. Buckley Jr.'s Crusade Against the John Birch Society," *National Review*, June 20, 2017.

10.   John Earl Haynes, Harvey Klehr, *Early Cold War Spies: The Espionage Trials that Shaped American Politics* (Cambridge: Cambridge University Press, 2006), 18.

11.   Simeon Larson and Bruce Nissen, *Theories of the Labor Movement* (Detroit: Wayne State University Press, 1987), 5.

12.   Harvey Klehr, "Lenin on American socialist leaders and on Samuel Gompers," *Labor History* 17 no. 2 (2008), 265-70.

13.   Industrial Workers of the World, "Preamble to the IWW Constitution," July 7, 1905. https://www.iww.org/PDF/Constitutions/CurrentIWWConstitution.pdf.

14.   Benjamin Gitlow, "How to Think About Communism," (New York: Graphics Group, 1949), https://archive.org/stream/HowToThinkAboutCommunism/Howtothinkaboutcommunism_djvu.txt.

15.   William H. Chartener, "Reds in Trade Unions," CQ Press, 1949, http://library.cqpress.com/cqresearcher/cqresrre1949072200.

16.   Ronald L. Filippelli and Mark D. McColloch, *Cold War in the Working Class: The Rise and Decline of the United Electrical Workers,* (Albany: State University of New York Press, 1995), 107.

17.   William H. Chartener, "Reds in Trade Unions," CQ Press, 1949, http://library.cqpress.com/cqresearcher/cqresrre1949072200.

18.   Ibid.

19.   Gary Donaldson, *Truman Defeats Dewey* (Lexington: University Press of Kentucky, 2000), 199–201.

20. Ibid., 201.

21. Paul D'Amato, "Labor and the Cold War," *Socialist Worker*, October, 1990.

22. Jen Kalaidis, "Bring Back Social Studies," *The Atlantic*, September 23, 2013.

23. Robert Townsend, "'No Child' Leaves the Social Studies Behind," American Historical Association, July 30, 2007.

24. Ken Shepherd, "37 percent of Americans can't name any of the rights guaranteed by First Amendment: Survey," *Washington Times*, September 13, 2017.

25. Emily Ekins, "82% Say It's Hard to Ban Hate Speech Because People Can't Agree What Speech Is Hateful," Cato Institute, November 8, 2017.

26. Arne Duncan, "The Social Studies are Essential to a Well-Rounded Education," National Council for the Social Studies, 2011, https://www.socialstudies.org/publications/a_well_rounded_education.

Index

P

Park, K-Sue, 1–3, 6

Pedagogy of the Oppressed, 148, 183

Pelosi, Nancy, 184

Perez, Carmen, 18

PolicyMic, 133

Polis, Jared, 24

Pope Pius IX, 40

Portland train attack, 195–96

Prohibition of offensive speech, 65

Protestant Reformation, 34

Purinton, Adam, 194

R

Race as criterion for admission, 106

Racial progress in America, 74–76

Racial segregation, 12–13, 54, 75, 98, 104, 178, 215

Radical Republicans, 45–46

Rape culture, 22, 24, 166

Rawls, John, 97–102, 106, 147

Red Scare, 221

Rerum Novarum, 36, 95–96

Roof, Dylann, 71, 123

Roosevelt, Franklin Delano, 52–53

Rosenfield, Kat, 120–21

Rubin Erdely, Sabrina, 23

Russification, 51–52

S

Sanders, Bernie, 70, 154, 191, 206

Schapiro, Morton, 12

Schutz, Dana, 130–31

Sexual assault on school campuses, 22–24, 167–72

Shakur, Assata, 17–18

Silicon Valley, 8, 66, 68

Sinyard, Shauna, 118–19

Slavery, 33, 36–37, 39, 41, 45–46, 95, 123–24

Smith, Adam, 34, 92

Social studies in schools, 227–28

Soviet infiltration of unions, 221–22, 224

Soviet Union/USSR, ix, 49, 51–52, 214, 220–24

Spencer, Richard, 176, 194

St. Louis, Connie, 10

State Street Global Advisors, 111–12

T

Tammany Hall, 42–43

Taparelli d'Azeglio Luigi, 34–36, 40, 95

Taylor, Matt, 9–11

Tea Party Movement, 57, 185, 219

Thiel, Peter, 176–77

Title IX, 167–68, 170–72

Torres, Eden, 56